GREAT STUFF

GREAT STUFF

Baseball's Most Amazing Pitching Feats

By Rich Westcott
Foreword by Paul Hagen

SPORTS
PUBLISHING

Sports Publishing books may be purchased in bulk at special discounts for sales promotion, corporate gifts, fund-raising, or educational purposes. Special editions can also be created to specifications. For details, contact the Special Sales Department, Sports Publishing, 307 West 36th Street, 11th Floor, New York, NY 10018 or sportspubbooks@skyhorsepublishing.com.

Sports Publishing® is a registered trademark of Skyhorse Publishing, Inc.®, a Delaware corporation.

Visit our website at www.sportspubbooks.com.

10 9 8 7 6 5 4 3 2 1

Library of Congress Cataloging-in-Publication Data is available on file.

ISBN: 978-1-61321-651-4

Printed in the United States of America

DEDICATION

To my loving wife Lois, for her constant companionship, encouragement, and help whenever needed. You are the beacon of my life and the reason I survive.

And

To all the pitchers who have ever gone to the mound and tried to get a batter out. As an old pitcher, I know firsthand how hard it is to perform that task.

ACKNOWLEDGMENTS

Many people have made substantial contributions to this book, and to them I would like to extend a special note of appreciation. In particular, I want to thank my friend Paul Hagen for writing the foreword. Tim Wiles and John Horne of the Baseball Hall of Fame in Cooperstown, NY have been especially helpful, as has baseball historian Bob Warrington. I also appreciate the tireless and extremely helpful work of editor Julie Ganz. And finally, a special thanks to Dick Allen, Harold Baines, George Brett, Jim Fregosi, Keith Hernandez, Wally Joyner, Mark McGwire, Lance Parrish, Ryne Sandberg, and Mike Schmidt for their insightful comments and expertise in helping me define some of the pitchers in this book who they played with or against.

FOREWORD

By Paul Hagen

When I moved from Texas to cover the Phillies in 1987, I had a lot to learn. How to pronounce Schuylkill Expressway—SKOO-kel—and to avoid it at all costs during rush hour. Where the best cheesesteaks could be found. To make sure I had cash for the Walt Whitman Bridge coming to and from Veterans Stadium from Cherry Hill, where I lived at the time. Back then it was 90 cents, and you paid both coming and going; E-Z Pass wouldn't come along for a few more years.

It didn't take long, though, to figure out that one of the most reliable sources for information on the history of one of the National League's charter teams was Rich Westcott. He was a regular presence in the press box and always had a fascinating fact to share or a story to tell.

That was many books ago. During his career, Rich has produced nearly two dozen volumes, many of which have illuminated the adventures and misadventures of one of baseball's most interesting franchises. *Great Stuff: Baseball's Most Amazing Pitching Feats* expands his scope, but is just as insightful and compelling.

It's one thing to attempt to identify the 50 most impressive pitching feats of all time. It's another to present each with anecdotes and details that raise the discussion beyond a dry recitation of facts. Westcott succeeds in doing just that.

This book, then, is kind of like those car insurance commercials on television. Everybody knows that in 1938 Cincinnati's Johnny Vander Meer became the only pitcher to ever throw back-to-back no-hitters. But, did you know:

That he had pitched a three-hitter in his start before the first no-no and didn't allow a hit in the first 3 1/3 innings of the one after?

That he declined the Reds' suggestion that he change his uniform number to 00 after completing his feat?

That he hurt his arm the following season but, 14 years later, pitching for Tulsa against Beaumont in a Texas League game, he hurled another no-hitter before an announced crowd of 335?

Everybody knows that Christy Mathewson pitched three shutouts for the New York Giants against the Philadelphia Athletics in the 1905 World Series. But did you know:

That he was nicknamed Big Six, possibly because that's what New Yorkers called the biggest, fastest fire engines? Westcott also unearthed a priceless, pithy quote from Mathewson summarizing his gameday approach. "Anybody's best pitch is the one batters aren't hitting that day."

Great Stuff is filled with interesting nuggets like that, making this a book that is both educational and entertaining. Along the way, we are introduced to many of the biggest names in baseball history. Walter Johnson, Greg Maddux, Babe Ruth, Bob Feller, Doc Gooden, Tom Seaver, Nolan Ryan, Sandy Koufax, Mariano Rivera, Bob Gibson, Steve Carlton, Cy Young, and Warren Spahn are all present and accounted for. But so are Fred Marberry, Lou Brissie, Leon Cadore, and Joe Oeschger. The latter are the stories that few people know and which demonstrate all over again what a maddeningly unpredictable game baseball can be.

And if that wasn't enough, Westcott ties it all up with a shorter list of 50 honorable mentions. It's almost impossible to imagine that there could be a more complete, detailed, and exhaustively researched list of the best pitching performances anywhere.

The presentation is sensibly broken into eras, and there's something in here for any baseball fan—the historian or the reader who enjoys the story behind the story, the old-timer or the youngster who is just discovering about the game. There's plenty of great stuff in *Great Stuff*.

INTRODUCTION

In all of sports, there is probably no position more difficult than that of the pitcher. A pitcher is more responsible for the outcome of a game than any other position player in team sports.

If a pitcher has a good game, his team often wins. If he does not, his team usually loses. To be successful, a pitcher must be at the top of his game. He not only has to be talented with the ability to throw good pitches with good command, but also he has to be knowledgeable, strong, tough, and smart. He must work hard, remain healthy, be able to deal with all kinds of different conditions, and stay focused on the job with a plan for approaching each hitter and each situation.

Quite obviously, it is no easy job being a pitcher. It is an even harder job being a good one. For those few who reach the highest level of their profession, the climb to the top is a magnificent achievement that is largely unparalleled in sports.

Sometimes, the pitchers who ascend to this level add special achievements to their glittering careers. It is these incredible feats performed by very special pitchers that form the content of this book.

During the long history of Major League Baseball, there have been many spectacular performances on the mound. Typically, these have been among the sport's most noteworthy achievements.

Some of these achievements involved a performance in a single game. Some occurred during a series of games or over the course of an entire season. Others were special records posted along the way of one's career. Some were an accumulation of related accomplishments performed over an extended period. Still others involved non-pitching endeavors that had a powerful effect on a pitcher's performance on the diamond.

These remarkable accomplishments are one of a kind. No one else had ever done them. And most likely, no one else ever will. In a few cases, the feats are the first of their kind. But each one stands alone as a singular achievement.

Indeed, these achievements are often the ones most vividly recalled by those who follow baseball. These stirring feats have carved an indelible mark in baseball history, and cannot easily be forgotten.

Johnny Vander Meer's back-to-back no-hitters stands at the highest level of pitching success stories. So does Christy Mathewson's three shutouts in one World Series. Carl Hubbell's 24 wins in a row, Robin Roberts' 28 straight complete games, Bob Gibson's 1.12 ERA in one season, Nolan Ryan's seven no-hitters, and Greg Maddux's miraculous decade are right there, too.

These and many other great feats comprise the contents of this detailed look at the special accomplishments of those who play one of the most exciting and important positions in baseball. As Connie Mack once said, "Pitching is 75 percent of the game." This book underscores that theory.

Because the game was previously played with notable differences, only those feats performed since 1893 when the pitching mound was moved back to 60 feet, six inches from home plate are covered. With the mound previously standing 50 feet from home plate, pitching was a wholly different function before 1893, and the achievements of hurlers before that date are not comparable to the ones performed in the "modern era." Moreover, only positive achievements were considered.

This is not a book that emphasizes a pitcher's career records. But there has been an attempt to inject information on a pitcher's entire career so that his special achievement can be placed in the proper perspective.

Each pitcher who's portrayed does not necessarily rank among baseball's all-time greats. Yet, each pitcher has demonstrated his own particular level of greatness by virtue of his inclusion herein. And because numerous other special achievements should not be ignored, an honorable mention section has been included.

The 50 top accomplishments that comprise the central focus of this book are ones I consider to be the greatest in the last 121 years of the game. The pitchers, many of whom I had the good luck of interviewing over the years (as well as some of the batters who hit against them), transcend the history of the modern-day game, all the way up to the present day.

Some of those cited threw hard, some threw soft. Some played with winners, some played with losers. Some had relatively short careers, others pitched for several decades. But despite their differences, all have one thing in common—when they took the mound, they all had great stuff.

—Rich Westcott

TABLE OF CONTENTS

CONTINUING THE TRADITION OF EXCELLENCE – 1930–1949

WHEN PITCHERS RULED THE GAME – 1950–1969

ANOTHER ERA OF SPECTACULAR HURLERS – 1970–1994

MODERN MASTERS OF THE MOUND – 1995 TO PRESENT

HONORABLE MENTION

STANDOUTS FROM THE EARLY YEARS – PRE-1930

1

AMOS RUSIE

CHANGED THE ART OF PITCHING

I f there is one person who, more than anybody, could be considered responsible for changing the art of pitching, it was Amos Rusie. In doing so, he changed the whole game of baseball.

In the early days, pitchers hurled huge amounts of games and innings. There were only a few hurlers on staff, and the word "relief pitcher" was for the most part an unknown phrase. Pitchers pitched long and hard, and when they were finished one day, they were ready to go again a few days later.

Significantly, the pitching mound stood a distance of 50 feet from home plate, having been moved back from 45 feet in 1881. Then along came Rusie, and largely because of him, the mound was moved back again in 1893, this time to 60 feet, six inches. Baseball would never be the same.

Pitchers had to contend with batters who now had a distinct advantage. A hitter could wait longer on a pitch, have a better chance of seeing what kind of pitch it was, and if it was a fastball, the pitch wouldn't arrive at the plate quite as fast as lightning.

When Rusie broke into the majors in 1889, pitchers—especially those who had blazing fastballs—had the upper hand. Amos personified the kind of hurler who thrived on the short distance from the mound to home.

The right-handed Rusie, who played mostly with the New York Giants, threw so hard that catcher Dick Buckley put a slab of lead covered by a sponge and then a handkerchief in his glove to soften the blow of Rusie's fastball.

A native of Mooresville, Indiana, where he was born in 1871, Rusie was called "The Hoosier Thunderbolt." Once, a line drive hit back to the mound struck him in the ear and permanently damaged his hearing. Another time, he beaned the Baltimore Orioles' Hugh Jennings, who then laid unconscious for four days.

"Words really fail to describe the speed with which Rusie sent the ball," said Chicago Cubs outfielder Jimmy Ryan. "The giant simply drove the ball at you with the force of a cannon. It was like a white streak tearing past you." To this, Orioles star John McGraw added, "You can't hit 'em if you can't see 'em."

The 6-1, 210-pound Rusie certainly had the size to throw a wicked fastball. He was also the owner of a nasty curve. And, as Ryan said, "he put every ounce of weight and sinew on every pitch."

Rusie had been a hard-thrower since his youth when his family moved to Indianapolis. He had quit school and gone to work in a factory while playing for a local semipro team. Originally an outfielder, it soon became apparent that the kid could throw a sizzling fastball, and he was converted to pitcher. Then, while still pitching for the semipro team called the "Sturm Avenue Never Sweats," he hurled shutouts in exhibition games against touring National League teams, including the Boston Beaneaters and the Washington Nationals.

That was enough to earn the 18-year-old Rusie a minor league contract with the Burlington Babies of the Central Interstate League. Shortly thereafter, he was signed by the Indianapolis Hoosiers of the National League. Rusie made his big league debut, striking out the first batter he faced on three pitches, but losing, 13-2, to the Cleveland Blues. He then went on to post a 12-10 record, but his ERA was 5.32 in 225 innings of work.

The following year, Rusie registered an incredible record of 29-34 (that's 63 decisions!) while pitching in 67 games and 548.2 innings. He led the league with 341 strikeouts and a still-standing record of 289 walks. Then, over the next two years, Rusie went 33-20 and 32-31 while working in more than 500 innings each season, including 541 in 1892. He recorded a league-leading 337 strikeouts in 1891, a year in which he pitched a no-hitter in a 6-0 pasting of the first-place Brooklyn Bridegrooms.

By 1892, Rusie had not only become one of the league's top pitchers, but he was also one of the wildest. At the time, he was in the midst of leading the league in walks five straight seasons, never going below 200 during that period.

Most batters were truly scared to face Rusie. He was fast—some said later that he probably threw in the 100 mph range—he was wild, and batters feared for their safety when they stepped to the plate against his terrifying overhand deliveries. Few hitters were willing to dig in at the plate, and as a result, few got good licks at his pitches. In fact, over his first four years, Rusie allowed just 28 home runs in 1,815.1 innings.

Prior to the 1893 season, major league officials decided that something needed to be done to help the hitter. To protect the batter and turn baseball into more of a hitters' game instead of one dominated by pitchers, the mound was moved back to 60 feet, six inches.

Because of the way he pitched, Rusie was deemed as the one most responsible for forcing this change. It was a change that would stand as the most significant one in baseball history, and one that would forever alter the way the game was played.

Nevertheless, to the surprise of baseball followers, the change hardly made a difference in Rusie's pitching. Amazingly, his effectiveness was not curtailed, and he continued to be one of the most dominant hurlers in the league. The year the mound was moved, Rusie posted a 33-21 record, while leading the league in games (56), games started (52), complete games (50), innings pitched (482), and strikeouts (208). He also topped the circuit in hits allowed (451) and walks (218).

Quite obviously, the change hardly affected Rusie. His crackling curve had more time to break, and his fastball raced across the plate just the same as it had. He went on to ring up a 36-13 record in 1894, leading the league in wins, ERA (2.78), games started (50), strikeouts (195), and walks (200). In what was then called the Temple Series when the National League's first- and second-place teams met in a postseason battle, Rusie won two games as the runner-up Giants swept the series in four games against the pennant-winning Orioles. In his two complete-game victories, Amos gave up just one run.

Rusie followed his spectacular 1894 season with a 23-23 mark while winning his fifth strikeout title. He then became involved in a bitter contract dispute with Giants owner Andrew Freedman in 1896, and incredibly held out the whole season, never appearing on the roster. He returned the following season and posted a 28-10 record, and 20-11 marks over the next two years. By then, Rusie and Cy Young were regarded as the premier pitchers in baseball. In addition, Rusie had become a popular figure on Broadway, with drinks named after him and big-time performers such as Lillian Russell wanting to meet him.

The big moundsman, who threw so fast that some batters said they couldn't see the ball, didn't play again in either 1899 or 1900. Hearing loss after getting hit in the head with a line drive, arm trouble that severely limited his speed, and what were described as "personal problems" were reportedly the reasons he stayed out of action.

Late in 1900, however, Rusie was back in the spotlight when the Giants traded him to the Cincinnati Reds for a promising young pitcher named Christy Mathewson. The 19-year-old right-hander had been sent back to the minors after a disappointing 0-3 start, and the Reds thought they had made a terrific trade. Instead, it was the other way around, as Mathewson went on to a Hall of Fame career with the Giants while Rusie quickly faded out of view.

Amos made three appearances with the Reds in 1901, but allowed 43 hits in 22 innings while losing one game and getting socked with an 8.59 ERA. The end had arrived for the once-storied pitcher, and this time he left the game for good.

After 10 years in the majors, Rusie finished his career with a 246-174 record, posting a 3.07 ERA in 463 games. He completed 393 of the 427 games he started while hurling 30 shutouts. In 3,778.2 innings overall, he struck out 1,950, walked 1,707, and allowed 3,389 hits.

In later years, Rusie, who died in 1942, would not be a name that was listed among baseball's all-time greatest pitchers. Undeniably, though, he would be at the top of the list of those who changed forever the way baseball was played.

2

RUBE WADDELL

WON 10 GAMES IN ONE MONTH

In the early years of the 20th century, it was not unusual for pitchers to work long and often. Some hurled complete games with regularity, even if that meant working well into extra innings. Some pitched on short notice and often with only a few days rest. Some even spent long hours on the mound with sore arms.

There was no better example of the old term "workhorse" than Rube Waddell. The zany southpaw, who toiled during his best years with the Philadelphia Athletics, was a classic example of an old-time hurler. Once he made it to the mound, he usually stayed there for the remainder of the game.

During a big-league career that was cut short by his eccentric personality, Waddell worked in just 10 full seasons (he appeared in three others). During that time, he completed 261 of the 340 games he started, three straight years pitching in well over 300 innings. He also relieved in 67 games.

When he finished his career in 1910, Waddell had a 191-145 record with a 2.16 earned run average that ranks as the sixth-best career mark in history. In 2,961.1 innings pitched, he yielded just 2,460 hits, 803 walks, and struck out 2,316 batters, leading the league in that category in six straight seasons and in

Bob Warrington

seven altogether. In 1904, Waddell set a major league record in strikeouts with 349, a mark that stood until it was broken by Sandy Koufax in 1965.

Waddell was labeled "a hitter's nightmare." Walter Johnson once said that "he had more pitching ability than any man I ever saw." To this, Connie Mack added that the lefty "had the fastest and deepest curve I ever saw." His curve was even better than his fastball, Mack claimed in a statement that was particularly amazing due to the presence of Rube's lightning-like fastball.

Of all the glittering career accomplishments that led to Waddell's induction into the Hall of Fame in 1946, none was more unusual that the record he compiled in 1902 in his first year with the Athletics.

That season, Waddell pitched in 12 games during the month of July, winning 10 of them. No pitcher in big league history has ever won 10 games in one month. It's a feat that far exceeds the boundaries of the imagination, especially in modern times when five-man starting rotations and 100-pitch counts are the norm.

Incredibly, Waddell's July record also included one loss. Three of his wins came while he was pitching in relief. Another game ended in a tie.

Just as amazing, Waddell wasn't even a member of the Athletics until late June.

He had started the season pitching for semipro teams in Illinois and Wisconsin before landing in Los Angeles to hurl for the Loo Loos in the independent and soon-to-be extinct California League. Ultimately, Waddell's elevation to the Athletics added another chapter in what had already been an exotic life.

Born George Edward Waddell in 1876 in Bradford, Pa., his baseball talent was visible at an early age. As a teenager, he pitched in a local semipro league, then for Volant College, where he played but never attended classes.

Rube, a nickname often used to describe farm boys, was signed in 1897 by the National League's Louisville Colonels. He lasted two games before being sent to the minors, where he played for several teams until returning to Louisville in 1899. Over the next three years, Waddell pitched for Louisville, the Pittsburgh Pirates (who had moved from Louisville), and the Chicago Orphans (later the Cubs), posting a combined 28-32 record while leading the National League in 1900 in ERA (2.37) and strikeouts (130).

Along the way, Pittsburgh suspended Waddell for what would become one of his many infractions. He then played briefly at Chicago and pitched in some semipro games, before winding up for a short spell with Milwaukee of the Western League, a team managed by Mack.

By 1902, the American League was one year old, Mack had become manager and part-owner of the Athletics, and Waddell was pitching in Los Angeles. Badly in need of pitching and remembering Rube's superior talents, Mack contacted the hurler, ultimately sending two Pinkerton guards to LA to escort him to Philadelphia.

Waddell's first appearance with the Athletics came on June 26. Now 25 years old, he lost a 7-3 decision to the Baltimore Orioles. At the time, the A's were six games out of first place.

The fortunes of both the A's and Waddell, however, were about to turn around. In his next start, Rube again faced the Orioles at the A's Columbia Park and fired a 2-0 shutout, striking out 13 and allowing just two hits.

Rube made his next start on July 4 against the Washington Senators. It didn't look good when Waddell gave up five runs in the first inning, but the Athletics rallied and Rube rode home with a 12-9 triumph.

Four days later, Waddell assumed a new role. With the A's leading, 9-6, in the fifth inning against the Boston Red Sox, Mack brought Rube in from the bullpen. After the A's scored 12 runs in the sixth, Waddell was taken out. Nevertheless, he was named the winning pitcher in a decision that later was unsuccessfully disputed.

One day later, Waddell was back on the mound against the Red Sox again. This time, he unfurled the most spectacular victory of the streak, working 17 innings to gain a 4-2 decision over Bill Dinneen, who also went the distance. Rube drove home the fourth run after a homer by Monte Cross.

Over a six-day span that followed, Waddell won three more games, defeating Boston, 3-2, Chicago, 9-3, and the White Sox again, 7-6. In 18 days, Rube had won seven games, and the streak was still alive.

On July 21, Waddell was back in his relief role, taking over for Eddie Plank in the eighth inning of a 10-10 game against the Cleveland Indians. Rube got the win when the A's scored in the ninth to gain an 11-10 verdict.

The next day, Waddell was again used in relief against Cleveland. This time, he hurled six scoreless innings to get the win as the A's rallied from a 4-1 deficit to take a 9-4 decision. Waddell had thus won two games in relief on two straight days.

Waddell's final win of the streak came on July 26 when he beat the St. Louis Browns, 3-1. That gave the ace hurler 10 wins in 26 days. He then lost, 3-1, to the Browns, and two days later pitched 10 innings against St. Louis in a game that was called because of darkness with the score tied at 4-4. During Waddell's spree, the Athletics had a 15-8 record for the month.

Rube went on to post a 6-4 record in August, one win being a 1-0 victory in 13 innings that was decided when Waddell tripled and scored on a single by Harry Davis. Rube posted a 9-2 record in September to end the season with a 24-7 mark and 2.05 ERA, leading the A's to their first American League pennant.

Over the next three years, Waddell went on to register marks of 21-16, 25-19, and 26-11, the latter including a league-leading 1.48 ERA. Rube, however, had long-ago established a reputation for his crazy antics. And that hurt his career.

The man who Mack once said was "the atom bomb of baseball long before the atom bomb was discovered," had an unpredictable, childlike personality that helped to turn him into a heavy drinker. Waddell wrestled alligators, tried to teach geese how to skip rope, shot marbles under the stands with children during games, did cartwheels on the mound, ran into the stands and sold hot dogs, led marching bands down the street, once stood in a store window as a mannequin, lived part of his time in Philadelphia in a firehouse, and played pro football and acted in the theater during his playing career. Said to have been married four times, he once went to jail for throwing flatirons at his in-laws. Another time, he shot a friend by accident.

Indeed, Waddell's life was full of craziness. After his last 20-win season, he had two more years with 19 wins, one that came after Mack finally decided he couldn't put up with him anymore and traded him to the Browns. Rube pitched three years in St. Louis before his career ended in 1910, four years before he died.

"Although he was known for his eccentricities," Mack said, "he was more sinned against than a sinner. He may have failed us at times, but I and the other owners of the Athletics owe him much."

Never was that debt more evident than in 1902, when as a newly minted member of the Athletics, Waddell performed the most incredible month that baseball has ever seen.

3

JACK CHESBRO

CAPTURED 41 WINS IN A SINGLE SEASON

The term "Iron Man" was once a popular label in baseball. It was a name used to define pitchers who went beyond the normal rigors of an everyday moundsman. Being called an Iron Man was a special compliment that applied only to the sturdiest of hurlers.

A pitcher had to have stamina to be an Iron Man. He had to have a strong arm, because he had to pitch more often and for longer distances than the average hurler. An Iron Man was the cornerstone of the pitching staff, a guy who could take the mound every couple of days, throw huge numbers of innings every season, and come away with records that went mostly unchallenged.

Iron men were numerous in the early days of big league baseball when pitching staffs included just a couple of hurlers. As time went on, with the sizes of pitching staffs increased and relievers eventually coming on the scene, the term Iron Man became obsolete. For the most part, iron men were no longer needed after the early decades of the 20th century.

Courtesy of the Library of Congress

Courtesy of the Library of Congress

By that time, though, iron men had made their mark on baseball with achievements that still stand in the record book. One of those names still in the book is that of Jack Chesbro, a short but sturdy right-handed hurler.

A 5-9, 180-pound native of North Adams, Massachusetts, Chesbro won 41 games for the New York Highlanders in 1904. That's the highest win total in baseball since the pitching mound was moved back to 60 feet, six inches in 1893.

The 1904 season was a spectacular campaign for Chesbro in many other ways, too. Verifying his description as an Iron Man, he worked in a league-leading total of 454.2 innings, which ranks as the third-highest in modern major league history. He also led the league in winning percentage (.774), games pitched (55), games started (51), and complete games (48), while striking out 239—a team record until broken 74 years later by Ron Guidry—walking just 88, and recording an ERA of 1.82. Chesbro's complete game total ranks as the second-highest in modern history, and his starts is tied for second.

Overall, the man called Happy Jack because of his pleasant and friendly demeanor had put together a season unduplicated in baseball annals and which played a major role in his getting elected to the Hall of Fame in 1946. He was the first Yankees pitcher to gain entry into the baseball shrine.

Chesbro had to toil long and hard to reach Cooperstown. Born in 1874 to a family that spelled its name Cheesbro, Jack pitched for several amateur teams in his early days. One was for a state mental hospital where he worked. While hurling for the team called the Asylums, his talent was discovered and in 1895 he signed a professional contract with Albany of the New York State League.

That season, Chesbro pitched for four different teams. During the season, Albany folded and he went to Johnstown of the same league. While there, the league shut down. He then moved on to Springfield of the Eastern League, but was released and wound up ending the season with a semipro team in Cooperstown.

Over the next few years, Chesbro's jagged career continued with stints at Roanoke of the Virginia League and Richmond of the Atlantic League where he posted a combined 23-15 record in 1898. The following year, he was sold to the Pittsburgh Pirates for $1,500 and as a 25-year-old rookie posted a 6-9 record. That winter, Jack was sent to the Louisville Colonels as part of a 12-player trade that included Honus Wagner. The Colonels, however, were dissolved, as the National League was cut from 12 teams to eight, and Chesbro was returned to the Pirates.

Chesbro then spent three more seasons in Pittsburgh, winning 64 games over that period. In 1901, he went 21-10 while leading the league in winning percentage (.677) and shutouts (six). The next year, Chesbro pitched the Pirates to the National League pennant as he surged to a 28-6 mark, again topping the circuit in winning percentage (.824) and shutouts (eight), which included three in a row. While registering what turned out to be the second-highest win total and second-best ERA (2.17) of his career, Chesbro completed 31 of the 33 games he started and worked in 286.1 innings. At one point, he won 12 straight games.

The pitcher who had now become one of the best in the league, was, however, not content to stay with the Pirates. So, in 1903, he jumped to the New York Highlanders of the two-year-old American League. Within a few years, Chesbro would become the first great pitcher of the team later called the Yankees.

In his first year in Manhattan in what was also New York's first year in the American League, Chesbro posted a 21-15 record for a team with a losing record (72-82). He lost the first game in Highlanders-Yankees history, falling to the Washington Senators, 3-1. Then he won the first home opener with a 6-2 victory over the Senators at Hilltop Park.

The following year, Happy Jack made history. By this time, Chesbro had become one of the first pitchers to throw a spitball. With long fingers and an overhand delivery, he was a natural for the pitch. Eventually, he could tell his catcher how far the ball was going to drop. It was said that Jack tossed the wettest ball ever thrown. That, however, had its drawbacks because a wet ball caused frequent errors by his teammates and was prone to wild pitches and hit batters.

Nevertheless, while becoming one of baseball's foremost spitball hurlers, Chesbro, whose arsenal also included an outstanding fastball and what was then called a "slowball," was about to etch his name in the record books.

Chesbro began the 1904 season spectacularly. In his first game, he gave up a leadoff single, then allowed no hits the rest of the way in a 2-0 win over the Washington Nationals. Jack started off with four wins in seven decisions. But then lighting struck. Beginning in early May, he won a then-record-setting 14 games in a row, including a victory on the Fourth of July to top it off.

From then on, Chesbro won 23 of his next 32 decisions, along the way completing 30 straight games before being knocked out by the Chicago White Sox on August 10. He won nine of 11 games in September. His 41st victory came on October 7 when, pitching with two days rest, he beat the Boston Pilgrims, 3-2, to send the Highlanders into first place with a half-game lead over Boston.

Jack started again the next day, but got knocked out for only the third time all season in a game won by Boston, 13-2. The Highlanders dropped out of first place, falling one and one-half games behind the Pilgrims.

Two days later, Chesbro started again in the fourth game of the five-game series. The results put an unfortunate stain on his spectacular season.

New York took a 2-0 lead into the seventh inning, but two errors allowed the Pilgrims to tie the score. Then in the ninth inning with two outs and a runner on third base, Chesbro uncorked a spitter that went over the head of catcher Jack Kleinow. The wild pitch allowed the runner to score, and Boston won the game and clinched the pennant.

Some years later, when a campaign led by Chesbro's wife, Mabel, attempted to overrule the wild pitch call, saying the ball should've been caught, Highlanders shortstop Kid Elberfeld was asked about the pitch. "Hell," he said. "The ball went so far over Kleinow's head that he couldn't have caught it if he'd been on a stepladder."

Despite the pitch, Chesbro had racked up some glittering numbers. He had hurled a one-hitter, a two-hitter, a three-hitter, eight four-hitters, and six five-hitters. He had become the first pitcher to lead both the National and American Leagues in winning percentage in a single season. He won three games in relief. And he established himself as one of the great baseball workhorses of all time.

The following season, Chesbro posted a 19-15 record and then went 23-17 in 1906, while leading the league in appearances (49) and games started (42). He slid to 10-10 in 1907 when hampered by an ankle injury, then dropped down to 14-20 the following year as the Highlanders lost 103 games and plummeted to last place.

After going 0-4 early in the 1909 season, Chesbro was traded to Boston, where he pitched in just one game before calling it quits after 11 years in the big leagues. During that time, Happy Jack registered a 198-132 record with a 2.68 ERA. He started 332 and completed 260 of the 392 games in which he pitched, giving up 2,642 hits in 2,896.2 innings. Chesbro struck out 1,265 and walked 690.

4

ED REULBACH

HURLED TWO SHUTOUTS IN ONE DAY

They hardly ever play doubleheaders anymore. Doubleheaders were once important elements of the baseball schedule, but they have now become something used only in desperate circumstances, namely when a game has been cancelled and there is simply no other way to play it except to double up on the same day of another game.

Even rarer is one pitcher starting both games of a doubleheader. That hasn't occurred in more than a half of a century, and it's highly unlikely that it will ever happen again. In an era when pitch counts have extinguished virtually every demonstration of stamina on the mound, such unusual feats today would be considered heresy.

Considered even more diabolical by today's standards, though, is the feat performed by Ed Reulbach way back before pitch counts and relief pitchers became fashionable. Not only did Big Ed start both games of a doubleheader, but he pitched complete game shutouts in each one of them.

It happened on September 26, 1908, with Reulbach hurling the Chicago Cubs to twinbill victories over the Brooklyn Superbas at Washington Park. In two games that lasted a combined time of two hours and 52 minutes before

a crowd of 15,000, the 6-1, 190-pound right-hander won 5-0 and 3-0 while allowing a total of eight hits.

Although it was not uncommon in those days for pitchers to work both games of a twinbill, no one had ever pitched shutouts in each contest. Reulbach's astounding achievement has not and never will be matched.

It had been clear dating back to his years as a teenager that Reulbach was going to be an outstanding baseball player. Born in Detroit, Michigan in 1882, by the time he was 17, Ed was playing minor league baseball under an assumed name at Sedalia of the Class D Missouri Valley League. He then enrolled at the University of Notre Dame, where he starred as a pitcher and outfielder for three years while continuing to play at Sedalia.

After meeting a girl from Vermont, Reulback transferred to the University of Vermont, where he spent his senior year. He then signed a contract with the Cubs for an amount that one newspaper said "would take the breath away from an average person." Four days later, after traveling to New York with a group of friends, he made his big league debut.

The 22-year-old hurler completed his rookie season in 1905 with an 18-14 record and a 1.42 ERA, the second-lowest for a rookie in major league history. In one game, he pitched all 20 innings in a 2-1 victory over the Philadelphia Phillies. Ed completed 28 of the 29 games he started while working in an amazing total (particularly for a rookie) of 292 innings.

Reulbach went on to post 19-4, 17-4, 24-7, and 19-10 records over the next four seasons, leading the National League in winning percentage three times and three times posting an ERA under 2.00. By then, Big Ed had become one of the most dominant pitchers in baseball and, with the New York Giants star Christy Mathewson, was considered one of the top hurlers in the game. He was, said an article in *Baseball Magazine*, "one of the greatest pitchers that the National League ever produced."

Owner of one of baseball's all-time best curveballs, Reulbach, whose delivery featured a high leg kick, but whose control was often bothered by a weak left eye that he chose never to reveal during his career, had some brilliant outings during his early years. In 1906, he hurled the first and one of only five all-time World Series one-hitters with a 7-1 win over the Chicago White Sox. That season, while posting a 1.65 ERA, the clean-living hurler threw 12 games in which he allowed five or fewer hits during the regular season.

In 1906, he gave up just 5.33 hits per nine innings, the fifth-best ratio in big league history. He also had a 17-game winning streak during the 1906–07 seasons, in 1908 tossed 44 scoreless innings, and in 1909 had a 14-game winning streak during which he gave up only 14 runs, fired five shutouts, and beat the Pittsburgh Pirates in their first game at Forbes Field.

All of these were history-making events at the time. But in 1908, Reulbach achieved his greatest feat with his two shutouts in one doubleheader.

That season, the Cubs were locked in a tight pennant race with the Pirates and New York Giants. All three had led the league at various times during the season, and on the morning of September 26, only a half-game separated the three teams.

By then, the Cubs' pitching staff, which also included Three Finger Brown (ultimately a 29-game winner), was beset by injuries and was totally worn out. The team that featured the famed "Tinker to Evers to Chance" infield was fighting desperately to hold on to its miniscule lead and capture its third straight National League pennant. But among the other starters, both Brown and Orval Overall had started twice in the previous four games.

Up stepped Reulbach into the breach. Manager Frank Chance had planned to start Big Ed in the first game, but had no idea who would work the nightcap. "I'll pitch both games," Reulbach suggested. Chance readily accepted the proposal.

In the first game, Reulback allowed five hits, struck out seven, and walked one to gain a 5-0 victory. In a game that stood at 1-0 entering the seventh inning, the Cubs lashed 10 hits, three each by Harry Steinfeldt and Johnny Kling, while the Superbas committed four errors. The game was completed in one hour and 40 minutes.

In the second game, Reulback pitched a three-hitter while capturing a 3-0 decision. He struck out four and walked one in a game that was played in one hour and 12 minutes. The Cubs, who had only five hits, including two by Kling, held only a 1-0 lead until the eighth inning.

Even though the Superbas were a team with no .300 hitters and who lost 101 games that year, Reulback was in the history books. In the midst of a streak in which he pitched 44 straight scoreless innings, he added to his laurels five days later when he blanked the Cincinnati Reds, 6-0. Two days after that, he ended his season with a 16-2 decision over the Reds and his 24th win of the year.

The Cubs and Giants finished the season in a tie for first place. In a special playoff, Chicago captured a 4-2 decision over Mathewson to advance to its third straight World Series. With Reulbach exhausted and largely ineffective in one start and one relief appearance, the Cubs went on to capture the Series in five games against the Detroit Tigers, thereby winning their second straight Series and last one in club history.

For Reulback, it was his most brilliant season. Along with winning 24 games during the season, he registered career highs in games (46), games started (35), innings pitched (297.2), and shutouts (seven).

Reulback would have one more stellar season before starting to decline. After his 19-10 campaign in 1909, he posted a record of 12-8 in 1910, a mark largely attributable to time spent with his seriously ill son. He then went 16-9 and 10-6 over the next two years. Then, during the 1913 season, he was dealt to Brooklyn for cash and a second-rate pitcher named Eddie Stack. Reulback finished the year with an 8-9 mark. He went 11-18 in 256 innings in 1914 before moving to the Federal League in 1915, when he fashioned a 21-10 record for the Newark Peps. Ed won the last game in Federal League history when he beat the Baltimore Terrapins, 6-0.

Back in the National League in 1916, Reulback spent that year and part of the next with the Boston Braves, recording a 7-7 log in 26 games. After getting released early in 1917, he spent the rest of his final season in baseball with the International League's Providence Grays.

When he retired, Reulback had posted a 182-106 record with a 2.28 ERA in 398 games. In 2,632.2 innings, he allowed 2,117 hits, struck out 1,137, and walked 892. Over his 13 years in the majors, Reulback, who later earned a law degree from Columbia University, gave up fewer hits than innings pitched each season. Opposing batters had a combined average of .224 off Ed during his career. He fired two one-hitters, six two-hitters, and 13 three-hitters

"He was five years ahead of his time in baseball thought," former teammate Johnny Evers once said.

As for Reulback's achievement in 1908, there was no allowance for time. It was a feat that would be the most momentous of its kind for all ages.

5

CHRISTY MATHEWSON

TOSSED THREE SHUTOUTS IN ONE WORLD SERIES

t is a foregone conclusion that Christy Mathewson was one of the greatest pitchers of all time. Only two other pitchers in baseball history won more games than the sturdy right-hander. Additionally, Mathewson holds a fistfull of pitching records that will never be broken.

During a 17-year career spent mostly with the New York Giants, Mathewson won 373 games, trailing only Cy Young (511) and Walter Johnson (416), and tying with Grover Cleveland Alexander. He won 20 or more games 13 times in a row, a major league record, and 30 or more games four times. He pitched more than 300 innings in 11 seasons. In five of those, his earned run average was under 2.00.

Elected to the Hall of Fame in the first class in 1936, Mathewson holds the modern National League record for most wins (37) in one season. He threw two no-hitters, won 14 games by 1-0 scores, twice won nine games in a single month, and once completed a game using just 67 pitches. He hurled 80 shutouts, third on the league's all-time list, his 2.13 career ERA ranks fifth, and his lifetime winning percentage of .665 places sixth. In 4,780 innings, Mathewson,

who lost 188 games during his career, walked just 844 batters while allowing 4,218 hits and striking out 2,502. He led the National League in strikeouts and ERA each five times, and in wins and shutouts four times apiece.

"He had everything—strength, intelligence, courage, and willingness," Giants manager John McGraw once said. "In addition to his physical ability, he had the perfect temperament for a ballplayer. I give a large share of the credit for my success with the Giants to Mathewson."

Big Six, as he was sometimes called—a name that was said to have been given to Christy because that's what New Yorkers called their biggest and fastest fire engines—did not have great speed. He relied more on his excellent control and uncanny knack of learning all there was to know about opposing hitters.

"A pitcher needs very little power, provided he has control and uses his strength intelligently," Mathewson claimed. "Great speed is always prized and so is a sharp-breaking curve. If these go with good control and good judgement, they are immensely valuable.

"Anybody's best pitch is the one batters aren't hitting that day," Mathewson added. "I always tried to learn about the hitters. Anytime someone got a hit off me, I made a mental note of the pitch. He'd never see that one again."

Mathewson was a native of Factoryville, Pennsylvania, where he was born in 1880. He attended Bucknell College for three years. There, he pitched and was an outstanding fullback and drop-kicker on the football team.

While at Bucknell, Mathewson signed his first pro contract in 1899 with Taunton of the New England League. One year later, having compiled a 20-2 record by June for Norfolk of the Virginia League, the 6-1½, 195-pounder signed with the New York Giants and went 0-3 before being returned to Norfolk.

That winter, the Cincinnati Reds claimed they had drafted Mathewson off the Norfolk roster, but then traded him back to the Giants for aging pitcher Amos Rusie. Meanwhile, Mathewson signed a multi-year $1,200 contract with the Philadelphia Athletics of the new American League. When the Giants claimed they would blackball Christy if he ever tried to return to them, the pitcher relented and rejoined them. He then settled in with the Giants, and in his first full season in 1901 posted a 20-17 record.

Two seasons later, Matty launched consecutive years of 30, 33, and 31 wins, pitching two no-hitters along the way. In the last of those three seasons, Big Six accomplished one of the greatest feats in the annals of big league pitching. It came in 1905, a year in which he led the league in wins (31), strikeouts (206), and ERA (1.27).

The first World Series had been played in 1903, but when the Giants won the National League pennant the following year, McGraw refused to send his team to the fall classic because of his and team owner John Brush's bitter dislike for the American League. In 1905, however, with the Giants winning 105 games and with the nastiness having subsided, the Giants decided to play in the Series.

That year, manager and part-owner Connie Mack had led the Athletics to their second American League pennant. With 92 wins, the Philadelphia club was a powerhouse. The Series figured to be a titanic clash between two of the greatest teams of the early 1900s. "It should be a fight to the bitter end," the Philadelphia *Public Ledger* proclaimed.

The Series would also become the stage for Mathewson's mammoth achievement. It was a feat that no one else has ever accomplished.

Other pitchers have won three games in one World Series. But nobody except Big Six ever fired three shutout victories in a World Series. Amazingly, all five games of the Series were shutouts.

Mathewson's streak began in the opener on October 9 at Philadelphia's Columbia Park. The Giants wore black uniforms in an attempt by McGraw to intimidate the less haughty A's. When the teams exchanged lineups before the game, the Giants manager was presented by A's captain Lave Cross with a package containing a model of a white elephant. The gift was intended as a rebuke to McGraw's disdainful remark that Mack had a "white elephant on his hands." During the meeting with the umpires, McGraw unwrapped the package and mockingly placed the elephant on his head. Forever after, it would become the symbol of Philadelphia Athletics teams.

Mathewson needed only 10 pitches to retire the Athletics in the first two innings. In the third inning, he was hit in the stomach by a hard line drive off the bat of Socks Seybold. After throwing the hitter out at first to end the inning, he retired to the dugout for some first aid. The next inning, Ossee Schreckengost reached base on an error before Topsy Hartsel got the first A's hit in the fifth.

By the end of the game, only one Athletics hitter had reached third base as the Giants won easily, beating Eddie Plank, a 25-game winner during the season, 3-0. Christy allowed four hits while striking out six and walking none. The game was played in one hour and 46 minutes with 17,955 jammed inside the ballpark and thousands of others perched outside on roofs, the tops of carriages, and in nearby trees.

Moving the next day to the Polo Grounds in New York, the A's won Game Two with Chief Bender tossing a four-hitter to beat Joe McGinnity by another 3-0 score. Two days later, following a rained out game at Columbia Park, which gave him an extra day of rest, Christy took the mound for Game Three.

Again, he pitched a four-hitter while striking out eight, walking one, and hitting one batter. Before a crowd of only 10,991, the Giants took advantage of five A's errors and seven unearned runs to capture a 9-0 victory. First baseman Dan McGann drove in four runs with two singles and a double while the Giants clinched the decision with a five-run fifth inning.

Back at the Polo Grounds on October 13, McGinnity kept the shutout streak alive with a five-hit, 1-0 victory. Plank fired a four-hitter, but an unearned run in the fourth inning gave him the loss. That set the stage for Game Five the next day at the Polo Grounds with Bender facing Mathewson.

McGraw had decided that Matty, who didn't want to take an additional day off, should pitch with just one full day of rest, theorizing that the Giants could clinch the Series and not have to return to Philadelphia where "Blue Laws" prohibited games from being played on Sunday. Mathewson had pitched before on such short notice, and McGraw was sure he could do it again.

He was right. With 24,187, the largest crowd of the Series, packing the stands, some standing 10 deep behind ropes in the outfield, Mathewson beat the Athletics, 2-0, while allowing six hits. It took Mathewson just one hour and 35 minutes to zip through the A's lineup. He struck out four, walked none, and retired the last 10 batters.

In three games, Mathewson pitched 27 innings, striking out 18 and walking only one. Only one Athletics player reached third base in the three games. The Giants players had no tough fielding plays throughout. "He [Matty] was the man who sparkled like a diamond in a coal mine," one writer declared. *The New York Times* wrote that "New York possesses the pitching marvel of the century."

From that glorious feat, Mathewson went on to a career that was led by his 1908 campaign, when he posted a 37-11 record with a 1.43 ERA while appearing in 56 games, starting 44, completing 34, and hurling in 390.2 innings with 259 strikeouts and 12 shutouts, all league-leading figures.

6

CY YOUNG

WON 20 OR MORE GAMES IN 15 SEASONS

I t is a well-known fact that Cy Young is the winningest pitcher in baseball history.

The bulging right-hander won 511 games during a career that spanned 22 years in the big leagues.

No one comes even close to matching Young in number of victories. Walter Johnson is next, but he is nearly 100 below Young at 416. Next in line are Christy Mathewson and Grover Cleveland Alexander, but they are even farther back with 373 apiece.

Clearly, Young is in a class by himself. But how did he get there? What did this member of the first Hall of Fame group of inductees accomplish to register such an overwhelming number of wins?

Of course, he had to win games. But the way he did it earns a place among baseball's most amazing feats.

Young won 20 or more games 15 times, including nine in a row, and more than 30 games five times. He pitched at least 400 innings in five different seasons, and went above 300 frames 16 times, including 15 in a row. He holds

several other all-time records: 7,356 total innings pitched; most years with 200 or more innings pitched (19); most years with 300 or more frames worked (16); 749 complete games; and 815 starts.

The man who was born in 1867 on a farm in Gilmore, Ohio, was a workhorse in every sense of the word. The 6-2, 210-pounder also kept himself in marvelous physical condition. That and his blazing fastball are what helped to bring him his records.

"A man who isn't willing to work from dreary morn till weary eve shouldn't think about pitching," Young once said. To that he added, "I had a good arm and legs. You have to have good legs to pitch, and I always took care of them. When I would go to spring training, I would never touch a ball for the first three weeks. Just do a lot of walking and running. I never did any unnecessary throwing. I figured the old arm had just so many throws in it, and there wasn't any use wasting them."

Young claimed he never took more than three to four minutes to warm up before a game. The few times he served as a relief pitcher, he never warmed up in the bullpen; instead, he went straight from the dugout to the mound.

As a young pitcher, Young was noted for his sizzling fastball. Later in his career, he developed several variations of a baffling curve ball.

"I had good control," he said. "I aimed to make the batter hit the ball, and I made as few pitches as possible."

With his outstanding control, he walked only 1,217 batters, which amounted to about one every six innings of work. He struck out a career total of 2,803 while allowing 7,092 hits and tossing 76 shutouts.

Young was also a man of many "firsts," having fired three no-hitters, including the first perfect game since the mound was moved to 60 feet, six inches. He was the American League's first Triple Crown winner and also hurled the first pitch in World Series history. Ultimately, his spectacular career was recognized in a way unlike that of any other major league player when in 1956, one year after his death, Major League Baseball chose to honor the top pitcher each year with the Cy Young Award.

Denton True Young dropped out of school after sixth grade to work on the family farm. He played sandlot ball until signing in 1889 with Canton, Ohio, of the Tri-State League, where he pitched for one season, posting a 15-15 record with a fastball that he said "almost tore the boards off the grandstand" when they were hit. The damage was said to make the area look like it had been hit by a cyclone, which then became Young's nickname until the media shortened it to "Cy."

Purchased for $500 in 1890 by the National League's Cleveland Spiders, the 23-year-old Young made his major league debut with a three-hit shutout over the Chicago Colts. He won both games of a doubleheader on the last day of the season, and wound up with a 9-7 record for the year.

His rookie season served as a warmup for what lay ahead. Although the mound was just 50 feet from home plate until 1893 (Young was one of the reasons it was set back because of his withering speed), he began his amazing streak with a 27-22 record in his sophomore season. He added a 36-12 mark in 1892 while working a career-high 453 innings with a 1.93 ERA, the first of six seasons when that figure would be below 2.00.

In 1893, it hardly mattered to Young that the mound had been relocated. He logged a 34-16 record, then went 26-21 and 35-10 over the next two years. In 1895, he won three games against the Baltimore Orioles in the Temple Cup, the post-game series played in the National League between the first- and second-place teams.

While going 28-15 in 1896, Young lost a no-hitter when Ed Delahanty of the Philadelphia Phillies smacked a two-out single in the ninth inning. Farmer Young, as he was sometimes called, got his first no-hitter the following season when he struck out three and walked none in a 6-0 victory over the Cincinnati Reds. During the game, the Reds' Bug Holliday hit two smashes that were ruled singles, but the calls were changed to errors before the game ended.

Over the next two years, Young, who liked to work every two or three days, continued his impressive pace with records of 21-19 and 25-13. Then in 1899, Spiders owner Frank Robinson bought the St. Louis Browns, and moved some of his players, including Young, from Cleveland to his new team. Young notched a record of 26-16 for the team called the "Perfectos," but his 20-win streak was broken the following year when he went 19-19.

When the American League was formed in 1901, Young jumped across the lines to sign for a salary of $3,500 with the Boston Americans. That year, he became the league's first Triple Crown winner with 33 wins, a 1.62 ERA, and 158 strikeouts. He followed that with 32-11 and 28-9 marks. In the first World Series in 1903, he threw the first pitch of the first game against the Pittsburgh Pirates.

Young lost that game, but went on to win his next two starts as Boston took the Series, five games to three.

In 1904, in the midst of a 26-16 record and another Boston pennant (there was no World Series that year), Young pitched the first perfect game since the mound was pushed back when he beat the Philadelphia Athletics and rival

Rube Waddell, 3-0, before a crowd of 10,267 at Huntington Avenue Grounds. In a game that took one hour and 25 minutes, Young struck out six. A's manager Connie Mack later called it "the finest-pitched game I have ever seen."

The perfect game was part of streaks set by Young of 45 consecutive shutout innings pitched and 25.1 innings pitched without allowing a hit. Although broken since then, the records stood for many years thereafter.

In subsequent years, Young posted 18-19 and 13-21 records for Boston teams that had dropped precipitously in the standings, then bounced back with 21-15 and 21-11 marks. At the age of 41, just one month after firing a one-hitter, Young pitched his third no-hitter in 1908, defeating the New York Highlanders, 8-0, before just 2,000 at Hilltop Park. A first inning walk kept Young from hurling another perfect game, but the batter was thrown out trying to steal second and Cy wound up facing just 27 hitters.

Cy was traded back to Cleveland in 1909, where he joined a team that had become known as the "Naps." He went 19-15 that year, but with his career nearing an end, dropped to 7-10 in 1910, although that year he won his 500th game when he beat the Washington Senators.

Getting just seven starts, Young went just 3-4 in 1911, and in mid-August he was released by the Naps. He then joined the Boston Braves but could only post a 4-5 record in 11 starts. On September 22, he beat the Pirates, 1-0, for his 511th career win.

The following year, Young tried to hang on with the Braves, but hampered by a relentless sore arm, he had nothing left. He retired in late May without having appeared in a single game that season.

Young was 45 years old. With his retirement came a record filled with magnificent seasons that will doubtless never be broken.

7

MORDECAI BROWN

PITCHED WITH ONLY THREE FINGERS

U nder normal conditions, it takes five fingers to throw a baseball from the pitchers' mound. Each finger has a special purpose, and although the way they grip the ball may vary among pitchers, no hurler with any designs on being successful would think of leaving one or two of his fingers out of the action.

And then there was Mordecai Peter Centennial Brown, so named because he was born in the centennial year of 1876. Brown was an astonishing exception to the theory that all pitching hands must contain five usable fingers.

Brown had only three usable fingers on his pitching hand. Accordingly, he had to hold the ball in a vastly different way than full-fingered hurlers. But for Brown, it was no particular liability. He could throw a ball as well as anybody in the game.

Nicknamed "Three Finger," Brown posted one of the finest records of his era. During 14 seasons in the big leagues, he recorded a 239-129 mark while appearing in 481 games. Brown's 2.06 career earned run average ranks as the sixth lowest in baseball history, and his 55 shutouts ties him for 14th place on the all-time list. Brown, who started 332 games, was also later credited with 48 saves.

Courtesy of the Library of Congress

Such a record was more than enough to get Brown elected to the Hall of Fame in 1949. Considering what he had to deal with, the 5-10, 175-pound moundsman probably could've walked into the Hall on merit alone.

Brown was seven years old when fate struck a horrendous blow. A native of Nyesville, Indiana, Brown was playing in the fields at his uncle's farm when his brother came along driving a corn shredder. Somehow, the youngster's right hand got stuck in the shredder. When he managed to pull it out, the index finger of his right hand was so badly damaged that it had to be amputated, leaving just a stub above the knuckle of his hand. Moreover, both his thumb and little finger were seriously injured, with the latter so badly hurt that it was of no use to Brown the rest of his life.

To make matters worse, just a few weeks after the accident, the young boy, wearing his right hand in a cast, was chasing a hog and fell down. The third and fourth fingers of Brown's right hand were both broken. Although the breaks eventually healed, each finger was twisted and would sit permanently bent on Brown's mostly disabled hand.

Life, however, sometimes takes unusual turns. In Brown's case, the injuries that he suffered as a boy played a defining role in his future as a man. Perhaps

Brown would have been a great pitcher anyway, but his success was ensured by his ability to utilize his handicap.

During his big league career, Brown had to put extra pressure on the ball with his middle finger. The unusual grip allowed him to throw a sharp-breaking curve that spun straight downward like it was rolling off a ledge. The pitch was enormously effective against both right-handed and left-handed batters.

"It gives me a bigger dip," Brown would say. When asked how he could pitch with such a handicap, the hurler said, "I don't know. I've never done it any other way."

Brown did not have a blazing fastball. But it was good enough to keep batters on edge, and he had excellent control. In 3,172.1 innings, he walked just 673 batters while striking out 1,375.

He was also an outstanding fielder who was particularly good at fielding bunts, and he was smart and a hard worker. "He had plenty of nerve, ability, and the willingness to work at all times under any conditions," said second baseman and teammate Johnny Evers. "Crowds never bothered him either. There was never a finer character—charitable and friendly to his foes and ever willing to help a youngster breaking in."

When Brown started playing baseball after his injuries healed, he was a third baseman. But while playing for a semipro team in Coxville, Indiana, Brown got his chance to pitch when the team's regular hurler was injured.

Brown's uncanny ability soon landed him a pro contract with Terre Haute in the Three-I League. He posted a 23-8 record in 1901, then followed that with a 27-15 mark with Omaha of the Western League. After the 1902 season, Brown was purchased by the St. Louis Cardinals. He went 9-13 in his rookie year for a last-place team that won only 43 games, but impressed Chicago Cubs manager Frank Selee so much that he persuaded his bosses to send ace pitcher Jack Taylor to the Cardinals in a four-player trade for the 25-year-old hurler. It was often reported that the Cards felt that Brown's disability would keep him from becoming a first-rate hurler.

With the Cubs, Brown disproved that theory, quickly establishing his worthiness. Called Three Finger by fans and press, but Brownie or Miner by friends and teammates because he had worked in a mine as a teenager, the solid right-hander posted a 15-10 record with a 1.84 ERA in 1904.

It was the start of a spectacular run by Brown. In 1905, he moved his record up to 18-12. Then, starting in 1906, he began a streak that placed him among the best hurlers in baseball. Brown posted records of 26-6, 20-6, 29-9, 27-9, 25-13, and 21-11. His 1.04 ERA in 1906 was the third-lowest since the pitching mound was moved back to 60 feet, six inches from home plate. His ERAs over the next four years were 1.39, 1.47, 1.31, and 1.86.

Twice Brown pitched in more than 300 innings, leading the league in 1909 with 342.2 innings pitched. That year, he also led the league in games (50) and starts (32). In 1910, he ranked at the top in starts (27), and in 1911 he led in games (53).

While teaming with the famed infield of "Tinker to Evers to Chance," Brown spearheaded a standout pitching staff that led Chicago to National League pennants in 1906, 1907, 1908, and 1910. The 1906 Cubs set an all-time major league record with 116 wins (36 losses), while the 1907 and 1908 Chicago clubs won the World Series.

Brown fired a two-hitter to beat the Chicago White Sox, 1-0, in Game Four of the 1906 Series, but lost both the first and sixth games as the Cubs bowed four games to two. Three Finger blanked the Detroit Tigers, 2-0, with a seven-hitter in the fifth and deciding game in 1907, then won twice in 1908 over the Tigers, earning one decision with two innings of relief in Game One and the other in Game Four with a four-hit, 3-0 victory. In 1910, Brown won Game Four with two innings of relief in a 4-3 victory over the Philadelphia Athletics in the Cubs' only win of the Series. He took the loss as a starter in the second and fifth games. Overall, Brown finished with a 5-4 record and a 2.81 ERA in nine World Series games.

Among Brown's other noteworthy feats were his legendary battles with the New York Giants' Christy Mathewson. The two arch rivals met 24 times. Brown won 13 of those games, including at one point nine in a row. In one game that Brown lost, both pitchers were hurling no-hitters after eight innings. In the ninth, however, two hits by the Giants gave them and Mathewson a 1-0 victory.

In another famous game in 1908, the Giants and Cubs were tied for first place when the two met after the season in a replay of an earlier battle in which the Giants' Fred Merkle had failed to touch second base while the potential winning run scored. With the run nullified and the game ruled a 1-1 tie after nine innings, the battle had to be replayed. Before a screaming mob at the Polo Grounds, Jack Pfiester started for the Cubs because Brown had pitched in 11 of the previous 14 games. But when Pfiester was kayoed in the first inning, Brown entered the game and allowed just four hits the rest of the way as Chicago beat the Giants and Mathewson, 4-2, to win the pennant.

Brown's last 20-win season came in 1911. Then, after suffering an arm injury, he slid to 5-6. The following year, he was traded to the Reds and went 11-12. In 1914, Brown jumped to the Federal League, where he spent two years, pitching for teams in St. Louis and Chicago and managing the former, while registering a 29-14 record on the mound.

Three Finger returned to the Cubs in 1916 and pitched in just 12 games, posting a 2-3 record. In his final start at the age of 39, he faced Mathewson, by then the manager of the Reds and also making his last start. The 36-year-old Matty got the win as the two old rivals sputtered through a 10-8 game.

8

WALTER JOHNSON

COMPILED AN ERA UNDER 2.00 11 TIMES

There is nothing unusual about starting pitchers giving up two or more earned runs in every game. It happens all the time. Always did. Always will.

Since the 1920s, pitchers who led their leagues in earned run average nearly always allowed more than two runs per game. In recent times, when shutouts have become virtually nonexistent and complete games are an extreme rarity, even the steady parade of pitchers who only work six innings per game almost always give up at least three earned runs in every outing.

Over the years, starting pitchers whose ERA is less than 2.00 in a given season are about as unheard of as 10-man pitching staffs. Only Bob Gibson, with a 1.12 ERA in 1968, has done it in the past 90 years.

This is why the record of Walter Johnson is so phenomenal. Over a 13-year period, Johnson recorded earned run averages of less than 2.00 11 times. Since the mound was set back to 60 feet, six inches, no one else has even come close to doing that.

True, the record was compiled in the deadball era before 1920, when home runs and high-scoring games were highly unusual and many pitchers posted ERAs of less than 2.00 for one season. But to do it 11 times is a remarkable feat.

Johnson's record ran from his rookie year in 1907 though 1919. He had a low of 1.09 in 1913. His high during that period was 1.89.

Of course, it helped that "The Big Train" was a prolific tosser of shutouts. Baseball's all-time leader in that category, he fired 110 shutouts over a 21-year career in which he appeared in 802 games, starting 666 and completing 531. Johnson also lost 26 games by 1-0 scores (while winning 38).

One of the hardest throwers in the game, the 6-foot, one-inch, 200-pound right-hander held the major league record for most strikeouts (3,509) in a career, a mark that stood for 62 years before it was broken by Nolan Ryan. On his way to becoming a member of the first group elected to the Hall of Fame in 1936, Johnson posted a 417-279 career record with a 2.17 ERA. He ranks second behind Cy Young as baseball's all-time leader in wins. Incredibly, Johnson's win-loss record included a 40-30 record in relief and with what many years later was calculated as 34 saves.

Johnson pitched throughout his career with the Washington Senators, a team that was often stationed in the lower regions of the American League standings. Nevertheless, Walter led the league in strikeouts 12 times, in shutouts seven times, in wins and complete games each six times, and in innings pitched and ERA five times apiece. Over a two-year period from 1912 to 1913, he posted a record of 68-19 in 98 games.

An extremely modest gentleman, Johnson always shared the credit for his success with others. "I guess I was lucky," he said. During his career, he "had five corking-good catchers."

While winning two Most Valuable Player (called Chalmers) awards (1913, 1924) and three triple crowns, Johnson pitched in 300 or more innings an incredible nine straight times. He led the league in strikeouts eight times in a row and 12 times overall. Twice he won more than 30 games in one season, recording a high of 36 in 1913. Once, he fired three shutouts against the New York Yankees in four days, hurling a four-hitter the first day, then a three-hitter followed by a two-hitter.

Johnson's blazing fastball, one of the fastest of all time and thrown with nearly a sidearm motion, was his trademark pitch. "I throw as hard as I can when I think I have to throw as hard as I can," he once said. As a product of this theory he whiffed as many as 313 batters in one season (1910).

"You can't hit what you can't see," Yankees outfielder Ping Bodie once said about Johnson's fastball. Ty Cobb said that Johnson's fireball "hissed with danger." And Babe Ruth once argued about a called strike, claiming "it sounded a bit low."

"I'm not ashamed to admit that I used to blink my eyes when I first saw Johnson's speed," claimed noted umpire Billy Evans. "He was just unbelievably fast. On dark days, ballplayers used to hope that the game would be over before they had to face him again."

Johnson also had magnificent control. One season, he walked 38 batters in 346 innings of work. Altogether, he issued base on balls to 1,363 hitters while pitching 5,914.1 innings. In his prime, Johnson also always allowed far fewer hits than innings pitched. For instance, he yielded 232 hits in 346 innings in 1913 and 241 hits in 326 frames in 1918.

Stack his record against his team's place in the standings, and it can be clearly stated that Johnson was the greatest pitcher in baseball history. During his time in Washington, he played with 10 second-division teams, including two that finished in last place, five that placed seventh, and all that were largely inept and prone to errors and other mistakes. Sixty-five of his losses came when the Nats were shut out. Johnson also pitched for 11 first division teams, two of them eventual pennant winners and one a World Series victor.

Johnson's pitching career began in high school in Olinda, California, near Los Angeles, where his parents had moved after he was born in Humboldt, Kansas in 1887. After high school, he got a job that paid him $75 per month to pitch and dig potholes for a telephone company in Idaho. In his second year there, Johnson was spotted by the Senators. Despite attempts by the Pittsburgh Pirates and Detroit Tigers to sign him, he inked a contract with Washington that gave him a $100 bonus and a salary of $350 per month.

It didn't take Johnson long to launch his sub-2.00 ERA record.

With no minor league experience, he posted a 1.88 ERA in 110.1 innings in his first season in the majors in 1907. The following year, he had a 1.65 mark in 256.1 innings while appearing in 36 games. The Big Train would go on to pitch in 35 or more games for 12 straight years and in 16 seasons altogether.

Johnson burst fully into the spotlight in 1910 when he rang up a 25-17 mark while leading the league with career highs in games started (42), complete games (38), strikeouts (313), and innings pitched (370). While also leading the league in games pitched with 45, he posted a 1.36 ERA.

In the following two years, Johnson had ERAs of 1.90 (25-13 record in 322.1 innings) and 1.39 (32-12 in 369 innings) in a year in which he recorded 16 wins in a row. Then in 1913, while registering a brilliant 36-7 record, which included 55.1 consecutive scoreless innings pitched, his ERA plunged to a career-low 1.14 during 346 innings of work. It would be the lowest ERA until Gibson's.

The Big Train, also nicknamed Barney because his fastball resembled the speed of Barney Oldfield's race cars, then posted ERAs of 1.72 (28-18 record in 371.2 innings), 1.55 (27-13, 336.2), and 1.90 (25-20, 369.2). A 2.21 ERA (23-16, 326) interrupted his sub-2.00 streak, but Johnson bounced back in 1918 with a 1.27 (23-13, 326), then followed that with a 1.49 (20-14, 290.1).

Johnson, who was the starting pitcher in 14 season openers, winning nine, including seven shutouts, would not have any more sub-2.00 ERA marks. By 1920, his arm was becoming tired and increasingly sore, and his performances on the mound began to slip.

But he did pitch a no-hitter in a 1-0 win over the Boston Red Sox in 1920 in a game in which he struck out 10 before a scant crowd of 3,000 at Fenway Park. It was Walter's eighth and last win of the season.

Then, in the midst of winning in double figures in each of the next six years, Johnson wound up with 23-7 and 20-7 records for Washington's pennant-winning teams in 1924 and 1925.

In 1924, Johnson lost two games in the World Series against the New York Giants, including the opener in 12 innings, but came back to get the clinching win in Game Seven with four innings of relief. The following year against Pittsburgh, he won the opener with a five-hitter and the fourth game with a six-hitter before taking the loss in Game Seven. In six World Series games, Johnson had a 2.34 ERA.

Johnson won his final season opener in 1926, beating the Philadelphia Athletics, 1-0, in 15 innings. One year later, he retired at the age of 40, after having won 107 games during the previous six years.

The great hurler left the game with numerous remarkable records.

One of them was certainly his amazing feat of having recorded sub-2.00 ERAs in 11 seasons.

9

GROVER CLEVELAND ALEXANDER

RECORDED 16 SHUTOUTS IN ONE SEASON

In the language of today's game, the phrase "complete game shutout" is one that's seldom used. That's because there's virtually no reason to make the phrase part of the current baseball vocabulary.

Under present conditions where multi-tiered pitching staffs are considered necessary and where pitch counts govern how far into a game a pitcher works, hardly anybody ever throws a complete game shutout. A complete game shutout is a distant relic that is mostly gone and fully ignored.

There once was a time, though, when shutouts had a different meaning. They happened regularly, and they were achievements that made one proud and that drew admiration to the pitcher who threw one.

Nobody ever hurled a shutout more regularly than Grover Cleveland Alexander did in 1916. That season, the pitcher known as "Ol' Pete" tossed 16 shutouts for the Philadelphia Phillies. The feat set a major league record that will stand forever.

Whole teams don't pitch as many shutouts in one season as Ol' Pete did. Indeed, whole leagues don't exceed that number by much. A pitcher who leads the league in shutouts might toss two or three of them.

Alexander fired 90 shutouts during a 20-year career that in 1938 saw him become one of the first members elected to the Hall of Fame. Only one pitcher—Walter Johnson, with 110—threw more.

Overall, Alexander posted a 373-208 record, pitching in 696 games, starting 598, and completing 439 while working in 5,190 innings, allowing 4,868 hits, and striking out 2,199. A control pitcher who walked just 953 batters during his career, the sidewheeling Alexander did not throw especially hard, but his arsenal of baffling pitches made him extremely unhittable. His superb control prompted sports writer Grantland Rice to say, "Alexander could pitch into a tin can. His control is remarkable, the finest I have ever seen."

Alexander, born in 1887 in Elba, Nebraska, was raised on a farm where he learned to throw by hurling rocks at squirrels and rabbits. He pitched an 18-inning shutout after less than two years in the minors. In 1911, he was purchased by the Phillies for the bargain-basement price of $750 from Syracuse of the Class B New York State League.

In the Nebraska Cyclones' first year in the majors, he posted a 28-13 record while leading the league in innings pitched (367) and shutouts (seven). Subsequently, he went 19-17, 22-8, and 27-15 before launching a run of three straight 30-win seasons. During his first seven years in the majors, Alexander led the league in innings pitched six times, and in compete games, shutouts, and strikeouts each five times.

In 1915, the 6-1 right-hander led the Phillies to the first pennant in club history with a 31-10 record, a career-low 1.22 ERA, and a career-high 241 strikeouts while hurling four one-hitters. In the team's first World Series game, Ol' Pete beat the Boston Red Sox, 3-1, in what would be the Phils' only win in the fall classic until 1980.

Alexander's 1915 season was a harbinger of things to come. In 1916, he had one of the most spectacular seasons ever staged.

The first whitewash was hurled in Alexander's second start of the season. After beating the New York Giants, 5-4, in the opening game, Alexander blanked the Boston Braves, 4-0, with a five-hitter. Three starts later, he fired his next shutout, blanking Boston, 3-0. Then, after working in two games, one in relief, Alex threw a three-hitter at the Cincinnati Reds, winning 5-0.

In his next outing, Alex zeroed the Pittsburgh Pirates, 3-0, with a four-hitter. Two starts later, he beat the Brooklyn Robins, 1-0, in a game in which he had a season-high nine strikeouts and the losers had men in scoring positioning four different innings, including the sixth when they had the bases loaded with one out. Alex escaped the jam when right fielder Gavvy Cravath snared a line drive and then threw Casey Stengel out at the plate.

As June began, Alex registered his fifth shutout with a 2-0 victory over the St. Louis Cardinals. Again, the Phillies' defense saved him. St. Louis had the bases loaded with none out in the fifth, but a force-out at home and then a sensational catch by left fielder Possum Whitted, who then threw a runner out at third, followed by spectacular plays by second baseman Bert Niehoff and center fielder Dode Paskert, saved the shutout.

The 29-year-old hurler pitched in seven more games without a shutout, allowing one run in three of them, including an 11-inning, 2-1 win over Boston, and then losing three in a row. On July 7, he logged his next shutout with a 1-0 victory over the Cardinals. Again, Paskert saved the game with a leaping grab of a ball headed over the fence.

Before July ended, Alex had again pitched back-to-back shutouts, beating the Pirates, 4-0, with a four-hitter and five days later, the Reds, 6-0, on a two-hitter. He also pitched three other games in which he allowed just one run. By the end of the month, his record was 19-7.

From August 1 to August 19, the Phillies won 13 of 15 games. The month began for Alex when he pitched 12 innings and gave up seven hits to beat the Chicago Cubs, 1-0. After a loss, he hurled three straight shutouts, beating Cincinnati 1-0 with a three-hitter, New York 8-0 with a four-hitter, and the Reds again 3-0, despite striking out just one batter. That blanking was Alexander's 13th of the season and broke the National League record previously held by Mathewson.

Alexander won two of his next three decisions, including an 8-2 triumph over the Cubs for which he received a $1,000 bonus for winning his 25th game of the year. Then on September 1, he beat Jack Coombs and the Robins, 3-0. Ironically, the shutout broke the major league record of 13 shutouts in one season—a record held by none other than Jack Coombs.

The win launched the Phillies on an eight-game winning streak during which time Alex won four of six games. On September 23 in the first game of a doubleheader, Ol' Pete gave up 13 hits, but beat the Reds, 7-3, for his 30th win. After the game, Phils manager Pat Moran approached Alexander. "I'll have to ask you to pitch the second game," he said. "We have only a little more than an hour to catch the train. Get it over fast."

Alex followed orders. In a game that lasted just 58 minutes, he beat the Reds, 4-0. After the game, fans swarmed onto the diamond at Baker Bowl and carried Alex across the field to the team's clubhouse in center field. Team owner William Baker gave him a bonus check of $100.

Ol' Pete split his next two decisions before pitching his final shutout of the season on October 2. Working with one day's rest and making his fifth start in the last eight games, he blanked Boston, 2-0, while yielding just three hits. It was Alex's 33rd win and fourth three-hitter of the season. The win put the Phillies back into first place, but they then lost their next three games and got knocked off the top perch for the rest of the season.

Alexander pitched in one more game, working 2/3 of an inning in relief in a 7-5 Phillies season-ending victory. It was his third relief appearance of the season. The Phillies, meanwhile, wound up finishing in second place, two and one-half games behind the Robins.

The amazing hurler finished the season with a 33-12 record, leading the league in wins, ERA (1.55), games started (45), complete games (38), innings pitched (388.2), hits (323), strikeouts (167), and, of course, shutouts. Nine came at Baker Bowl, a hitter's paradise where the right field wall stood just 272 feet down the line.

Alex posted a 30-13 record in 1917, but was traded after the season to the Cubs in the worst swap in Phillies history. Fearing that Alex would be drafted into World War I, Baker dealt him and starting catcher Bill Killefer for two mediocre players, catcher Pickles Dillhoefer and pitcher Mike Prendergast, who played in a combined total of 46 games with the Phillies.

Alexander served in the War, then came back and pitched for the Cubs and Cardinals before returning briefly to the Phillies in 1930. With the Cubs and Cards, he had three more 20-win seasons and 10 more seasons in which he won in double figures. Alex, by then suffering from physical and drinking problems, won special accolades for preserving a Cardinals win by striking out the New York Yankees' Tony Lazzeri with two outs and the bases loaded in the seventh inning of the deciding game of the 1926 World Series.

Named after United States president Grover Cleveland Alexander, Alex was portrayed by a future president, Ronald Reagan, in the 1952 film *The Winning Team*.

10

BABE RUTH

WENT FROM ACE PITCHER TO HOME RUN KING

It has often been said that if Babe Ruth hadn't made the Hall of Fame as a hitter, he surely would've made it as a pitcher. There can be no doubt as to the accuracy of that statement.

Ruth went from being one of the best pitchers in the major leagues to one of the best hitters of all time, all in the space of a few years.

One season, Ruth was a 20-game winner. The next year he led the majors in home runs. Such an astounding feat makes the Babe's transition rank as the most spectacular switch in positions that there's ever been.

Others have gone from pitcher to position player with a great deal of success. Still others have shifted from hitter to pitcher with glowing results. In almost every case, though, the change took the player from mediocre to outstanding.

But no one ever did it the way Ruth did, going from the top to the top during a career that led to his being in the first group inducted into the Hall of Fame.

Of course, Ruth's success as a hitter is the reason he's in the baseball shrine. Until Hank Aaron broke his record in 1974, Ruth had hit more home runs (714) than any player in baseball history. He led the league in homers 12 times, in runs scored eight times, in RBI six times, and in slugging percentage 13 times. His lifetime batting average of .342 ranks 10th on the all-time list. And he was the first player to hit 60 home runs in one season.

It was "The Bambino" who as a hitter brought baseball out of the dead-ball era, changed it into a game featuring the "lively ball," and in the process brought attention and prosperity to baseball that was unlike anything ever seen before. When it comes to ranking pioneers who brought everlasting changes to their sport, Ruth holds a spot at the top of the list.

But that occurred after Ruth made his own change. In 1917, he posted a 24-13 record, bringing his three-year mark to 65-33 with his second straight 20-win season. The following season, he led the league in home runs with 11. That number expanded to a record-breaking 29 in 1919 and 54 one year later.

Just five years before he hit his 29 homers to break a record that had stood since Ned Williamson had set the record with 27 in 1884, Ruth had been a rookie pitcher seemingly on the way to a glittering career on the mound.

From the age of seven until he was 19, Ruth had lived at St. Mary's Industrial School for Boys, an orphanage and reform school for wayward boys in Baltimore, Maryland. Described as "incorrigible," the youngster, who was born in 1895, had been sent there apparently because of his parents' inability to control his reckless behavior.

At St. Mary's, Ruth began playing baseball, first on the street where he broke house windows with his ferocious smashes, and then on the school team where he started out as a left-handed catcher with occasional stints as a third baseman, shortstop, and outfielder. "It was all the same to me," Ruth said many years later. "All I wanted was to play. I didn't care much where."

It soon became apparent that Ruth could throw a baseball with a considerable amount of ability, and he spent increasing amounts of time as a pitcher. By 1913, he had become so good that he was allowed to leave St. Mary's and play on local sandlot teams.

Ruth's pitching prowess was spotted by Baltimore Orioles owner and general manager Jack Dunn, and in 1914 he signed the Babe to a contract for a salary of $250 per month. Ruth hurled impressively in spring training games, at one point inspiring Philadelphia Phillies manager Pat Moran to accurately predict that "within a few years, Ruth will be one of the best southpaws in baseball." He continued to pitch well in early-season games, but the International League team had developed financial problems, and Dunn was forced to sell off his top players. He peddled Ruth to the Boston Red Sox.

Babe, then known as "Gig," made his major league debut on July 11, 1914 against the Cleveland Indians at Fenway Park. Pitching seven innings, he earned the victory as Boston won, 4-3. But Ruth was ineffective in his next start and was demoted to the bench, where he sat until mid-August, when he was sent down to the International League's Providence Grays. There, he helped the Grays win the pennant. At the end of the season, Ruth was recalled by the Red Sox and hurled a complete-game victory over the New York Yankees to finish his debut year with a 2-1 record.

The following season, Ruth's talent as a pitcher exploded across the map. He rang up an 18-8 record with a 2.44 ERA, starting 28 of the 32 games in which he pitched and completing 16 of them. At one point, he won three games in nine days. Although the Red Sox won the pennant that season, Ruth did not pitch in the World Series.

Ruth was even more successful in 1916, when he went 23-12 while leading the league in ERA (1.75), shutouts (nine), and games started (41). In 323.2 innings, Babe gave up just 230 hits while striking out 170. He beat Walter Johnson in four of five meetings, once in a 13-inning, 1-0 game.

Again, Boston won the pennant, and, for the second straight year, the World Series. In Game Two, Ruth and Sherry Smith met in one of the great Series pitching performances ever staged. The game lasted 14 innings, and both pitchers went the distance (Smith 13 and Ruth an all-time Series record 14), with Babe yielding just six hits and capturing a 2-1 victory.

Ruth continued his great success on the mound in 1917 with a 24-13 record, a 2.01 ERA, and a league-leading 35 complete games (in 38 starts). Again allowing far fewer hits than innings pitched, Ruth gave up 244 base hits in 326.1 innings. In one of the most noteworthy games in baseball annals against the Washington Senators, Ruth walked the leadoff batter, but was then ejected for arguing the calls and throwing a punch at the umpire. Ernie Shore entered the game, and while the batter was thrown out stealing, he retired 26 hitters in a row for what was considered a perfect game until the rules were changed eight decades later.

The Babe continued to pitch in 1918, and went 13-7 with a 2.22 ERA in 20 games (he completed 18 of his 19 starts). That year for the first time, Ruth also played in the outfield and at first base. He wound up appearing in 59 games as a position player; in 317 at-bats, he led the league in home runs with 11 while hitting .300.

Ruth's pitching heroics weren't over yet, though. That fall, Boston won its third World Series in the last four years, and in the opener, Ruth pitched a six-hitter to beat the Chicago Cubs, 1-0. He also won Game Four, driving in the eventual winning run while working eight innings in a 3-2 triumph. That game was noteworthy because Babe had pitched 29 2/3 straight scoreless innings until the streak was broken in the eighth inning. The streak was a major league record that stood until broken by Whitey Ford in 1961.

Ruth pitched in 17 games in 1919, compiling a 9-5 record. On days when he wasn't pitching, he played in the field, where he appeared in 115 games. Babe again led the league in homers with 29 while hitting .322 with league-leading totals in RBI (114) and runs (103).

By then, the strain of pitching every fourth day and playing the field in between was getting to Ruth. "I don't think a man can pitch in his regular turn, and play every other game at some other position and keep that pace year after year," he said.

It was also becoming evident that his bat was more important than his arm. For a variety of reasons, owner Harry Frazee sold Ruth early in 1920 to the Yankees for $125,000. It was the start of a whole different career for Ruth, who wound up with a 94-46 record and a 2.28 ERA in 163 games.

During his 15 years with the Yankees, Ruth pitched in just five games. Meanwhile, he became a full-time outfielder and in 1920 hit .376 with league-leading totals in homers (54), RBI (1,137), and runs (158). He followed that with a .378-59-171 record in 1921.

Ruth was well on his way to becoming arguably the greatest hitter of all time. That was the result of a transition never seen before or since in the game of baseball.

11

LEON CADORE/JOE OESCHGER

EACH PITCHED 26-INNING GAME

Back in the day before there were such things as pitch counts, back before a pitcher was treated like royalty if he went six innings, back before hordes of relievers dotted every roster, there was once a game that lasted 26 innings and each of the starting pitchers went that entire distance.

Their names were Leon Cadore and Joe Oeschger. While they may not be among the most familiar names in the elite pitching ranks of baseball, this duo holds a place in the history books that has never been and never will be challenged.

By today's standards, the performances of the two on that cloudy, drizzling day in Boston are simply unfathomable. No one would even remotely believe such a superhuman feat could happen.

But it did. On May 1, 1920 at Braves Field in a game between the pennant-bound Brooklyn Robins and the Boston Braves, the teams played to a 1-1 tie before a crowd estimated to be about 4,500. No major league game has ever

Joe Oeschger. Courtesy of the Baseball Hall of Fame & Museum

Leon Cadore. Courtesy of the Baseball Hall of Fame and Museum

lasted that many innings, and certainly no pitchers have ever come close to hurling 26 innings.

The two pitchers had some things in common. Both were right-handers. Both were 29 years old. Both weighed 190 pounds (Oeschger was 6-1 and Cadore was 6-0). And both were said to have been born in Chicago, although much later it was determined that Cadore really came from Muskegon, Illinois.

The two had also previously pitched a memorable game against each other.

Just 10 days earlier, the Robins, led by Cardore, had beaten Oeschger and Boston, 1-0 in an 11-inning game in which both went the distance, with the former giving up seven hits and the latter allowing 12.

Oeschger had broken into the big leagues in 1914 with the Philadelphia Phillies. A football and baseball star in high school, he had attended St. Mary's College in Oakland, where he earned a bachelor's degree in engineering. Later, he earned a master's degree at Stanford University.

In his first year with the Phillies, Oeschger was used infrequently and posted a 4-8 record with a 3.77 ERA in 10 games. Joe began and ended the 1915 season with the pennant-winning Phillies—winning just one game—but spent most of the summer with Providence of the International League, where he pitched a no-hitter and fashioned a 21-10 record with a 2.50 ERA.

Oeschger spent most of the 1916 season on the disabled list after taking a line drive off his hand in spring training. The next year he went 15-14 with a career-best 2.75 ERA, at one point pitching 14 innings in a 0-0 game against Brooklyn. The following season, as the Phillies took a dive into the second division, he tumbled to a 6-18 log, which nonetheless included five one-run losses.

Early in the 1919 season, Oeschger was involved in another long game. This time, before just 1,300 at the Phillies' Baker Bowl, he and Burleigh Grimes of the Robins matched pitches for 20 innings before the game was called because of darkness with the teams tied, 9-9. A few weeks later, the Phillies traded Oeschger to New York, where he pitched in only five games before the Giants shipped him to Boston, where he appeared in only seven more games (4-2 record) that season.

Meanwhile, Cadore had experienced a jagged path of his own. Having been a student at Gonzaga University, he signed his first pro contract in 1912. Leon spent his first three seasons in the minors, playing in Trenton and Wilkes-Barre three different times before appearing in Jersey City and Buffalo, both of the International League. He was finally summoned to Brooklyn in 1915.

Cadore pitched in just seven games that year and one the next while spending most of the 1915 and 1916 campaigns back in the International League at Montreal. Overall, Cadore had an 81-63 record in 186 minor league games.

In 1917, Cadore returned to the Robins and logged a 13-13 mark with a 2.45 ERA in 37 games (30 as a starter). But it was back to the minors in 1918 with Atlanta of the Southern Association. He returned to Brooklyn the next year, and posted a 14-12 record and a career-best 2.37 ERA while starting 27 of 35 games.

Both pitchers were on their ways to respectable years as the 1920 season began. But no one could have expected what would happen a little more than one month into the season.

Oeschger went into the game with a 2-1 record, having beaten the Giants, 1-0, with a six-hitter and then seven-hit the Phillies in a 10-3 rout, after which he had lost the 11-inning game to Cadore. In addition to that win, Cadore had also downed the Phillies on eight hits, 9-2, and lost to the Giants, 5-2.

The weather was raining and a cold wind was blowing off the Charles River as the game got underway at 3 p.m. Shivering fans were wrapped in raincoats, but shortly after the start of the game, the rain stopped.

Neither team could do much until the fifth inning when Brooklyn scored. Ernie Krueger walked, then Cadore smacked a hard grounder up the middle. The ball bounced off Oeschger's glove, and instead of getting a double play, the Braves had to settle for the out at first. Krueger then scored on a single by leadoff batter Ivy Olson.

Boston came back with the tying run one inning later. Wally Cruise tripled. Zack Wheat made a shoestring catch of a liner by Walt Holke and almost doubled off Cruise at third before Tony Boeckel laced a hit to center that scored Cruise.

There were no more threats until the ninth when Boston loaded the bases with one out. The Braves' Charlie Pick drilled a hard bouncer to second. Olson made a sparkling stop, then tried unsuccessfully to tag baserunner Ray Powell as he advanced to second before throwing to first to nip the batter. Boston's Rabbit Maranville scored, but umpire Eugene Hart ruled that Powell was out for running out of the baseline and the run didn't count.

Nothing more happened until the 17th inning when the Robins loaded the bases. With one out, Rowdy Elliott sent a grounder back to the mound where Oeschger fielded it and threw to the plate to force out Wheat. Catcher Hank

Gowdy then fired the ball wildly to first, but Holke knocked it down and threw home, where Gowdy tagged the sliding Konetchy.

After that, there were no more scoring threats. As the hitters swung for the fences in hopes of breaking the tie, Oeschger and Cadore pitched brilliantly. In the 23rd inning, the National League record for most innings played in one game was broken. The Major League mark fell two innings later.

Finally, with darkness falling, umpire Bill McCormick stopped the game. Players protested the call. Among them was Olson, who begged, "wait one more inning. I want to be able to tell my grandchildren I played the equal of three nine-inning games in one afternoon." "Not without a miner's cap," McCormick replied.

The record-setting game was over. Amazingly, it was played in just three hours and 50 minutes. Oeschger gave up nine hits, struck out seven, and walked four. Cadore yielded 15 hits, fanned seven, and walked five. Many years later, it was speculated that Cadore threw 345 pitches while Oeschger served up an estimated 319 offerings. First basemen Holke registered 43 putouts and Konetchy 30.

"The game," Oeschger said many years later, "was one of those when the pitchers had the hitters at their mercy. After the game, Pick said, 'my children are probably going to ask me if I used a bat that day.' I was tired," he added, "but I pitched some other games when I was more exhausted."

Cadore, who got the first massage of his career after the game, said that because of the enormous strain put on their arms, many writers figured their careers were over. "I couldn't raise my arm for a couple of days," he said.

Oeschger finished the season with a 15-13 record, while Cadore ended up at 15-14. Cadore posted a 13-14 log in 1921, then hurled a little more than two more years in the majors, ending his career with the Chicago White Sox and Giants with a 68-72 overall record and a 3.14 ERA in 192 games, 147 as a starter. Oeschger posted a 20-14 record in 1921, then went 6-21 and 5-15 before ending his career in 1925 with stints his final two years with the Giants, Phillies, and Robins. His career record was 82-116 with a 3.81 ERA in 365 games, 197 of them as a starter.

No matter what their records were, though, they paled in comparison to that one great day in 1920 when each pitcher performed in a way that defied belief.

CONTINUING THE TRADITION OF EXCELLENCE – 1930–1949

12

LEFTY GROVE

NOTCHED THREE RECORDS THAT HAVE NEVER BEEN EQUALED

There can be no doubt that Lefty Grove ranks among the greatest pitchers of all time. During a sparkling 17-year big league career, he posted a record that ranks among the best in baseball annals.

He is just one of 24 pitchers ever to win 300 games, and one of only six left-handed hurlers to have reached that exclusive plateau. He ranks among baseball's all-time leaders in career winning percentage (.680) and complete games (298), and over three seasons between 1929 and 1931 his record was an unmatchable 79-15, which at one point included 16 straight wins.

Elected to the Hall of Fame in 1947, Grove was so good that Babe Ruth once proclaimed that "when this guy is right, there isn't a team and never has been a team that could lick him." Mickey Cochrane said that Grove "could throw a lamb chop past a hungry wolf." "He pitched with the most beautifully coordinated motion I ever saw," added Ted Williams.

The 6-foot, three-inch, 190-pounder once struck out Ruth, Lou Gehrig, and Bob Meusel on nine pitches. Another time, he won four games in seven days. And he snapped the New York Yankees' streak of 308 games without a shutout with a 7-0 win.

Among his many achievements, Grove's record is bolstered by three feats that are unmatched in baseball history. At the start of his career in the majors,

AP Photo

he led the league in strikeouts seven straight times. He also topped the league in ERA nine times. And he led the league in winning percentage five times.

Although Walter Johnson led the league in strikeouts eight times in a row and Dazzy Vance did it seven straight times, no one ever duplicated Grove's mark of winning seven consecutive strikeout crowns beginning in his rookie season.

And no one else ever won nine ERA titles or led his league in winning percentage in five different campaigns.

In an era when many batters tried to meet the ball and didn't swing for the fences, Grove's dazzling fastball often got the best of opposing hitters, even though he threw it most of the time and until later in his career lacked the usual repertoire of breaking balls and changeups.

Lefty, it was said, "threw with terrifying intensity." "It's hard to believe that anyone could throw faster than Lefty Grove," Charley Gehringer said. Even Grove himself acknowledged his devastating fastball. "If I ever hit a guy on the head with my fastball," he said, "he'd be through."

He won his first strikeout title as a rookie in 1925, and then won again every year through 1931. Although his totals weren't high by today's standards, he usually reached the upper 100s, achieving a career high in 1930 with 209 strikeouts. Along the way, his highest one-game total was 12. Once, Grove ended a game by striking out the final six batters on 19 pitches.

Lefty's ERA titles began in his sophomore season in 1926 when he went 2.51. He posted a career-low 2.06 in 1931, and won his final title with a 2.54 in 1939 at the age of 39. That year, he also led the league for the final time in winning percentage, a title he had first claimed in 1928. Grove's figures in that category were .769 (20-6), .848 (28-5), .886 (31-4), .750 (24-8), and .789 (15-4).

Amazingly, Grove didn't begin his big league career until he was 25 years old. Had he started sooner, there's no telling what heights his records could have reached.

Lefty, who was born Robert Moses Grove in 1900, came from Lonaconing, Maryland. As a youth, he didn't play baseball in earnest until he was 17 years old. By then, he had quit school and was working in a silk mill, earning $7 per week. He went from there to a glass factory, where he played sandlot ball for the factory team, mostly as a first baseman.

Grove's ability to unfurl a sizzling fastball—developed, he said later, by throwing rocks "at anything moving or stationary"—soon became apparent, and in 1920, he signed a contract with Martinsville of the Class D Blue Ridge League. Shortly afterward, Grove was spotted by Jack Dunn, owner and manager of the Baltimore Orioles. Dunn, who had signed Ruth, bought Grove from Martinsville for a reported $3,500.

The budding fireballer spent four and one-half years with the Baltimore powerhouse, at the time, the winners of five straight International League pennants. Over that period, he posted a 108-36 record, and was pursued by numerous big league teams. Eventually, Grove was sold to the Philadelphia Athletics for $100,600, an amount set so Connie Mack could accede the price the Yankees had paid for Ruth.

Grove began with a 10-12 record, but led the league in strikeouts with 116. Two years later, he had his first 20-win season (20-13), then followed that with his first of two 24-8 records. Ultimately, he would be a 20-game winner in seven straight seasons and eight altogether.

From 1929 to 1931, the Athletics fielded some of the greatest teams in baseball history, all three times winning more than 100 games, including 107 in 1931, and capturing three pennants and two World Series. Over that period, Grove posted 20-6, 28-5, and 31-4 records. In the World Series, he went 4-2 with a 1.75 ERA and two saves. His wins were highlighted by an 8-1, five-hit victory over the St. Louis Cardinals in Game Six of the 1931 Series.

The 1931 season was the high-water mark in Grove's illustrious career. That year, he compiled one of the best seasons in baseball history when he won his second straight triple crown (wins, ERA, strikeouts), and also garnered first-place finishes in complete games and shutouts.

Along the way, Grove beat the Boston Red Sox in 12 innings with a complete game shutout, and hurled a two-hitter against the St. Louis Browns. Two days later, he beat Boston with seven innings of relief. Grove's .886 winning percentage stood as a major league record until broken in 1978 by Ron Guidry. Since Grove did it, no other American Leaguer has won 30 or more games, except Denny McLain in 1968.

Grove's totals in 1931 included 16 straight wins, which at the time vaulted his record to 25-2 and tied a major league mark held by Johnson and Joe Wood. Lefty's streak came to an end when he lost a 1-0 decision to the Browns, the winning run scoring when A's substitute outfielder Jimmy Moore misjudged a fly ball that sailed over his head. At the end of the season, Grove was the first American Leaguer chosen as Most Valuable Player by the Baseball Writers' Association of America.

Throughout his career, Grove was noted for his temper tantrums. He raged against teammates who botched plays and reporters who asked too many questions. Often, he punched lockers, always making sure to use his right hand, threw chairs, gloves, and bats, and even screamed sometimes at the stoic Connie Mack. "All he had was a fastball and a mean disposition," Mack said. "I took more from Grove than I would from any man living."

Grove posted 25-10 and 24-8 logs in 1932 and 1933, running his record over a seven-year period to 172-54. Mack, however, was dismantling the Athletics, selling off his top players, and running the team into the depths of the American League.

After the 1933 season, he peddled Grove to Boston for $125,000. Lefty pitched in eight more seasons, his best year being in 1935 when he went 20-12 and a league-leading 2.70 ERA. In 1936, he led the league with a career-high six shutouts. With the mediocre Red Sox, Grove still led the league four times in ERA while also posting 17-9, 14-4, and 15-4 records.

In 1941, with his fastball gone and his tired arm unleashing mostly breaking balls, Grove became baseball's first 300-game winner since Grover Cleveland Alexander won that many in 1924. Pitching against the Cleveland Indians, Lefty yielded 12 hits, but gained a 10-6 decision. It would be the last win of his career.

Grove retired during the 1941 season, going 14-13 over his last two years. His final record was 300-141 with a 3.06 ERA in 616 games, 456 of them as a starter. In 3,940.2 innings, Grove struck out 2,266, walked 1,187, and allowed 3,849 hits. He hurled 300 complete games, 35 of them shutouts. His .680 winning percentage is the highest of all 300-game winners. Grove was also used in 139 games in relief. As a result, 33 of his wins came from the bullpen, and he was later credited with 55 saves.

Of all his glittering records, though, his marks in winning percentage, earned run average, and strikeouts were ones that have never been matched.

13

FRED MARBERRY

BECAME FATHER OF ALL RELIEVERS

Long before there was a pitcher who was called a closer; long before there was anybody known as a setup man; and long before there was a moundsman labeled a mid-distance hurler, there was Fred (Firpo) Marberry. He was all of them and then some.

It didn't matter if it was the second inning, the fifth, or the ninth. Marberry could be summoned to the mound anytime. And how long he pitched wasn't a factor.

Neither was the situation that bought him to the mound. Left-handed batter, right-handed batter, the need for a ground ball, or a final out, it didn't matter. He was available at any time and in any situation.

There was no special name given to Marberry's position. He was simply a relief pitcher. Not just any relief pitcher, of course. The fireballing right-hander is regarded as the father of all relievers, the first hurler to spend much of his career coming out of the bullpen.

Marberry set in motion a trend that today has reached a point where relief pitchers are regarded as being among the most valuable players on a team. Unlike

in Marberry's day, each reliever today has a very specific duty. But without a good bullpen, a modern team has little chance of being a consistent winner.

In the days prior to Marberry, although there were times when starting pitchers failed to complete games, relief pitchers were usually either starting pitchers in between starts or washed-up hurlers trying to hang on to their jobs. There was no special category of relief pitcher. Generally, a reliever was used only when the starter was getting clobbered. And there was certainly no such statistic as a save.

Marberry was the first outstanding pitcher to be a reliever. Unlike some others who had previously thrown in relief, he was particularly talented and employed a blistering fastball that later became a vital tool in the arsenal of many successful relievers. As such, he set records that stood for many years.

Although there was no such thing as a save until 1969, retroactive studies determined that Marberry was the first reliever to reach 100 career saves. He is credited with being the first reliever to record 20 saves in one season. He is also the first pitcher to lead his league in saves five times. And he is the first pitcher to make 50 relief appearances in a single season and 300 in a career.

In a career that extended from 1923 to 1936, Marberry wound up pitching in 551 games, 364 of them in relief. As a reliever, he posted a 53-37 record with 101 saves. He led the league in games pitched six times, including an astounding 64 games pitched in 1926.

During parts of his career, primarily in some of the early days and much of the final years, Marberry also served as a starting pitcher. Hence, he registered an overall 147-89 record with a 3.63 ERA in 2,067.1 innings of work. He struck out 822 and walked 686 while completing 86 games and hurling eight shutouts.

But it was as a reliever that Marberry made his mark, and it was as a reliever that he is credited with pioneering a whole new dimension to the game of baseball. Indeed, relief pitching was seldom a major factor in baseball games until it began to gain acceptance in the 1940s.

Born in 1898 in Streetman, Texas, Marberry was raised on a farm, and because of his duties there, played little baseball as a youth. Eventually, though, he began playing with a town team, where he was mainly an infielder.

Marberry did not throw his first pitch from the mound until he was 21 years old. When he did, though, he demonstrated a raging fastball. It was more than enough to attract local scouts. Ultimately, he signed with Mexia of the Texas-Oklahoma League. Before the season was over, Marberry was promoted to Jackson of the Cotton States League and then Little Rock of the Southern Association. Although he was not particularly effective at either place, he returned to Little Rock in 1923 and posted an 11-10 record.

By then, Marberry was on the radar of the Washington Senators, and late in the 1923 season, they acquired him and brought him to the big leagues. Although he was now 24 years old and had nothing else but a blazing fastball, Marberry went 4-0 while starting four of 11 games and posting a 2.82 ERA.

A 6-foot, one-inch, 210-pounder, Marberry was soon given the nickname of "Firpo," because his appearance and demeanor resembled Luis Firpo, a boxer from Argentina known as "The Wild Bull of the Pampas." Firpo had fought (and lost to) Jack Dempsey in a heavyweight bout in 1923.

Marberry didn't like the name, but it didn't affect his pitching. And in 1924, he became mostly a reliever, working in 50 games, 35 of them in relief.

Later, it was calculated that he saved 15 games while posting an 11-12 record over. Often, Firpo pitched three or more innings and sometimes as many as six or seven.

That season, the Senators won the American League pennant. In the World Series against the New York Giants, Marberry recorded saves in the second and fourth games. He started and lost the third game, and pitched three innings of relief in Game Seven, as the Senators won both the game and the Series, 4-3.

Neither Firpo nor the Senators was as successful the following year when Washington again went to the World Series. Marberry pitched only twice, recording one save as the Nats bowed to the Pittsburgh Pirates in seven games.

Although Allan Russell was also primarily a reliever on the Senators and had registered several fine seasons, Marberry was now the club's main fireman. For much of the rest of his career, he would be known as a relief pitcher. In that post, Marberry was cited by statistician and historian Bill James as being as valuable a pitcher in the American League as anybody except Lefty Grove. "He was a modern reliever," James said. "A hard-throwing young kid who worked often and was used to nail down victories."

Between 1924 and 1929, Firpo led the league in games pitched five times, climaxed by a high of 64 in 1926. In retrospect, he also led the league in saves four straight times, recording a high of 22 in 1926. During 1925 and 1926, Marberry made 59 straight relief appearances.

Marberry had the perfect temperament for a reliever. He would march briskly in from the bullpen with a confident air. When he got to the mound, he'd stand there scowling at the hitter and throw and kick dirt. Then he'd rear back and with a high kick, fire a withering fastball that, if it was late in the day, would be hard to see in the building shadows.

While distinguishing himself as a reliever, Marberry was also occasionally drawing starting assignments. In 1925, however, he pitched in 55 games, all in relief, and in 1926, 59 of his 64 games were in the role of a reliever. Before Firpo, no other pitcher had ever come out of the bullpen as often as he did.

In 1929, Marberry logged a 19-12 mark and had a league-leading 11 saves, but 26 of his 49 appearances were as a starter. Firpo's role was changing, and he was increasingly being used as a starter.

By then he had developed a curveball and a changeup, and he was enjoying his role as a starter. "Relief pitching is a job for a young pitcher," he said. "His arm can stand the wear and tear of uncertain work. In my case, I feel that I have earned the right to a change."

Most of Marberry's future seasons were spent with well over half of his games coming in the role of a starter, although in 1932 he took the mound in 54 games and started just 15 times while leading the league with 13 saves.

Firpo was traded after the 1932 season to the Detroit Tigers. Starting 32 of his 37 games, he posted a 16-11 record. He was 15-5 the following year while starting half of his 38 games.

A sore arm kept Marberry on the sidelines through most of 1935, and he was eventually released. He played in one game with the Giants the next season before returning to Washington, where he ended his big league career after appearing in five games.

Marberry then pitched in a little more than four seasons in the minors, with stops at Dallas and Fort Worth in the Texas League and Toledo in the American Association. His career ended in 1941. By then, Mayberry was the acknowledged founder of the art of relief pitching. He set the stage for a specialty that would become one of the most important facets of baseball.

14

CARL HUBBELL

WON 24 GAMES IN A ROW

For a guy who was initially forbidden to use his best pitch and who was ready to quit baseball after his second year in the minors, Carl Hubbell did quite well. Not only did he become one of the greatest left-handed pitchers of all time, but also his career is filled with accomplishments that in some cases are still unmatched.

During a 16-year big league career spent entirely with the New York Giants, Hubbell won 253 games, including 20 or more five years in a row.

He won in double figures 15 times, leading the National League in wins and earned run average each three times.

One of baseball's most highly acclaimed screwball pitchers, Hubbell was twice named the National League's Most Valuable Player and was selected for nine All-Star teams. The Hall of Famer won four World Series games, including two in 1933 when the Giants beat the Washington Senators. Joe DiMaggio once called Hubbell "the toughest pitcher I ever faced."

Hubbell, nicknamed "The Meal Ticket," still ranks as the owner of one of the most amazing performances in All-Star Game history. In 1934, he struck out Babe Ruth, Lou Gehrig, Jimmie Foxx, Al Simmons, and Joe Cronin—all future Hall of Famers—in a row.

AP Photo/Tom Sande

That feat, though, is only second best to Hubbell's other history-making performance. "King Carl," as he was also called, won 24 games in a row, an astounding record that has never been approached. It came during the 1936 and 1937 seasons.

Hubbell's life began in Carthage, Missouri, where he was born in 1903. Carl grew up on a pecan farm in Meeker, Oklahoma, where as a youth he threw stones at knotholes in a barn door. He pitched for the high school team and then worked for an oil company before joining a team in 1923 in Cushing in the Oklahoma State League. Two years later, after he compiled a 17-13 record at Oklahoma City of the Western League, Hubbell's contract was purchased by the Detroit Tigers.

By then, Hubbell had developed his screwball, a pitch thrown by turning the hand over in the reverse direction used to throw a curveball. "It's an unnatural pitch," Hubbell said many years later. "Nature never intended a man to turn his hand like that. It's like throwing rocks at a bear."

Detroit manager Ty Cobb didn't like Hubbell throwing that pitch. He thought that it created arm problems, and thus he forbid Hubbell to throw it. That destroyed Carl's effectiveness as well as his confidence. Sent back to the minors, Hubbell had two mediocre seasons and threatened to quit the game. Instead, he was sold to Beaumont of the Texas League.

Encouraged to use his screwball again, Hubbell soon blossomed, and in 1928, he was sold to John McGraw's club at mid-season. Hubbell posted a 10-6 record the rest of the way. Over the next four years, the 6-foot, 170-pounder won 67 games, twice capturing 18 in one season. In 1929, he hurled a no-hitter against the Pittsburgh Pirates in an 11-0 victory.

In 1933 he posted a 23-12 record and led the league in wins, ERA (1.66), innings pitched (308.2), and shutouts (10). He pitched a perfect game for 12 innings before finishing with a six-hit, 18-inning shutout in a 1-0 win over the St. Louis Cardinals. Later in the season, he pitched 46 1/3 consecutive score-less innings, a streak that included four shutouts. That fall, the Giants beat Washington in five games in the World Series, with Hubbell winning the first game with a five-hitter, 4-2, and the fourth, 2-1 in 11 innings. Carl was named Series MVP.

Hubbell had a devastating screwball and marvelous control. "The source of his skill is his matchless control in using his curveball to set up his screwball," New York Yankees pitcher Waite Hoyt said.

In 1934, Carl made history in the second All-Star Game, played at the Polo Grounds. Hubbell started for the National League, and after yielding a leadoff single and a walk, he struck out Ruth, Gehrig, and Foxx in the first inning, and Simmons and Cronin in the second before allowing a single to Bill Dickey. Sports writer Grantland Rice, who called Carl "The Carthage Catapult," wrote that the feat was performed "with a baffling assortment of curves, screwballs, and zigzags that stood five of baseball's greatest hitters on their well-known heads."

The performance, though, wasn't Hubbell's greatest. That began two years later.

After going 21-12 and 23-12 in the preceding seasons, 1936 turned into a year in which he was the winning pitcher in the All-Star Game, posted a 26-6 record with a league-leading 2.30 ERA, won his second MVP while becoming the award's first unanimous pick, and beat the Yankees, 6-1, in the first game of the World Series, which the Giants ultimately lost in six games.

That season, Hubbell also started on a path to a record that may never be broken. It began on July 17, when Carl beat the Pirates with a five-hitter, 6-0. He followed that with a 4-3 victory in 2.2 innings of relief over the Cincinnati Reds and a 2-1 triumph over the Cardinals in 10 innings. He then won 13 more games in a row, beating every team in the National League except the Boston Braves. Hubbell defeated the Philadelphia Phillies four times, and the Cardinals and Chicago Cubs each three times. Although he threw only one shutout, he gave up one run in a game seven times and two runs four times. His complete games included four four-hitters and only two games in which he gave up 10 or more hits. The highest number was 11 in a game in which he beat the Reds, 6-5.

During the streak, Hubbell pitched in 19 games, once getting no decision as a starter and twice hurling in relief without a decision. He completed 14 games. His last win of the season came on September 23 when he beat the Phillies, 5-4.

The streak had reached 16 by the end of the season, but it was hardly over. Hubbell launched the 1937 campaign with a three-hit, 3-0 verdict on Opening Day against the Braves. He followed that with an 11-2 victory over the Brooklyn Dodgers and a 7-6 win over the Reds in a game in which he struck out 10, the most in the streak.

Hubbell won his eighth straight game of the season on May 27, a 3-2 triumph, pitching in relief against the Reds. By then, he had closed five games, and had allowed one run in two games and two runs twice, while facing all the teams in the league except the Phillies. "A fellow doesn't last long on what he has done," Hubbell rationalized. "He has to keep on delivering."

The streak finally ended in a Memorial Day doubleheader before 61,756, the second largest crowd in the history of the Polo Grounds. In the first game against the Dodgers, Hubbell was kayoed with one out in the fourth inning. Ironically, Hubbell was presented with his 1936 MVP Award between games.

When his run ended, Hubbell had won 24 straight games. He had pitched in 207.2 innings, allowing 159 hits and 45 runs while striking out 104 and walking 35. Overall, Carl had started 22 games during the streak, and relieved in five others.

Hubbell finished his 1937 season with a 22-8 record. In the World Series, the Yankees again defeated the Giants, this time in five games. Hubbell lost the opener, but came back to give the Giants their only win with a six-hit, 7-3 victory in Game Four.

Hubbell won 13 games in 1938 and 11 in each of the next four seasons.

In 1940, he pitched a one-hitter against the Dodgers, allowing only a bloop hit to John Hudson, who was then erased on a double play. Carl faced only 27 batters while throwing just 81 pitches. "Every pitch went where I wanted it to go," he said. "I never had such control either before or afterward."

Carl retired in August, 1943 after posting a 4-4 record in 12 games. His final record was 253-154 with a 2.97 ERA in 3,589.1 innings. He pitched in 535 games, starting 432, recording 1,678 strikeouts, and walking just 724. Hubbell pitched more than 300 innings in four consecutive seasons. Had they been counted back then, he would've been credited with 33 saves.

Hubbell had to pay for owning one of the most devastating screwballs ever thrown. His left arm, permanently damaged from years of twisting, dangled in a deformed position with the palm of his hand pointing away from his body. He also had bone chips and pain. Nevertheless, the screwball was the pitch that allowed him to record some of the game's greatest feats.

15

BOB FELLER

ACHIEVED AN UNMATCHABLE BIG LEAGUE DEBUT

A pitcher, if he's good enough, does not lack for opportunities to perform noteworthy feats. Some take advantage of the situation. Some don't.

Bob Feller was an example of one who did. During a career in which he pitched in all or parts of 18 big league seasons, Feller performed numerous spectacular feats en route to etching his name in the annals of baseball's greatest pitchers.

The sturdy right-hander, who spent his entire big league career from 1936 to 1956 with the Cleveland Indians and who was elected to the Hall of Fame in 1962, was a pitcher with a consistently better record than anyone else in his era. He could throw a fastball at least as fast as anyone ever did, and he had a terrifying curve and just enough wildness to make him on most days virtually unhittable.

Feller posted a 266-162 record while playing mostly for poor to mediocre Indians teams. Most likely, he would've easily been a 300-game winner had he not spent nearly four years in the Navy during World War II. Feller wound up

with 2,581 strikeouts recorded during 3.827 innings pitched. While starting 484 of the 570 games he pitched, Feller compiled a 3.25 earned run average, allowing 3,271 hits and walking 1,764.

In addition to career records, Feller's seasons were often filled with other glittering accomplishments. The 6-0, 185-pound flame-thrower led the American League in strikeouts seven times, including 348 in 1946, which broke a record that had been set in 1904 by Rube Waddell. He fanned 18 in 1938 against the Detroit Tigers, then the highest single-game total in the modern era.

Feller was a 20-game winner six times, leading the league in wins each time. In 1946, he pitched 371.1 innings, one of five times he led the league in that category. He topped the AL in games started five times, once reaching 42, and in complete games three times, once reaching as high as 36.

"Rapid Robert," as they called him, pitched three no-hitters. One (in 1940) is the only Opening Day no-hitter ever pitched (Leon Ames of the New York Giants pitched an opening day no-hitter for nine innings in 1909, but lost in extra innings, and under present rules is not credited with a no-hitter). Another came in 1946 in Feller's first full season after his military duty. The third was registered in 1952.

Feller also pitched 12 one-hitters. He won 107 games before he was 23 years old. He was the first player to be paid as much as $80,000 for one season. He pitched before one of the biggest crowds in baseball history (86,000) at Cleveland's Municipal Stadium in the 1948 World Series. And he was the first pitcher ever to be clocked at throwing a fastball more than 100 miles per hour.

Of all his scintillating achievements, though, one that rates at the top of the list occurred in 1936 in a game against the St. Louis Browns. It was Feller's first start as a big league pitcher. He was 17 years old and just approaching his senior year in high school. And he won the game, 5-3, with the incredible total of 15 strikeouts.

No 17 year old ever did that either before then or since then. It was an amazing feat that was arguably the most spectacular of Feller's memorable career.

Bob was a farm boy, born in 1918, and living in a small Iowa farm town of Van Meter in a house that originally had no electricity, no indoor plumbing, and a telephone that had a party line consisting of 17 families. His grandfather had been known as the best pitcher in town in the 1870s. As a youth, Feller had to walk three miles to school, sometimes through snow and temperatures well below freezing.

Feller began throwing baseballs to his dad when he was five years old. He would gain strength by milking cows and cleaning out the barn. Bob eventually became a star pitcher on local teams that played games in other towns around Iowa. By the time he had pitched five no-hitters and struck out 22 in one game, young Bob had attracted the attention of legions of big league scouts. One was the Indians' Cy Slapnicka. A former big league pitcher, Slapnicka watched Feller intently and finally signed him to a contract for $1.00. His bonus was an autographed baseball. Slapnicka then returned to Cleveland where he told his employers that he had found "the greatest pitcher in history."

"I had wanted to be a big league pitcher since I was about five years old," Feller said. "I didn't care about the money. All I wanted was the opportunity to play."

Just finishing his junior year in high school, Feller joined the parent club during the summer of 1936. At first, he traveled with the team as a non-roster player, working out every day. Despite having no minor league experience, Feller was sent into a mid-season exhibition game against the St. Louis Cardinals, and in three innings of relief struck out eight and gave up one hit.

Umpire Red Ormsby claimed that Feller was faster than both Lefty Grove and Walter Johnson. And after two strikes during his first at-bat, Cardinals shortstop Leo Durocher walked away from the plate, telling the umpire that he could call the third strike on his own. When asked if he would pose for a picture with the teenage hurler, Dizzy Dean reportedly said, "Maybe you'd better ask him if he'll pose with me."

Two weeks later, he was placed on the active roster and made his big league debut with a one-inning relief stint against the Washington Senators. Feller then made several more relief appearances before drawing his first starting assignment.

It came on August 23 against manager Rogers Hornsby's Browns, owners of a 44-76 record. Despite their record, the Browns featured a lineup that included six hitters with batting averages of .280 or above.

Feller struck out leadoff hitter, Lyn Lary, on three pitches. He then gave up a single to Harland Clift, but ended the inning with two more strikeouts. The Browns scored their only run of the game in the sixth inning on cleanup hitter Beau Bell's RBI single. By the end of that inning, Feller had 12 strikeouts.

Meanwhile, Cleveland, with Hal Trosky leading the way with four hits and two RBI, knocked out St. Louis starter Earl Caldwell while heading to an easy 4-1 victory.

Feller wound up going the distance, while striking out Lary and Moose Solters each three times and fanning every member of the Browns' starting lineup at least once. Young Bob's 15 strikeouts were two short of the then-major league record and the most strikeouts for an American League pitcher since 1919, when Bob Shawkey whiffed 15. Bob gave up six hits and walked four, but also threw four wild pitches. He was the youngest pitcher ever to start, win, and pitch a complete game on the same day. It was an incredible debut that may never be matched.

"After the game, some kids were waiting for me at the dressing room door and asked me for my autograph," Feller recalled. "Funny thing was, some of them were older than I was."

Feller's success took a temporary detour when he lost his next two starts, bowing to the Boston Red Sox, 5-1, then getting knocked out in the first inning by the New York Yankees. He bounced back with a 7-1 over the Browns. Then on September 13, the teenage schoolboy fired a two-hitter to beat the Philadelphia Athletics, 5-2. Feller struck out 17 batters, which broke the American League record set in 1908 by Waddell and tied the major league mark set three years earlier by Dean.

Master Bob, as he was now being called, finished the season with a final record of 5-3 with 76 strikeouts in 62 innings.

After the season, Feller returned to Van Meter for his senior year in high school.

"It was October by then," Feller said, "so my classmates, all 16 of them, had a five-week head start on me. But I didn't mind. I was just glad to be back home."

Feller, who was elected class president, stayed in school until a spring barnstorming tour with the Indians and New York Giants. Then, after being slowed by a sore arm, he completed the season with a 9-7 record in 26 games while striking out 150 in 148.2 innings. The youngster was on his way.

Over the next four years, Feller would have seasons with 24, 27, and 25 wins while pitching a no-hitter and leading the league in strikeouts three times. Then, after his tour with the Navy, Feller returned to the majors and posted seasons with 26, 22, and 20 wins while carving his name among the ranks of baseball's greatest pitchers. It all began, though, with his amazing debut as a 17 year old from a tiny town in Iowa.

16

JOHNNY VANDER MEER

FIRED BACK-TO-BACK NO-HITTERS

In any discussion of no-hitters, one of the first names always mentioned is Johnny Vander Meer. With good reason, too—Vander Meer holds a place among no-hit pitchers that has never been matched.

Since the pitching mound was moved back to 60 feet, six inches from home plate in 1893, there have been 238 no-hitters thrown by individual pitchers. Yet only Vander Meer ever threw two no-hitters in a row.

In 1938, the left-handed pitcher performed the spectacular feat of throwing no-hitters four days apart in what was his first full season in the major leagues. Hurling for the Cincinnati Reds, Vander Meer blanked the Boston Bees and then the Brooklyn Dodgers on successive starts.

As a postscript to that amazing feat, Vander Meer pitched three and one-third innings of hitless ball in his next start, giving him 21 1/3 straight innings without allowing a hit, a record that is likely to stand until they stop playing baseball.

Amazingly, he wound up allowing three hits in that game, the same number he'd yielded in the game before his first no-hitter. Thus, Vander Meer gave up a total of six hits in 36 innings.

AP Photo/stf

It was a spectacular run, but even that didn't compare to the two games in the middle that earned Vander Meer the nickname "Double No-Hit." Even today, nearly eight decades since the events took place, the 6-foot, 1-inch, 190-pound hurler is one of the most frequently mentioned no-hit pitchers.

Among candidates for back-to-back no-hitters, Vander Meer probably wouldn't have ranked near the top of the list. He was neither a high-strikeout hurler nor a control pitcher, and for the most part, he had not been a big winner in his years in the minor leagues. In his only year in Triple-A in 1937, he had won just five of 16 decisions before moving to the Reds later that year and posting a 3-5 mark.

Vander Meer, a native of Prospect Park, New Jersey, where he was born in 1914, had entered pro ball in 1933. He went 29-28 during his first three years in the minors before recording a 19-6 log at Durham in the Piedmont League in 1936 and being named Minor League Player of the Year by *The Sporting News*. By the time he got to Cincinnati in 1937, the Reds were about to finish in last place, 40 games out of first.

But change was on the way. In 1938, with Vander Meer joining Paul Derringer and Bucky Walters in the starting rotation, Cincinnati leaped all the way up to fourth place. Vander Meer had a 5-2 record when the Reds met Boston on June 11 at Crosley Field. Just 10,311 fans were in the stands. Only four days earlier, in a game against the New York Giants, Vander Meer was touched for only two first-inning hits and a broken-bat single in the ninth.

Ironically, the fifth-place Bees were the last team to knock Vander Meer out of the box. But this time was different. Johnny retired the first nine Bees in order with the help of a sensational catch by center fielder Harry Craft on a line drive by Gil English. Vander Meer walked one batter in the fourth inning and two in the fifth, but no other Boston hitters, not even Vince DiMaggio or Johnny Cooney, reached base.

Meanwhile, the Reds scored once in the fourth and twice in the sixth on catcher Ernie Lombardi's two-run homer. In the ninth, with two Reds pitchers warming up in the bullpen, Vander Meer retired three straight pinch-hitters to end the game with a 3-0, no-hit victory. Vander Meer wound up with four strikeouts. The game was played in one hour, 48 minutes.

Four days later on June 15 at Ebbets Field in Brooklyn, Vander Meer faced the Dodgers in their first night game and with the second-largest crowd (38,784) in club history in the stands, Johnny pitched another no-hitter, the first ever thrown in a night game.

Prior to the start of the game, thousands of people were turned away at the gates, and the game was delayed for an hour by a balky light fixture and a ceremony commemorating the Dodgers' new lights. But with his parents in the stands, Vander Meer shut down the eventual seventh place Dodgers, a team that included future MVP Dolph Camilli and Kiki Cuyler.

"The Dutch Master," as he later became known, retired the first five batters before issuing a walk. In the third inning, the Reds scored four runs with two outs with the help of a two-run homer by Frank McCormick.

Although some players were having trouble getting used to the lights and Johnny was wild throughout the game, Brooklyn fans began cheering loudly as the no-hitter continued. After the Reds scored single runs in the seventh and eighth innings, there was no doubt for whom Dodgers fans were rooting.

With one out in the bottom of the ninth, Vander Meer loaded the bases with three walks on just 18 pitches. Reds manager Bill McKechnie rushed to the mound to try to calm his jittery pitcher. It worked, as Johnny retired the last two batters, getting Leo Durocher on a fly to center field for the final out.

As the fans went crazy with cheers and Reds players pounded their heroic pitcher, Vander Meer struggled to get off the field, finally reaching the clubhouse where he flopped, exhausted, on a bench. The Reds had won, 6-0, and Vander Meer had etched his name into the record books.

Vander Meer walked eight batters while striking out seven. "In the first game," he said many years later, "I threw a lot of fastballs. I had good control that day, and Boston hit a lot of ground balls. In the second game, I was real quick, real fast, but my curveball was hanging. I only threw three curves in the first seven innings. By the eighth, I was starting to lose my fastball, but the curve came back to me. In both games, I figured, if they're gonna beat me, they're gonna beat my good stuff. I didn't go for a no-hitter in either game until the ninth inning. Before then, I was just going for the shutout.

"One of the things I remember most about those games," Vander Meer added, "was the second game when it was probably the only time in the history of Ebbets Field that the fans weren't pulling for the Dodgers. Brooklyn fans were probably the most loyal fans in baseball, but when they saw what was going on, they pulled for me. That really gave me a thrill."

While the nation celebrated Vander Meer's momentous feat, Johnny declined an offer from the Reds to change his number to 00. Four days later, before a wildly hopeful crowd of 34,511 at Boston, he allowed no hits until Debs Garms slammed a two-out single in center in the third inning. The safety snapped Vander Meer's hitless streak at 21 and two-third innings. Ultimately, the Reds won the game, 14-1.

Vander Meer was the starting and winning pitcher in the All-Star Game, yielding one hit in three innings of a 4-1 National League victory. Johnny then went on to finish the season with a 15-10 record and a 3.12 earned run average while pitching in 32 games and 225 innings, allowing 177 hits, striking out 125, and walking 103. At the end of the season, he was named the Major League Player of the Year by *The Sporting News*.

Johnny hurt his arm in 1939, and was stunningly sent back to the minors at Indianapolis. He was reactivated late in the season and won the pennant-clinching game for the Reds with a 3-2, 13-inning victory over the Philadelphia Phillies. Vander Meer finished with a 5-9 record, but did not pitch again, as the Reds were swept by the New York Yankees.

"The no-hitters are what I'm most known for," Vander Meer said in an interview 50 years later, "but to me, that (pennant-clinching) game was the biggest thrill of my career. I was still going strong in the 13th inning. I knew my arm was back. To me, that was my greatest game."

Vander Meer went on to pitch in 13 big league seasons, ending his career in 1951 with a 119-121 record while appearing in 346 games. Overall, he posted wins in double figures five times, with a high of 18 in 1942. He led the league in games started (36) once, in strikeouts three consecutive times, and in walks twice.

Released after going to the Cleveland Indians early in the 1951 season, Vander Meer went back to the minors, and while hurling for Tulsa in the Texas League in 1952—some 14 years after his famous games—he pitched a no-hitter in a 12-0 win over Beaumont. Just 335 people were in the stands to watch a guy who had authored one of pitching's greatest achievements.

17

HAL NEWHOUSER

VOTED MVP TWO CONSECUTIVE YEARS

In the days before the Cy Young Award was invented, postseason honors for pitchers were extremely limited. A pitcher could be a candidate for Most Valuable Player honors, but he had to compete with position players, and as one who did not play every day, he was seldom considered for the award.

Between 1922 when the MVP award officially began until 1956 when the first Cy Young winner was selected, pitchers won MVP honors just 13 times—seven in the National League and six in the American League.

Of those pitchers, none duplicated the amazing feat of Hal Newhouser. The stylish, cunning left-hander won two MVP awards in a row. In the midst of a spectacular three-year run, Newhouser captured the reward as the best player in the American League in 1944 and 1945.

A 1992 Hall of Fame inductee, "Prince Hal," as he was often called, posted a 29-9 record in 1944 and a 25-9 mark in 1945. Adding his 26-9 log in 1946, when he placed second in the voting for MVP, Newhouser went 80-27 over that three-year period, a record that no pitcher since then has come close to matching.

Overall, Newhouser had a 207-150 record with a 3.06 ERA during his 14 full seasons in the big leagues (he also appeared in a few games during three other seasons). While pitching in all or parts of 15 seasons with the Detroit Tigers, he won in double figures seven times while appearing in five All-Star Games.

But it was his work in the mid-1940s that etched the name of the 6-foot, 2-inch, 190-pounder among one of pitching's greatest success stories.

In his early years, Newhouser was mostly interested in ice hockey and football. The son of a gymnastics instructor from Germany, Hal spent long hours as a boy training with his father, a practice that he later said was a major influence in his pitching career.

Born in Detroit in 1921, Newhouser had started playing baseball as a left-handed shortstop, and didn't pitch until he was 15 years old. Although a self-described "hot-headed kid," he became a brilliant hurler in American Legion baseball as a teenager, and was signed by the Tigers at the age of 17. Detroit scout Wish Egan said that he had just signed "the greatest left-handed pitcher I ever saw."

Hal spent slightly less than two seasons in the minors at Alexandria of the Evangeline League and Beaumont of the Texas League before reporting to the Tigers as an 18 year old at the end of the 1939 season.

Over the next four years, Newhouser never won more than nine games in a single season, and only once did he register as much as a .500 season. He had gone 9-9, 9-11, and 8-14 in his first three full seasons with Detroit. Then in 1943, he went 8-17, at one point losing 13 straight games, including six by one run. Hal was so discouraged that he demanded to be traded. If that didn't happen, he said, he'd go home and get a job in industry.

Detroit nearly did trade their then-erratic hurler, citing, along with his lack of effectiveness, his bad attitude and clubhouse tantrums as key reasons to get rid of him. But Tigers manager Steve O'Neill, who believed that Newhouser had good potential, halted a proposed swap with the Cleveland Indians.

At the time, World War II was at its peak, and many athletes were being drafted into military service. But Newhouser was afflicted with a leaking heart valve, and this congenital problem kept him out of the service.

As the 1944 season got underway, Newhouser won back-to-back decisions, first downing the Indians, 4-3, for his first win of the year with a three-inning relief stint. Then, four days later, he worked 12 innings, giving up just four hits in a 2-0 decision over the Chicago White Sox.

On May 27, Newhouser went 10 innings and allowed just five hits to beat the Philadelphia Athletics, 2-1. Three days later, he pitched a complete-game seven-hitter in a 4-3 victory over the New York Yankees.

More stellar games followed. In June, Newhouser hurled 11 innings while beating the Athletics, 3-2, and conquered the White Sox with a two-hit, 2-0 victory. He beat the Washington Senators with three innings of relief in a 6-5, 11-inning game. Shortly afterward, he became a 20-game winner for the first time in his career with seven-hit, 3-0 shutout of the Boston Red Sox.

Starting in late August, Newhouser won six consecutive games. Hal's 29th win came while pitching on just two days' rest on September 30, a 7-3 triumph over the White Sox.

Newhouser finished the season with a 2.22 ERA, working 312.1 innings and leading the league in wins and strikeouts (187). Altogether, he pitched in 47 games, starting 34 and recording 25 complete games. Four of his wins came in relief for the fifth-place Tigers.

Although just 23 years old, it seemed that Newhouser had turned his career around. His curveball was extraordinary, and with his high-kick delivery, he threw a good fastball. He quit blaming his teammates for his losses and also stopped throwing tantrums in the clubhouse. "What turned me around," Newhouser recalled, "was that I got a little older and I began to do some thinking about my temper. Steve O'Neill had become the manager, and he was just like a father to me. And he brought in Paul Richards to catch, and he helped settle me down."

After the season, Newhouser and teammate Dizzy Trout were the leading candidates for the MVP award. Trout had posted a 27-14 record while leading the league in ERA (2.12), innings pitched (352.1), complete games (33), and shutouts (seven). But Hal beat him by four votes to win top honors.

Newhouser continued his hot pace the following season. This time, he was pitching for a pennant contender. On April 21, he went all 11 innings to beat the Indians, 3-2, with a five-hitter. He also tossed a one-hitter in a 3-0 victory over the St. Louis Browns, and hurled a complete game, 11-inning, 2-1 victory over the Browns, the defending champions and Detroit's main competition in the American League pennant race. Although not a strikeout pitcher, Newhouser set a season high with 11 whiffs in a 7-1 victory over Philadelphia in May.

Hal won seven straight games in June. Then on August 20, he captured his 20th victory of the season with a 4-0 win, a seven-hitter over the A's. Four days later, in one of the great pitching duels of the era, Newhouser lost to Bob Feller at Cleveland, 4-2, before a crowd of 46,477 in the Indians' pitcher's first start since returning from military service.

Late in the season, Newhouser fanned 10 in an 11-0 victory over Cleveland. On the last day of the season, Detroit clinched the pennant with a 6-3 victory over the Browns, with Newhouser getting his 25th win in 2.2 innings of relief work.

Hal finished the season with four four-hitters and two-five hitters. This time, Newhouser won the Triple Crown, leading the league in wins, ERA (1.81), and strikeouts (212), and also in innings pitched (313.1), games started (36), complete games (29), and shutouts (eight).

In the World Series against the Chicago Cubs, Hal was kayoed in the third inning of the Tigers' 9-0 loss in the opener, but came back to win Game Five with a complete game, 8-4 victory. In the seventh game, Newhouser again beat the Cubs, working all nine innings of a 9-3 win that gave Detroit the World Championship, and for Hal "a thrill that can't be explained."

Soon afterward, Newhouser was again voted the American League's Most Valuable Player. No other pitcher ever won two straight MVP awards, and up to that point, only two—Walter Johnson and Carl Hubbell—garnered as many as two during their careers. Hal was also named Major League Player of the Year by *The Sporting News.*

Newhouser, though, wasn't through. In 1946, he went 26-9 while leading the league in ERA (1.94), tying for the lead in wins, and placing second to Ted Williams in the MVP voting. He followed that with 17-17, 21-12, 18-11, and 15-13 records before being slowed by arm trouble.

In 1954, he was released by Detroit and signed with the Indians by his former teammate and now Cleveland general manager, Hank Greenberg. Newhouser joined a staff that included Bob Feller, Bob Lemon, Early Wynn, and Mike Garcia. Pitching mostly in relief, he had a 7-2 record for an Indians team that set an American League record with 111 wins.

Cleveland released Newhouser early in the 1955 season. Long after his playing days were over, though, Newhouser was still remembered for his accomplishments during a two-year stretch in the mid-1940s.

18

LOU BRISSIE

RETURNED TO PITCH AFTER WAR HEROICS

Baseball history is filled with examples of men who overcame huge obstacles to play the national pastime.

Some were required to surmount serious injuries or illnesses, while others had to hurdle the effects of accidents. Still others needed to conquer some form of personal tragedy. Lou Brissie was one of these players.

Brissie, a left-handed pitcher who did his best work with the Philadelphia Athletics during a seven-year career in the majors, pitched with a shattered leg that had nearly been blown off during World War II. The injury earned him two Purple Hearts and a Bronze Star. Despite such a crushing disaster, Brissie was at one point considered one of the top southpaws in the American League.

A native of Anderson, South Carolina, where he was born in 1924, Leland "Lou" Brissie had enlisted in the Army in December, 1942, and reported for duty in April, 1943. One year later, he was shipped to Europe as a member of the 88th Infantry Division, which subsequently fought in numerous battles and suffered numerous casualties. Along the way, a promising pitching career was nearly dashed on a battlefield in the Apennine Mountains of northern Italy.

"In December, 1944, I was hit with shell fire," Brissie, a corporal at the time, recalled. "Our unit had been on the line, but they pulled us off one night, and took us back to get a hot shower and breakfast. On the way back to the front, artillery shells started landing a couple of hundred yards out. We had to get everybody out of the truck. I yelled to the guys to jump back, and as I did, a shell landed nearby. If I had been six feet back, it would have killed me."

As it was, the shell broke Brissie's feet and shattered his left leg, which was split open from the ankle to the knee. Also hit in the hands and right shoulder with mortar fragments, Brissie had to crawl for cover through the mud, and in the process bacteria lodged in the wound.

Found lying unconscious, Brissie was rushed to a field hospital and given emergency treatment. Although doctors wanted to amputate one of his legs, Brissie convinced them not to. What followed was an odyssey during which he spent time in scores of hospitals in Europe and the United States. It took 23 operations and the insertion of a metal plate to piece the leg back together.

"A Major Brubaker saved my leg," Brissie said many years later. "I'll never be able to thank him enough. He wired some bone fragments back into my leg. There were some empty spots in my leg, and he decided just to let the bones grow back together. Basically, what he did was reconstruct my leg with wire.

"When he told me I was going to be okay, I felt it was just a matter of time before I got back on my feet. But I wound up going to hospitals all over. I was the first guy in the Mediterranean Theater who was put on penicillin therapy. I even smelled like penicillin, I had so much of it."

After returning to the United States, Brissie finally got out of the hospital. For more than a year, he hobbled around town on crutches. Finally, in September, 1945, he traveled to Philadelphia to check in with the team that had originally signed him in 1942 and to show Connie Mack that he could throw the ball.

But osteomyelitis, a bacterial infection of the bone marrow, had settled into Brissie's leg, causing him to miss the 1946 season, and it would give him trouble the rest of his career. If it gets into the blood, it can be deadly, but Brissie controlled it with antibiotics.

"I told Mr. Mack that I felt I'd be ready for Spring Training in 1947," Brissie said. "I just wanted to let him know I was okay."

That, of course, was a big concern of the A's. They had gone to great lengths to sign the strapping left-hander. In 1941, the day after Brissie had finished high school, scout Chick Galloway brought the young pitcher to Philadelphia, where he met Mack and agreed to sign with his club. By then, the 6-4½, 210-pound hurler had become one of the most talked-about players in South Carolina. Brissie had started out on the sandlots of Greenville, where he had begun playing at the age of 13.

Lou finally got to his first Spring Training in 1947. On the way north, the A's dropped him off at their Class A team in Savannah. That year, Brissie's 23 wins (he had just five losses), 1.91 ERA, and 278 strikeouts led the South Atlantic League. In 254 innings, he gave up just 167 hits. Although he couldn't run well, Brissie was called up to the Athletics at the end of the 1947 season. He started one game, but lost, 5-3, at Yankee Stadium on the first Babe Ruth Day.

The following spring, Brissie was back in camp with the A's. This time, he not only made the major league club, but was also a starter on Opening Day at Fenway Park against the Boston Red Sox.

Brissie pitched a sparkling four-hitter to beat the mighty Sox, 4-2, even though at one point Ted Williams lined a drive off his bad leg. With a respectable fastball, a sharp curve, and a deceptive changeup, he compiled a 14-10 record and was fourth in the league in strikeouts with 127, while appearing in 39 games.

"I worked awful hard to get to that point," said Brissie, who always wore a protective guard over his left leg. "I had a lot of therapy. I did a lot of walking. My leg was wired together, and part of my ankle was gone—even today it bends only 30 percent of what it should.

"The injury changed my pitching style. I couldn't throw as hard or with as much control as I did before. I threw stiff-legged. But I just tried to work around such things. Some days I hurt, and some days I didn't. You just have to make the adjustment. It was kind of like going to the office. Some days you don't feel like doing it, but you do it anyway. I just looked at it day to day. I knew I was realizing a dream that I had for a long time. And I enjoyed every minute of it."

Brissie had another fine season in 1949, although he missed most of September when the osteomyelitis flared up in his leg. He posted a 16-11 record while completing a career-high 18 games. At mid-season, he was named to the American League All-Star team. Lou pitched the middle three innings, giving up five hits in his team's 11-7 victory over the National League.

In 1950, as the Athletics lost 102 games, Brissie appeared in more games (46), started more games (31), and had a better ERA (4.02) than he had in his previous two seasons. Although Lou led the A's staff in games pitched and innings (246), his record had slipped to 7-19. As he had done in previous years, he also spent time in the bullpen and registered eight saves while relieving in 15 games.

The following season, Lou became part of a three-team trade with the Cleveland Indians and Chicago White Sox in a deal in which the A's got out-fielders Gus Zernial and Dave Philley. The Indians landed Brissie, ending a storied run for a guy who had become an enormously popular player in Philadelphia.

Brissie started in just four of 54 games for the Indians, winning four and losing three (overall record was 4-5). In 1952, Lou posted a 3-2 record while starting just one of 42 games.

In 1953, Brissie's playing time was drastically reduced. He appeared in just 16 games, all in relief, and had no decisions. That fall, the Indians sold him to Indianapolis, but Lou refused to report. Hence, his big league career was over. He wound up with a 44-48 career record with a 4.07 ERA while appearing in 234 games. Overall, he pitched in 897.2 innings, allowed 867 hits, struck out 436, and walked 451. He completed 45 games and had 29 saves.

Many years later, Brissie could look back and celebrate his amazing baseball career. "After what I'd lived through and seen," he said, "I was just glad to be there. I figured I was the luckiest guy in the ballpark. I wasn't supposed to be there. I had rheumatic fever at the age of 10, and wasn't sup-posed to live to be 25. I carried two buckets of sand for two years so my arms could open up.

"I guess," he added, "a man who goes to war and sees what he sees learns something about life. I always felt thankful just to be around."

WHEN PITCHERS RULED THE GAME – 1950–1969

19

ROBIN ROBERTS

HURLED 28 STRAIGHT COMPLETE GAMES

On the baseball diamond, seemingly long ago, a complete game was like a badge of honor. It was a meritorious achievement that earned a commendable mark on a pitcher's resume.

Complete games weren't unusual. Under normal conditions, pitchers were expected to work the entire game. Even into the 1970s, some of the top pitchers recorded 30 or more complete games in a season.

Eventually, as moundsmen were celebrated for lasting six innings and throwing 100 pitches, and bullpens the size of small armies became fashionable, complete games virtually disappeared. Today, if a pitcher has three or four CGs in one season, he is roundly applauded.

All of which makes the work of Robin Roberts with the Philadelphia Phillies particularly noteworthy. From August 1952 to July 1953, the 6-1, 190-pound right-hander threw 28 consecutive complete games. Over that period, Robin won 21 games, lost six, and tied one while pitching in 264 innings. Along the way, he also worked two-thirds of an inning in relief.

Roberts' mark is not a major league record. That is held by Jack Taylor, who completed 39 games in a row in 1904. But Taylor's record came in the deadball

era, long before the platoons of relievers arrived and back when complete games were delivered regularly. Roberts, though, hurled in the lively ball era when home runs were abundant and relief pitchers were beginning to surface with some frequency.

"In those days," Roberts said about his era, "you just went out there and pitched. You started the game and just kept going. I never wanted to be taken out. I always wanted to pitch the whole game. I was either a rock head or a strong guy, but I never considered coming out until the manager came out and took the ball away from me."

In Roberts's case, managers didn't come out too often. During a career that stretched from 1948 to 1966, he started 609 games and completed more than half of them, a remarkable 305. He led the league in complete games five times, never going lower than 37 and reaching a high of 41 in 1953. Fourteen times during his 18 full seasons in the majors, he completed 30 or more games.

Complete games, of course, weren't Roberts' only strength. A hurler with impeccable control, he posted a career record of 286-245 with a 3.41 ERA while pitching in 676 games overall. In 4,688.2 innings, he gave up 4,582 hits, struck out 2,357, and walked 902. Roberts, who tossed 45 shutouts, led the league in games started six times, in innings pitched five times, and in wins four times.

The crowning achievements of Roberts 'career came between 1950 and 1955 when he registered six straight 20-win seasons, totaling 138 victories altogether. In 1950, pitching for the third time in five days, he went 10 innings to beat the Brooklyn Dodgers, 4-1, on Dick Sisler's three-run homer in the 10th inning, in the final game of the season, to give the Phillies their first pennant since 1915.

Roberts, who was elected Major League Pitcher of the Year (a forerunner of the Cy Young Award) in 1952 and 1955 and who made seven National League All-Star teams, was born in 1926 in Springfield, Illinois. Known more for his basketball exploits than his baseball prowess, he attended Michigan State University on a basketball scholarship after serving in the military during World War II. During the summers, he played amateur baseball in New England before signing a contract with the Phillies that called for a $25,000 bonus. Robin spent two months in the minors before getting called up to the Phillies in 1948.

By 1950, he had become a 20-game winner. Then in 1952, he posted a 28-7 mark that earned him *The Sporting News* Player of the Year Award, while just missing out in the voting for National League's Most Valuable Player.

Yet Roberts' '52 season was magnificent in many other ways, too. On August 28, he began a 28-game winning streak when he beat the St. Louis Cardinals,10-6. Just two games earlier, he had won his ninth straight game with a 10-5 victory over the St. Louis Cardinals. That game was followed by a 3-0 loss to the Chicago Cubs in a game in which he was lifted in the eighth inning.

The second game of the streak occurred on September 2 when he beat the Dodgers, 8-2. Then came the streak's most memorable contest. In the first game of a doubleheader on September 6 at Shibe Park against the Boston Braves, the game was tied, 6-6, after nine innings. The contest was finally decided in the 17th on a home run by Del Ennis. Incredibly, Roberts pitched the whole game, allowing 18 hits.

That game, which lasted just three hours and 50 minutes, was followed by five more wins in September, the last of which was a 7-4 decision over the San Francisco Giants that gave Roberts his 28th win of the season, a mark that no National League pitcher has reached since then. At that point, Roberts had completed eight games in a row, although none was a shutout, and 30 of his 37 starts that season. He worked in 330 innings and compiled a 2.59 ERA with three shutouts for the season.

Robbie had won eight games in a row as the 1953 season began, but he lost the opener, 4-1, to the Giants and Larry Jansen, despite going the distance. He came back six days later and fired a three-hitter to beat Jansen and the Giants, 2-1. Then, with just two days of rest, he trumped the Dodgers, 6-1. With just two days rest again, he sank the Pirates, 7-6. April ended with Roberts getting no decision in a game against the Cardinals that was called after five innings on account of rain.

The streak continued as Roberts beat the Cubs with a six-hitter, 5-1, then topped the Dodgers, 7-6, holding on after Roy Campanella socked a two-run homer with two outs in the bottom of the ninth. A six-hit, 1-0 victory over the Cubs and a 6-3 win over the Reds, despite fourth-inning home runs by Willard Marshall and Ted Kluszewski, came next. Then on May 23, Roberts tossed a four-hitter, but lost to the Dodgers, 2-0.

The streak was still alive, though, and in the next game, Robbie fired his third three-hitter in the last 24 days in a 14-2 rout of the Pirates. By then, the streak had reached 18 games. "But I never heard anybody talking about it," Roberts recalled. "I certainly wasn't thinking about it. In fact, I had no idea the streak was happening."

But it was, and on June 2, the hurler known as "The Springfield Rifle" fired his second shutout of the season with a 5-0 whitewash of the Cardinals. Four days later, he won the 100th game of his career, a 6-2 verdict over the Milwaukee Braves. Then came a 9-1 triumph over the Cubs.

Roberts lost the next game, 7-4, to the Cubs. Two days later, incredibly, he was used to pitch one and two-thirds innings of relief against the Braves. He then beat the Reds, 10-3, and the Cubs, 6-1, before losing 7-4 to the Cardinals in a game in which he surrendered 14 hits, and 5-4 to the Dodgers in 10 innings. He returned to the win column with a two-hit, 2-0 victory over Pittsburgh in 10 innings for his 20th complete game of the season.

The streak finally ended on July 9 in a seesaw battle with the Dodgers. With Brooklyn winning, 5-4, Roberts was replaced by a pinch hitter in the bottom of the eighth. Ultimately, the Phils went on to win, 6-5. His consecutive complete game streak wound up at 28.

Roberts had gone nearly an entire year without being removed from a game in which he was pitching. After the streak ended, he came back to pitch four consecutive complete games. Robbie finished the season with a 23-16 record, completing 33 of his 41 starts while setting career highs in innings pitched (346.2) and strikeouts (198).

Fortunately, the Phillies had a lead in many of the games in the streak. "That made it easier for me to stay in the game because they didn't have to pinch-hit for me," Roberts said many years later. "Plus, I could hit a little bit, so they could leave me in the game instead of sending in a pinch-hitter."

Despite pitching for mediocre teams, Roberts won at least 23 games three years in a row. Eventually, he won in double figures 12 years in a row and 15 years altogether while finishing the last five years of his career with the Baltimore Orioles, Houston Colt .45s, and Cubs.

Robbie had a brilliant career that was recognized when he was inducted into the Hall of Fame in 1976. His remarkable record of 28 straight complete games certainly held a place among his major achievements.

20

DON LARSEN

FIRED PERFECT GAME IN THE WORLD SERIES

There are many memorable dates in sports history. But October 8, 1956 stands in a class by itself.

That is the date when everyone who was a sports fan remembers where he or she was. It is the date when virtually the entire sports world, indeed most of the nation, came to a stop to follow the event that was unfolding.

On that most memorable of dates, an angular, fun-loving 27-year-old right-handed pitcher with the New York Yankees named Don Larsen pitched the greatest game in baseball history.

As a nationwide audience became riveted to their radios or television sets, and with 64,519 watching hysterically in Yankee Stadium, Larsen pitched a perfect game in Game Five of the World Series, beating the Brooklyn Dodgers, 2-0, in what would be the fourth Series meeting between the two teams in the last five years.

It was the only perfect game ever pitched in a World Series, the first perfect game pitched in the majors in 34 years, and only the fourth perfect game hurled in baseball since the pitching mound was moved back to 60 feet, six inches.

The feat, probably the greatest single achievement in sports history, was especially remarkable not only because it came amid the heavy pressure of a World Series, but because it came against a team that had one the best offensive lineups ever to appear on the diamond. It included four future Hall of Famers— Jackie Robinson, Duke Snider, Pee Wee Reese, and Roy Campanella—plus three other outstanding hitters in Gil Hodges, Carl Furillo, and Junior Gilliam. What's more, the opposing pitcher was the venerable Sal Maglie, who that day fired a five-hitter and who just two weeks earlier had thrown his own no-hitter.

Larsen, who had compiled an 11-5 record during the season and who just two years earlier had been stung with a 3-21 mark with the first-year Baltimore Orioles (losers of 100 games), had also been the starting pitcher in Game Two of the Series, but had been kayoed in the second inning after allowing four unearned runs.

"I didn't even know I was going to start the fifth game until I got to the ballpark that day," Larsen recalled many years later. "Casey [Stengel] told me, and I went out and warmed up. I knew I had good stuff."

A native of Michigan City, Indiana, where he was born in 1929, Larsen had grown up in San Diego. Although more noted in high school as a basketball player, he was signed by the St. Louis Browns in 1947 and broke into pro ball with Aberdeen of the Northern League. After four years in the minors and two in military service, he reached the big leagues in 1953 with St. Louis, where he went 7-12 in the team's last year in Missouri. Larsen was sent to the Yankees in 1955 as part of a blockbuster 18-player trade in which he and Bob Turley, among others, went to the Yanks and Gene Woodling, Gus Triandos, and others landed with the Browns.

That year, after reporting to Spring Training in less than peak condition, he was sent to Denver of the American Association, where he posted a 9-1 record and hit .360 with 10 home runs. He was recalled at mid-season and went 9-2, which included beating the Boston Red Sox on the next to last day of the season to give the Yanks the American League pennant.

During Spring Training in 1956, the 6-4, 215-pound hurler was in an auto crash at 4 a.m., his car hitting a telephone pole, when Larsen claimed he had fallen asleep at the wheel. But he bounced back to have his best season during 14 years in the majors. Don, who decided at mid-season not to use a windup, was primarily a fastball pitcher with a hard slider. Coming down the stretch in 1956, he fired four straight four-hitters to lead the Yankees to the flag.

Larsen's history-making Series game, coming with the teams tied at 2-2, started with him striking out Gilliam and Reese, and retiring Snyder on a liner to right. Robinson gave Larsen a scare leading off the second, when he drilled a smash that ricocheted off the glove of third baseman Andy Carey. The ball bounced to shortstop Gil McDougald, whose throw to first beat the fleet Robinson by one step.

As the game wore on, everybody in the park became tenser. About the only person who didn't was Larsen himself. "I wasn't really nervous," he said. "The Dodgers added to the suspense by needling Don throughout the game, although he said later that he wasn't aware of it.

In the fifth inning, Hodges hit a smash to deep left-center on which Mickey Mantle, whose home run had given the Yanks a 1-0 lead in the fourth, made a spectacular backhanded catch. "It probably would've been a home run in any other park," Larsen recalled. Then the next batter, Sandy Amoros, clubbed a hard liner to left that swerved foul by one foot just as it reached the stands.

In the seventh, Mantle made another sparkling catch on Reese's smash to center. An inning later, Carey snared a vicious liner hit a few inches off the ground by Hodges, and Mantle gloved another long clout by Amoros.

As the ninth inning began, the crowd was going crazy. Larsen began the inning by retiring Furillo on a fly ball to Hank Bauer in right. Campanella then grounded out to Billy Martin at second. Pinch-hitter Dale Mitchell, a fine hitter, was the next batter.

"By then, I was really pumped," Larsen remembered. "He was a helluva hitter. I said to myself, 'You've come this far, so you better get this last out.'"

Larsen threw a ball, then a called strike. Mitchell swung and missed the next pitch before fouling off a fastball. With a 1-2 count, Larsen uncorked another fastball. Mitchell made a checked swing, but umpire Babe Pinelli, who like Mitchell was in the last game of his career, called "strike three."

Catcher Yogi Berra raced to the mound and flung himself into Larsen's arms. Other Yankees rushed to the mound, and fans leaped out of the stands in one of the most jubilant celebrations ever seen on an athletic field.

"When Yogi jumped on me, my mind just went blank," Larsen said. "Earlier in the game, I was very conscious of what was happening. I knew it was a no-hitter, but I didn't realize it was a perfect game. On the bench, nobody would talk to me. That made me really nervous. The only time I felt comfortable was out on the mound.

"When the game was over, everybody was going wild. But we hadn't even won the Series, yet. We still had two games to play."

Larsen wound up throwing 97 pitches. He struck out seven. And he etched his name into one of the most amazing spots in baseball history. Even Maglie and Robinson came over to the Yankees clubhouse to congratulate Larsen, and President Dwight D. Eisenhower sent him a telegram.

The Yankees went on to lose the next game, then win the Series in Game Seven on a three-hitter by Johnny Kucks. It was the Yanks' seventh Series victory in the last 10 years.

Larsen went on to pitch 10 more seasons in the majors. In the three years after 1956, he posted just a 25-17 record. He won three more World Series games with the Yankees. In the 1957 Series, he worked seven and one-third innings of relief to gain a 12-3 win over the Milwaukee Braves. The following season, he tossed seven shutout innings in a 4-0 win over the Braves. Then in 1962, he got the win while hurling for the San Francisco Giants with one-third of an inning of relief in a 7-3 decision over the Yankees.

After leaving the Yanks in 1959, he pitched with the Kansas City Athletics, the Chicago White Sox, the Giants, the Houston Astros, the Orioles again, and the Chicago Cubs. In going to Kansas City, Larsen was part of a trade that brought Roger Maris to the Yankees.

Larsen finished his career with an 81-91 record and a 3.78 earned run average. He posted a 26-23 record in relief with 23 saves. Don pitched in 412 games, starting 171 of them and completing 44 with 11 shutouts. In 1,548 innings pitched, he gave up 1,442 hits, struck out 849, and walked 725.

It was, though, the perfect game for which Larsen will always be remembered. It is unquestionably regarded as the greatest game ever pitched.

"I like to think it was," Larsen said. "I guess every pitcher is entitled to a good game. I don't know why this particular one happened to me. I guess the Man Upstairs was with me."

So, too, were his teammates and legions of fans who were scattered from one end of the country to the other.

21

DON NEWCOMBE

VOTED MVP AND CY YOUNG IN SAME YEAR

Winning the Cy Young Award is unquestionably a noteworthy feat to which all pitchers aspire. Winning the Most Valuable Player Award is also an exceptional accomplishment that is the goal of every player in baseball.

For one player to win both awards is an incomparable achievement. It's even more amazing if a player wins both awards in the same year.

Don Newcombe did it in 1956. Newcombe won both the Cy Young Award and the Most Valuable Player Award, becoming the first pitcher ever to accomplish that distinction after completing a season that ranks as one of the finest in the annals of major league pitching.

The feat is particularly noteworthy because of the fact that in Newcombe's playing days, the Cy Young award was bestowed on only one pitcher each season. In 1956, when Newcombe became the first pitcher ever to win the award, the winner was either from the National League or the American League, but not both. The award for a pitcher in each league was not instituted until 1967.

The big right-hander who was nicknamed "Newk" had numerous other firsts during his career. He was the first player to win the Cy Young, MVP, and

Rookie of the Year awards (an honor he captured in 1949). He was also the first African American to start in a World Series game and the first black pitcher to win 20 games.

Indeed, Newcombe was a true pioneer in the game of baseball. In fact, once, while having dinner with Martin Luther King, the renowned civil rights leader told Newk, "Don, you'll never know how easy you and Jackie [Robinson] and Roy [Campanella] and Larry [Doby] made it for me to do my job by what you did on the baseball field." Just 28 days later, King was assassinated in Atlanta.

What Newcombe did on the baseball field began at the professional level in 1944 when as a 17 year old, he played with the Newark Eagles of the Negro National League. In two seasons and 29 games with the Eagles, he was credited with a 9-7 record.

By 1945, Dodgers president Branch Rickey was looking for players to break the color barrier in professional baseball. At the end of that season, the Eagles played an exhibition game at Brooklyn's Ebbets Field. While Newcombe pitched two innings, Brooklyn coach Clyde Sukeforth watched from the stands. Suitably impressed, he asked the 6-4, 225-pound hurler to come the next day to the Dodgers' office. When he did, Newcombe was signed to a contract worth $375 per month with a $1,500 bonus.

Newcombe, who was born in 1926 in Madison, New Jersey, was assigned to play for the Nashua Dodgers in the New England League, a circuit that at the time was one of the few to accept black players. One of four black players signed by the Dodgers (the others were Robinson, Campanella, and pitcher Roy Partlow), Newcombe posted 14-4 and 19-6 records over the next two years at Nashua. In 1948, he joined the Dodgers' International League team at Montreal, where he compiled a 17-6 record.

Newcombe began the 1949 season back at Montreal, but after five games was summoned by the Dodgers. "They liked me because I was so big and could throw the ball hard," he said.

That season, Newk tied for the league lead with five shutouts, at one point pitching 32 straight scoreless innings, and was selected to his first of three straight All-Star teams while ending the season with a 17-8 record with a 3.17 ERA. After the season, he was named Rookie of the Year by both *The Sporting News* and the Baseball Writers' Association of America, just the second African American player (the first was teammate Jackie Robinson in 1947) to win the award.

Newk started the first game of the 1949 World Series, and pitched a five-hitter before losing to the New York Yankees, 1-0, on a ninth inning home run by Tommy Henrich. He also lost the fourth game of a Series as the Dodgers bowed in five games. From there, he posted a 19-11 record while throwing the home run pitch to Dick Sisler that gave the 1950 Philadelphia Phillies the National League pennant on the last day of the season. That season, he also tried the by-then unheard of chore of pitching both games of a doubleheader against the Phillies, winning the first game, then lasting through the seventh inning in the nightcap.

Newcombe became the first African American pitcher to win 20 games when he went 20-9 in 1951. Afterward, he was drafted and spent two years in the military during the Korean War. After getting discharged, he fell back to a 9-8 mark in 1954, then rebounded with a 20-5 log the following year. An outstanding batter, Newcombe also hit .359 with seven home runs, a National League record. While the Dodgers won their first World Series in club history, Newcombe started but got no decision in the first game.

Then in 1956, Newk reached the height of his career. While posting a 27-7 record in 38 games (36 starts) for a Dodgers team that registered a 93-61 mark for the season, he led the majors in wins and winning percentage (.794), striking out 139 and allowing just 219 hits in 268 innings with a 3.06 earned run average.

During the season, Newcombe got off to a 2-1 start in April, then posted a 5-2 record in May. His 7-3 record by then included five straight wins and a three-hit shutout victory over the Chicago Cubs.

In June, Don won two out of four games with a no-decision game thrown in. He didn't lose a game in six decisions in July, including another shutout of the Cubs on a five-hitter. Then, with a seven-game winning streak underway, he began August with a four-hit, 10-strikeout shutout of the Braves and a six-hit blanking of the Pirates, while building a streak of seven straight complete games and three consecutive shutouts. Altogether, Newcombe won seven games in August, which also included a two-hitter against the Phillies, a three-hitter against the New York Giants, and a victory in relief over the Cubs.

Newcombe flew into September with a 22-6 record. But he didn't stop there.

The hard-thrower, who infielder Junior Gilliam once called "the hardest worker around," won five more games while losing just once. Again, Don blanked the Cubs with a three-hitter, and in another game beat the Giants with an 11-strikeout six-hitter.

When the season ended, Newcombe ranked fourth in the league in complete games (18), shutouts (five), and innings pitched. Although the Dodgers again won the pennant, this time by one game over the Braves, no other Brooklyn pitcher had more than 13 wins.

While Newcombe's World Series misery continued—he lost one game and got no decision in the other—his regular season performance was justly rewarded. He became the only pitcher ever to win the MVP Award and the Cy Young Award when it was presented annually to just one hurler (65 years later, Justin Verlander won both awards, the Cy Young by then going to pitchers from each league). Adding to his honors, Newk also was named the National League Pitcher of the Year by *The Sporting News*.

It was a truly magnificent season for Newcombe, but it would be his last big year. Don slipped to an 11-12 mark in 1957. Then, after getting off to an 0-6 start the following year, he was traded to the Cincinnati Reds for first baseman Steve Bilko and pitcher Johnny Klippstein.

Newcombe, who by then was having problems with alcohol, which he later overcame, had only one more winning season, a 13-8 mark with the Reds in 1959. The following season, after going 24-21 in parts of three seasons with the Reds, he was sold to the Cleveland Indians, who at the end of the year gave Newcombe his unconditional release.

After sitting out a season, Newcombe became the first major league player to sign with a Japanese team when he inked a pact with the Chunichi Dragons. In one season in Japan, Newk was noted moreso as a hitter than as a pitcher. At the end of the season, he returned home.

Newcombe's final big league record stood at 149-90 with a 3.56 ERA in 344 games. He posted 136 complete games and 24 shutouts while throwing 2,154.2 innings, allowing 2,102 hits, striking out 1,129, and walking 490. As a batter, Newk had a career average of .271 with 15 home runs with 108 RBI.

22

HARVEY HADDIX

WAS PERFECT FOR 12 INNINGS

Every once in a while a little guy squeezes in among the giants of the mound, and shows he can throw a baseball pretty well, too. Harvey Haddix was one of those guys.

The diminutive left-hander's size was usually listed at 5-9, 150 pounds, but even that was widely viewed as an exaggeration. In his early days, the wee hurler was often mistaken for a batboy.

Although he was nicknamed "The Kitten," Haddix was no pussycat on the mound. He was more like a tiger. Few batters ever wanted to be in the same jungle with him. Haddix won 38 games in his first two full seasons in the majors, and he won in double figures eight times during a 14-year career in which he posted a 136-113 record and was a three-time National League All-Star.

But all those records paled by comparison to the game he pitched in 1959 with the Pittsburgh Pirates against the Milwaukee Braves. Haddix hurled a perfect game for 12 innings, the longest hitless game ever pitched. He gave up a hit in the 13th inning, which, as it turned out, drove in the game's only run. The Kitten lost the game, but his magnificent effort earned a place as one of the greatest games ever pitched.

It was a performance that may not have been expected of a little guy like Harvey. But that should not have been the case. The Kitten, so named because the nickname "The Cat" was already taken by pitcher Harry Brecheen, was a well-established moundsman who was highly capable of pitching such a game.

Born in 1925 in Medway, Ohio, Haddix didn't sign a pro contract until he was 21 years old. He spent four seasons in the minors, winning in double figures each time, including a 19-5 mark in 1947 at Winston-Salem, an 18-6 log in 1950 at Columbus with a 10-inning no-hitter. He served nearly two more years in the military before reaching the big leagues late in 1952 with the St. Louis Cardinals.

One year later in his first full season in the majors, Haddix rang up a 20-9 record, which included a near no-hitter against the Philadelphia Phillies. Harvey followed that season by going 18-13, then won in double figures each of the next three years, including the 1956 season, when the Cardinals traded him to the Phillies. After the 1957 campaign, the Phillies dealt him to the Cincinnati Reds, where he spent one season before getting swapped again, this time to the Pirates.

In his first season at Pittsburgh, Haddix made baseball history. It happened on May 26 at Milwaukee's County Stadium against the first-place Braves, the National League pennant-winners the two previous years. Entering the game, the 33-year-old Haddix carried a 2-3 record for the third-place Pirates. His opponent was Braves standout Lew Burdette. A crowd of 19,194 was in attendance.

The odds were not in Haddix's favor. In addition to the fact that it had rained during the day, and at game-time dark clouds hovered over the ballpark and lightning flashed in the distance, Haddix, as someone said, "was sick as a dog" from a bad cold and was stuffing his mouth with cough drops. He had spent much of the afternoon in bed at the hotel. Even when he arrived at the ballpark, he went straight to the trainer's room and took a nap. Added to that, three Pirates regulars—Roberto Clemente, Dick Groat, and Dick Stuart—were not in the lineup. The Braves had one of the league's strongest batting orders that included future Hall of Famers Hank Aaron and Eddie Mathews, plus Andy Pafko, Wes Covington, and Joe Adcock.

Nevertheless, The Kitten started by retiring Johnny O'Brien on a hard grounder to short. The brilliant performance was underway. Harvey then went to a 3-2 count on Mathews before inducing him to line out to first. It would be the only time all night that Haddix threw three balls to one batter. Aaron flied out to center to end the inning.

The Braves hit five more fly balls over the next four innings, but none came close to being a hit. Few balls were hit hard off Haddix, although Johnny Logan smashed a liner in the third inning that Bucs' shortstop Dick Schofield pulled down with a leaping catch. Logan also sent a grounder into the hole at short and after it took a bad hop, Schofield made a barehanded stop and threw the batter out at first.

Meanwhile, Pittsburgh had several scoring opportunities. The Bucs loaded the bases with two outs in the third inning, but failed to score. Bob Skinner, who earlier had drilled a shot down the left field line that went foul by three or four inches, laced a fly to deep right in the seventh. It would have left the park, but heavy winds held it back and Aaron caught it against the fence. The Pirates also had men on first and third with two outs in the ninth.

Haddix was as sharp as he'd ever been. Mixing a fastball and slider with an occasional changeup, Harvey sent down one Brave after another, although it was later revealed that Milwaukee pitchers had been stealing signs from the club's bullpen. Even that didn't matter, though.

"I was doing the best I could and my fastball was really jumping," Haddix said many years later. "But I wasn't aware that it was a perfect game. I didn't know whether I had walked anybody or not."

By the end of nine innings, Haddix had thrown just 78 pitches. He had fanned two batters in the same inning just once. Burdette had given up 12 hits.

In the 13th inning, the Pirates had a runner on base, but couldn't get him home.

Then in the bottom of the frame, Haddix's masterpiece came to an end after he had retired a record 36 straight batters on just 90 pitches.

Felix Mantilla, a .215 hitter who had entered the game in the late innings, poked a high bouncer to third. Don Hoak fielded the ball, but his throw to first pulled Rocky Nelson off the bag. Hoak was charged with an error, and Haddix's perfect game was over.

Mathews bunted Mantilla to second and then Aaron was intentionally walked.

That brought Adcock, who five years earlier had smacked a drive off Haddix's knee that nearly ended his career, to the plate. The Braves' cleanup hitter slammed Haddix's second pitch to deep right center, where it cleared the fence for an apparent game-ending three-run homer. But Aaron, thinking the ball had not cleared the fence, touched second and then headed back to the dugout figuring that Mantilla had scored to give the Braves a 1-0 win.

Meanwhile, Adcock raced to third. At the urging of their teammates, Aaron returned to second and Adcock to first, where they rounded the bases and scored. No one was sure of the final score. But the next day, National League president Warren Giles declared the Braves 1-0 winners, ruling that Adcock was automatically out for passing Aaron on the bases. Adcock was credited with an RBI double.

It was a heartbreaking loss for Haddix. "That's what I remember the most," Haddix said. "We didn't win. Nothing, of course, can make up for not winning a perfect game, but anytime you win, it's a different feeling."

Exhausted by the end of the game, Haddix finished with eight strikeouts. Thirteen balls were hit to the outfield. The Pirates left eight men on base in a game that took 2:54 to play. Burdette, who also went the distance, gained his eighth win in 10 decisions.

Harvey went on to post a 12-12 record in 1959. Then in 1960, after registering an 11-10 mark and helping manager Danny Murtaugh's Bucs win the National League pennant, he was the winning pitcher in two games of the World Series. He posted a 5-3 Pirates victory in Game Five, before getting the decision in relief in the seventh game when Pittsburgh clinched the Series on Bill Mazeroski's ninth-inning home run.

Haddix wound up pitching five years for the Pirates before getting traded to the Baltimore Orioles. He played two years with the Orioles before retiring after the 1965 season.

Because he had not given up any hits during the regulation nine innings, Haddix had always been credited with a no-hitter. But in 1991, a statistical committee formed by Major League Baseball decided that to be credited with a no-hitter, a pitcher had to pitch one throughout the entire game, no matter how long it lasted. Since Haddix hadn't done that, even though he had hurled 12 hitless innings, his remarkable feat, along with those by numerous others pitchers, was erased from the record book.

It didn't really matter, though. Along with his excellent career in the big leagues, Haddix is remembered as the owner of one of the greatest games ever pitched.

23

WHITEY FORD

HOLDS KEY WORLD SERIES RECORDS

In every era, there are certain players who thrive on performing in the World Series. No matter what the circumstances might be, they always rise to the occasion. And whether they play in one Series or many, their records indicate that they have what it takes to perform at the highest level in a pressure-packed event that ranks at the top of the sports world.

While there is seldom anything predictable about a World Series, these are players who have no problems with basking in the spotlight. While favored teams sometimes lose, and star hitters and pitchers falter, the World Series is their special place in the sun.

No one fits this description better than Ed (Whitey) Ford. In the years when he played in the World Series, the blonde hurler pitched with unmatched success. The crafty 5-10, 178-pound left-hander compiled a stack of records that put him at the top of the list of World Series stars.

Ford spent all of his 16 years in the major leagues with the New York Yankees. During that time, the Yanks went to the World Series 11 times and won eight of them. Although he missed two of those Fall Classics because of military duty, Ford won 10 Series games, the most in baseball history.

Baseball Digest. Courtesy of Wikimedia Commons.

The hurler known as "The Chairman of the Board" because of his ability to handle pressure situations calmly and without fluster also holds World Series records for most games pitched (22), most games started (22), most games as the opening-game starter (eight), most innings pitched (146), most strikeouts (94), most walks (34), and most losses (eight). He is the only hurler ever to start four straight World Series openers.

Ford's biggest claim to World Series fame, however, is his scoreless streak. Whitey pitched 33 2/3 scoreless Series innings, an all-time record that broke the previous mark of 29 2/3 innings set in 1918 by Babe Ruth.

Ford broke Ruth's record in 1961 when he pitched his third straight World Series shutout. Although that falls well short of the all-time season record of 59 straight scoreless innings held by Orel Hershiser, considering it was achieved in the World Series, it is a most impressive feat.

The plucky southpaw, of course, had many other impressive feats. He won more games (236) than any other Yankees pitcher. He is the all-time leader in winning percentage (.690) among hurlers who have at least 300 career decisions. He was a member of 10 All-Star teams, won the Cy Young Award in 1961, and was inducted into the Hall of Fame in 1974.

Overall, Ford's win-loss total was 236-106 with a 2.75 earned run average. Although often held out by manager Casey Stengel so he could pitch against the best teams, Ford appeared in 498 games, starting 438, completing 156, and firing 45 shutouts, including eight by 1-0 scores. In 3,170.1 innings pitched, he yielded 2,766 hits, struck out 1,956, and walked 1,086.

"Slick," as he was called by teammate Mickey Mantle, won in double figures 13 years in a row while leading the American League in wins and winning percentage three times apiece, in ERA, innings pitched, and games started each twice, and in complete games once. Twice in his career, Ford struck out six straight batters. He also fired two straight one-hit games in 1955.

Unlike most others, Ford didn't have to go far to become a Yankee. He was born just a few miles from Yankee Stadium in 1928, in Queens, NY. After graduating from high school, he signed off the sandlots with the Yankees in 1947 for a bonus of $7,000.

In slightly more than three years in the minors, starting in 1947 with Butler of the Mid-Atlantic League, he posted a 51-20 record, including a 16-5 mark in 1949 in the Eastern League's team at Binghamton. Called up to the Yankees in 1950, he won his first nine games before losing to the Philadelphia Athletics. That fall, while being named Rookie of the Year by *The Sporting News*, he won his first World Series game with a 5-2 decision over the Philadelphia Phillies in the fourth and deciding game, allowing no earned runs in eight and two-thirds innings.

Although lacking an overpowering fastball, Ford relied on a collection of breaking balls and stellar control. Sometimes, he later admitted, some of his pitches were "doctored." No matter what he threw, though, Ford always delivered his pitches with a cocky, self-assured demeanor. "When he's got the ball, the game's over," someone once said.

Ford missed both the 1951 and 1952 seasons while serving in the Army during the Korean War. When he returned to baseball, he logged records of 18-6, 16-8, and 18-7 before jumping up to a 19-6 mark in 1956, when he led the league with a 2.47 ERA and a .760 winning percentage.

After losing a game to the Brooklyn Dodgers in 1953, Ford's World Series highlights began in 1955, when he beat the Dodgers twice. Although the Yanks lost the Series, Ford won Game One, 6-5, and Game Six, 5-1, with a four-hitter.

Then in 1956, he was ousted after three innings in a first-game loss, but came back to pitch a complete game 5-3 victory in the third tilt as the Yankees took the Series from the Dodgers in seven games.

Ford, who said he pitched with "his arm, heart, and head," and who became noted for his after-hour exploits with Mantle and Billy Martin, registered records of 11-5, 14-7, 16-10, and 12-9 over the next four years. Most likely, he would've won more had Stengel used him in the regular rotation instead of saving him to face the best teams and pitchers.

In the 1957 Series in a losing battle against the Milwaukee Braves, Ford beat Warren Spahn in the first game, 3-1, but lost in Game Five, 1-0. The following year, he lost the opener to Spahn, 4-3, and got no decision in two other games. Then in 1960, he blanked the Pittsburgh Pirates, 10-0, with a four-hitter in Game Three and 12-0 in Game Six with a seven-hitter.

Although the Yanks lost the Series to the Bucs, Ford's streak was now underway.

So were his finest years during the regular season. In 1961, Whitey had the best year of his career. With new manager Ralph Houk using Ford on a regular basis, the hurler posted a dazzling 25-4 record while leading the league with career bests in wins, winning percentage (.862), innings pitched (283), and games (39), and winning the Cy Young Award.

In a year dominated by teammate Roger Maris's home run spree, the Yanks beat the Cincinnati Reds in the Series with Ford hurling a two-hit, 2-0 victory in the first game. In Game Four, he added five more scoreless innings before he was removed in the sixth inning after suffering an ankle injury in what became a 7-0 Yankees win. Ford had now broken Ruth's record, and his scoreless streak stood at 32 innings.

After Ford recorded a 17-8 mark in 1962, the Yanks returned to the Series with a winning effort over the San Francisco Giants. Ford won the opener, 6-2, but his streak came to an end when he gave up a run with two outs in the second inning.

Ford's World Series heroics were not over yet. In 1963, he fashioned a 24-7 record while leading the league in wins, percentage (.774), starts (37), and innings pitched (269.1). The Yankees went back to the Series against the Los Angeles Dodgers, but while his team was getting swept, Ford lost two games to Sandy Koufax by scores of 5-2 and 2-1.

Whitey had one more shot in the Series in 1964 after posting a 17-6 record during the regular season. But again, he lost the opener, pitching just 5.1 innings against the St. Louis Cardinals, eventual winners of the Series in seven games.

Although his World Series appearances were finished, Ford went 16-13 in 1965. Shoulder and later elbow problems set in the following year, and surgery limited the lefty's duties. That year and the next, he would spend a substantial amount of time on the disabled list and total just four wins (with nine losses) in 29 games.

Ford retired in May 1967 at the age of 38. During his career, he had been one of the most dominant pitchers of his era. That was especially true of his work on the mounds of World Series games.

24

WARREN SPAHN

WON 23 GAMES AT 42 YEARS OLD

Rare is the player who pitches into his 40s in the big leagues. Even rarer is the pitcher who at that age compiles a successful record.

There have, however, been some notable exceptions. One was Warren Spahn. Near the end of a storied career in the majors, the brilliant left-hander added one more laurel to his record when at the age of 42, he won 23 games.

No one in baseball history ever won 20 or more games at that age. And only four other pitchers—Cy Young, Jack Quinn, Murry Dickson, and Jamie Moyer—even won in double figures at 42 years old.

In Spahn's case, the mark was remarkable not only because of his age, but because it climaxed a career in which he had won in double figures 17 times during his 19 full seasons in the majors. In 13 of those years, he won 20 or more games.

Spahn is also the winningest left-handed pitcher in baseball history with a 363-245 record compiled in 750 games, of which he started 665. In 5,243.2 innings on the mound, he gave up 4,830 hits, struck out 2,583, walked 1,434, and posted a 3.09 earned run average.

The stylish southpaw ranks fifth on the all-time list of winners. He hurled more complete games (382) and more shutouts (63) than any left-handed pitcher in National League history. No other NL pitcher ever started more games (665), pitched more innings, or worked more years (21) than Spahn, who ranks eighth on the all-time list of innings pitched, sixth in shutouts, and 16th in strikeouts.

During a career that led to his induction into the Hall of Fame in 1973, Spahn pitched two no-hitters, was baseball's second Cy Young Award winner (1957) when the honor was bestowed on just one pitcher each year, and was named to 17 All-Star teams. He led the league in complete games nine times, and in innings pitched and strikeouts each four times. Amazingly, Spahn had not won a single game before the age of 25, and he won 75 times after he was 40.

"I always felt," he once said, "that some people mature older than others. I was one of those people. Because of the time I spent in the service, I had a better perspective of what this game was all about. Your vision becomes stronger when you're in jeopardy, and you find out that the human animal is pretty strong and determined. It's like the animal that is hunted in the wild. It's survival. I felt like that during my baseball career. And no writer was going to write my epitaph. I was a different breed."

It was Spahn's career in the military that had delayed his arrival in the big leagues. Born in 1921 in Buffalo, New York, he had turned down a scholarship to Cornell University so that he could sign with the Boston Braves at the age of 19. He pitched in the minors for three years, then was brought up by the Braves late in 1942 and pitched in four games. After that season, he joined the Army and served in Europe during World War II, at one point getting wounded during heavy fighting along the Rhine River, receiving a Purple Heart, and eventually earning a battlefield commission as a second lieutenant.

After serving three years in the military, the slender 6-0, 175-pound hurler rejoined the Braves in 1946 and posted an 8-5 record. Then, over three of the next four years, he won 21 games each season. When the Braves moved to Milwaukee in 1953, he won 23 and then two years later launched a streak in which he was a 20-game winner in six straight years. Over that period, he led three Braves teams to the World Series, posting a 4-3 record in eight starts. He also hurled no-hitters against the Philadelphia Phillies in 1960 and the San Francisco Giants in 1961 when at the age of 40 he became the second-oldest pitcher up to that point to toss a hitless game.

As his career got longer, the ageless hurler had changed his style from being a power pitcher with a good fastball and a wicked curve, plus superb control and an unusual delivery that featured a high kick, to one whose strength became guile and whose assortment of pitches, including a baffling screwball, often fooled the hitter. "I was never satisfied with what I did the year before," he said. "I always wanted to improve."

Spahn, who was often described as one of the smartest pitchers in the game and a "consummate artist," by Branch Rickey, won 126 games and 20 or more each season between 1956 and 1961. The streak was interrupted when he dropped to 18 victories in 1962. But he was back in the magic circle in 1963 when he won 23 as a 42 year old.

On Opening Day in 1963, Warren set a NL record by pitching for the same team for 19 years. He beat the New York Mets with a six-hitter, 6-1. Five days later, he notched his first of seven shutouts that season with a four-hit, 8-0 victory over the Phillies. Then, following a 3-1 loss to the Mets, Spahn won two games, beating the Giants and Juan Marichal in the second one, 3-1, while allowing 11 hits. A good hitter who helped his own cause on numerous occasions, Warren drove in the go-ahead run in the eighth inning.

Spahn ended April with a 4-1 mark, but didn't win another game until May 14, when he beat Bob Gibson and the St. Louis Cardinals, 5-2, despite being hit by a line drive off the bat of Stan Musial. Always a big fan of Spahn's, Musial later said, "There's never been any question in my mind. Spahn was the greatest pitcher I ever hit against."

Nevertheless, Spahnie had yielded 11 hits to the Cards. In his next game, he gave up 11 hits for the third time, but downed the Chicago Cubs, 8-2. After that, he lost once, then won five games, the highlight being a three-hit, 3-0 triumph over the Phillies, with two no-decisions along the way. He pitched another three-hitter in a 1-0 victory over Don Drysdale and the Los Angeles Dodgers to end June with a glittering 11-3 record.

July began for Spahn with his participation in one of the great pitching matchups in baseball history. Spahn once again faced the Giants and Marichal at Candlestick Park with a crowd of just 15,291 in the stands. Both pitchers moved through the first nine innings virtually unscathed. The outcome wasn't decided until the bottom of the 16th, when Willie Mays slammed a one-out home run to give the Giants a 1-0 victory. Both Spahn and Marichal went the distance. In working 15 1/3 innings, Spahn gave up nine hits, struck out two, and walked one. He later estimated that he threw about 250 pitches.

Five days later, Warren blanked the Houston Colts, 4-0, with a five-hitter. Unfortunately, after making all those pitches in San Francisco, his arm had weakened and Spahn was shut down because of a sore arm. He missed his next three starts, but came back and after losing, 3-1, to the Cardinals, captured eight straight wins in the next month. He worked the full nine innings in each game while allowing just 15 runs. In the game on September 4, Spahn hurled a four-hitter in a 1-0 victory over the Pirates. Then he captured a 3-2 victory over the Phillies.

Spahn's streak was ended on September 13 when he was knocked out in the second inning and took a 7-0 loss to St. Louis. Next, he pitched three innings in an 11-3 defeat by San Francisco. Spahn then won his last three starts of the season. All were complete games and two were shutouts, a 4-0 three-hitter and a 2-0 four-hitter, both against the Cubs.

The win clinched not only Spahn's place in the history books, but earned him a congratulatory telegram from President John F. Kennedy. And Spahn didn't just end the season with a 23-7 record, but he also led the league in complete games for the seventh straight year, with 22. Warren posted a 2.60 ERA while starting 43 games, working in 259.2 innings, giving up 241 hits, and striking out 102.

It was a great season for a pitcher who had that much success at his age. "Like always, I strived to do the best job I could," he said. "I used every tactic I knew to hold the upper hand."

Spahn tumbled to a 6-13 mark the following season, after which he was sold to the Mets and then the Giants, where he finished his career in 1965 at the age of 44. It had been a career full of spectacular achievements, not the least of which was his amazing 1963 season.

25

GENE CONLEY

PLAYED TWO PRO SPORTS SIMULTANEOUSLY

In the world of professional athletes, there has seldom been a case in which a player performed in two sports at the same time. It is not a practice that is either predictable or practical, and even if the person is an accomplished athlete in more than one game, a double dose of sports at the same time is a rarity that only a few have ever attempted.

There have, of course, been some noteworthy exceptions. One is certainly Gene Conley, a slender, 6-8, 225-pound athlete who performed successfully in both pro baseball and pro basketball.

In so doing, Conley put himself in a class of two-sport athletes who played at the major league level, including the immortal Jim Thorpe, plus Lou Boudreau, Bo Jackson, Dick Groat, Dave DeBusschere, Deion Sanders, Ron Reed, John Brodie, Danny Ainge, Chuck Connors, and a collection of others ranging from the well-known to the unknown.

Conley not only played two sports professionally, but also he is the only athlete ever to perform on championship teams in two pro sports.

"I guess I was in the right place at the right time," Conley once said with a considerable degree of modesty. "When I think back, I don't know how I did it. I think I was having so much fun that it kept me going."

A native of Muskogee, Oklahoma, where he was born in 1930, Conley played six seasons in the National Basketball Association and 11 years in Major League Baseball. Some of his years were spent in Boston, where he is recognized as the only athlete ever to play for three of the city's professional teams.

While performing in Boston with the Celtics in basketball and the Braves and Red Sox in baseball, Conley also earned the distinction of playing with future Hall of Famers, including Warren Spahn, Hank Aaron, Ted Williams, Bill Russell, Bob Cousy, Bill Sharman, and Ed Macauley.

During his career in basketball, Conley played for the Celtics for four years and the New York Knicks for two. In those six years, he appeared in 351 games while scoring 2,069 points and playing for three NBA championship teams.

In his baseball career, Conley spent one season with the Boston Braves, continued after they moved to Milwaukee for five years, then concluded with two years with the Philadelphia Phillies and three with the Red Sox. During those years, Conley compiled a 91-96 record with a 3.82 earned run average while working in 276 games.

Always a well-rounded athlete, Conley moved as a youth with his family to Richland, Washington. There, he made the high school all-state team in both baseball and basketball, and was the state champion in the high jump. He then attended Washington State University, where he not only excelled in basketball, but also starred on the Cougar team that reached the finals of the College World Series before losing to Texas. In basketball, Gene was a two-time honorable mention All-American and one year led the Pac 8 in scoring with a 20 points per game average.

With two years still to go in college, Conley was offered pro contracts by two NBA teams, the Minneapolis Lakers and the Tri-Cities Blackhawks. He also attracted the attention of pro baseball scouts, many of whom offered him a contract. Conley, however, turned down all offers, claiming that his family wanted him to finish college.

It became increasingly difficult, however, to shun the offers, which got bigger as time went on. Finally, late in the summer of 1950, Conley accepted a $3,000 bonus and signed with the Boston Braves. Assigned to the Hartford Chiefs of the Eastern League, Conley regaled onlookers with his sizzling fastball, while posting a 20-9 record in 33 games, leading the league in innings pitched (263), earning a spot on the league All-Star team, and being named the circuit's Most Valuable Player and the Minor League Player of the Year by *The Sporting News*.

That got Conley a call to the parent team in 1952, but after posting an 0-3 record, he was sent down to the Milwaukee Brewers of the American Association, where he went 11-4 for the season. Then the next year with the Toledo Mud Hens of the same league, Conley recorded a 23-9 mark, leading the league in wins, ERA (2.90), strikeouts (211), and innings pitched (261). For that, Conley was again named Minor League Player of the Year.

Conley moved back to the big leagues to stay in 1954, rejoining the Braves, who had now moved to Milwaukee. He would pitch there for five years, winning 42 games and losing 40, his best mark being a 24-9 spot in 1954. In 1955, he was the winning pitcher in the All-Star Game. After striking out Al Kaline, Mickey Vernon, and Al Rosen in order in the top of the 12th inning, Conley got the win when Stan Musial homered in the bottom of the frame to give the Nationals a 6-5 victory.

Early in 1959, Conley was traded to the Phillies as part of a six-player swap that ironically included infielder and former basketball All-American Johnny O'Brien. Gene again made the All-Star team that year, pitching two innings in the second game. He ended the season with a 12-7 record, then posted an 8-14 log the following year, after which he was traded to the Red Sox for 6-7 pitcher Frank Sullivan, also a former basketball player. Conley called it "the biggest trade in baseball history."

Gene spent three seasons with the Red Sox, his best year being 1962, when he logged a 15-14 mark. After incurring more arm trouble, Conley retired from baseball after the 1963 season.

The 1963–64 season also marked Conley's last campaign in basketball. Conley had originally joined the Celtics in 1952 after being the 90th pick in the NBA Draft. Playing for a Boston club that included Cousy, Sharman, and Macauley, he appeared in just 39 games as a reserve on a team that was one of the better ones in the league. After the season, however, the Braves persuaded him to forgo basketball and focus on his baseball career.

Gene didn't appear again in the NBA until the 1958–59 season. Suffering from a sore arm in 1958, when he went 0-6 in an abbreviated season with the Braves, the team offered Conley a contract with a 20 percent pay cut. Instead of signing it, Gene called Celtics coach Red Auerbach. "Could he return to the Celtics?" Conley wanted to know.

Auerbach, a loyal fan of Boston sports, said no. He'd prefer that Gene stick with the Braves, rather than disrupting the roster of another local team. Ultimately, however, Auerbach relented, and Conley signed to play with the

Celtics. Once again, Gene would be playing two major league sports at the same time.

It was a good decision for Conley. By then an NBA powerhouse, the Celtics won three straight championships between 1959 and 1961, defeating the Minneapolis Lakers, the St. Louis Hawks, and the Los Angeles Lakers in the Finals. Conley, playing as a reserve forward and sometimes as Russell's backup, scored a total of 1,114 points during those three seasons. Gene was known as an outstanding rebounder and defensive player.

"It was hard, both physically and mentally because you never get a rest," he said. "I did it because I needed the money. I had a family to raise."

Indeed, Conley went from one season to another with virtually no time off in between. Basketball season would end in March, and Conley would immediately report to his baseball club for Spring Training. Then in October, when the baseball season ended, it would be time to head back to basketball. It was a tough life, but if anybody could deal with it, Gene was the right person. "He was the toughest guy I ever had," Auerbach once said.

In 1961, the NBA added a new team to its lineup, the Chicago Packers. Conley was picked in the expansion draft by the Packers (soon to be called the Zephyrs). Around the same time, he was also drafted by the New York Tapers of the new and short-lived American Basketball Association.

Conley never played for either team. The Packers traded him to the Knicks, and he played two years in New York for a team that was one of the worst in the NBA. Gene was a regular during much of the 1962–63 season, scoring 630 points. The following year, he returned to a reserve role and scored 192 points.

After the 1963–64 campaign, Conley, who at various times with the Knicks had played with Tom Gola, Richie Guerin, Len Chappell, and Johnny Green, retired from basketball.

And with that, he ended one of the most successful two-sport campaigns in the history of professional sports.

26

SANDY KOUFAX

HAD AN ASTONISHING SEASON

On the list of great pitching performances, hurling a perfect game ranks at the very top. Winning a Cy Young Award is also an extraordinary achievement. So is winning 20 or more games in one season, earning the Triple Crown of pitching, and being named a World Series Most Valuable Player.

If a pitcher accomplishes any of these feats during the course of his career, he earns a special place on the list of baseball's greatest achievers.

Like many of the pitchers who have been named the greatest in baseball history, Sandy Koufax accomplished all of those feats. Unlike the others, though, he did it in one season. Moreover, he did it in the next to last season of his career, and with a painful, arthritic elbow that required special treatment throughout the campaign.

Koufax's astonishing performance in 1965 ranks as one of the most incredible feats in baseball history. That season, he posted a 26-8 record and pitched what was then a record fourth no-hitter with a perfect game against the Chicago Cubs. Koufax was the winning pitcher in the All-Star Game. He set a then all-time record for strikeouts in one season. He was a unanimous winner of his

second Cy Young Award, and runner-up in the Most Valuable Player voting. And he led the Dodgers to their first World Series victory since moving to Los Angeles with two wins, including one in the seventh game, which earned him the Series MVP award.

It was all part of a season in which the brilliant left-hander led the league in wins, winning percentage (.765), earned run average (2.04), complete games (27), innings pitched (335.2), and strikeouts (382). He appeared in 43 games, starting 41, allowing just 216 hits, walking 71, and hurling eight shutouts. Batters had a combined .179 average against him. He even recorded two saves.

Koufax, who was inducted into the Hall of Fame in 1971, at 36, the youngest player ever elected, had other magnificent seasons. He finished with a career record of 165-87 with a 2.76 ERA. Sandy appeared in 397 games, including 314 as a starter, of which he completed 137 of them, with 40 of them shutouts. In 2,324.1 innings, he allowed 1,754 hits, with 2,396 strikeouts and 817 walks. He was also credited with nine saves (he had a 6-2 record in relief).

Five straight times, he had the best ERA in the league. And he struck out more than 300 three times. Not bad for a player who had no minor league experience, was not very effective during his first six years in the majors, and as a youth was more interested in basketball!

Born in 1935 in Brooklyn, New York, Koufax was an All-City basketball player in high school, and went to the University of Cincinnati on a basketball scholarship. There, he also pitched on the baseball team. When scouts saw his blazing fastball, he relinquished his intentions of having a career as an architect, and at 19, signed for a $40,000 bonus with his hometown Dodgers.

In those days, bonus babies had to spend their first two years with the major league club. So in 1955, Koufax stayed with the Dodgers. He pitched infrequently, although in his second of five starts that season, he hurled a two-hitter. But he was excruciatingly wild. He ended the season with a 2-2 record in 12 games.

Sandy's wildness continued in the ensuing seasons. In his first six years, he posted a combined record of 36-40, his best year being 11-11 in 1958, the Dodgers' first year in LA. But Koufax was not ignored by his opponents. "Whenever we talked trade, his was the first name mentioned," said Dodgers manager Walter Alston. The Dodgers knew they had something special, and after catcher Norm Sherry gave the young pitcher special advice on his motion, Koufax started to emerge as a topflight moundsman.

The 6-2, 210-pound lefty perfected his blazing fastball, combining it with a devastating curve that was said to break from the nose to the ankles. By 1961, his pitches and control had become so good that he went from an 8-13 record the year before to an 18-13 mark while leading the league with 269 strikeouts.

Koufax's success continued in 1962, when he struck out 18 in one game for the second time (the first was in 1959) and pitched a no-hitter in another against the New York Mets. But hand and finger problems surfaced at mid-season, and Sandy finished with a 14-7 record.

He was back on track again in 1963, hurling a no-hitter against the San Francisco Giants, posting a 25-5 record with a 1.88 ERA and 306 strikeouts, and winning both the Cy Young and Most Valuable Player awards. He also won twice in the World Series as the Dodgers swept the New York Yankees, and was named Series MVP. The following year, he went 19-5 with another no-hitter, this one against the Philadelphia Phillies, but his season ended early after he injured his elbow while sliding.

Koufax was now established as one of the premier hurlers in baseball. "Hitting Koufax is like mining hard coal with a toothpick," former catcher-turned-broadcaster Joe Garagiola proclaimed.

The 1965 season began on a down note when in early Spring Training his arm hemorrhaged and his elbow became badly swollen. He was told that his pitching career might not last much longer. The constant pain in his elbow put Koufax on a regular schedule of taking medication and immersing his elbow in a tub of ice after each game.

Sandy was able to pitch by the fourth game of the season and fired a six-hitter to beat the Phillies, 6-2. Four days later, he nudged the Mets with a four-hit, 2-1 victory. "I went out there every day to pitch a perfect game," Koufax said.

In May, Koufax pitched a three-hitter and struck out 13 Houston Astros in a 3-0 shutout. He then beat the Astros again, allowing five hits and fanning another 13 while working 10.1 innings in a 5-3 victory. Four days later, he beat the Chicago Cubs, 3-1, with 12 strikeouts for his fourth straight game with strikeouts in double figures.

Koufax took a 7-3 record into June. He began the month with a 14-3 victory over the Phillies. That began a streak of 11 straight wins, which at one point included a 5-0 victory over the Mets, and two starts later, a 2-1 verdict over the same New Yorkers, this time yielding just one hit. The streak continued into July with a four-hitter in a 3-1 win over the Cubs, and a three-hit, 3-2 triumph over the Astros. Koufax also got the win with one inning of relief in a 6-5 National League victory in the All-Star Game.

Sandy won his 20th game of the season on August 10, when he beat the Mets, 4-3. In his next start, Koufax beat the Pittsburgh Pirates, 1-0, in 10 innings. Three straight losses followed before his season reached its pinnacle.

That came on September 12, when Koufax fired a perfect game against the Cubs, only the sixth perfect game in the modern era. With a crowd of 29,139 watching at Dodger Stadium, Sandy fanned 14, including the last six batters. In a historic game in which the Cubs' Bob Hendley allowed just one hit, the Dodgers triumphed, 1-0, with Ron Johnson singling and scoring an unearned run in the fifth inning.

It was Koufax's fourth no-hitter in four years, which at the time, gave him the most no-hitters ever thrown by one pitcher. At that point, Sandy was virtually unhittable. "Because he had such good control and was easy to see because he threw over the top, you were very comfortable going to bat against him, except you never hit him," said All-Star shortstop Jim Fregosi. "Whatever he wanted to throw was his best pitch."

Despite a painful, degenerative elbow, Koufax finished with four straight wins, including three straight shutouts, one a two-hit, 5-0 victory over the Cincinnati Reds. Then, for the second time in three years, the Dodgers won the National League pennant.

In the World Series against the Minnesota Twins, Koufax declined to pitch in the opening game because it was Yom Kippur. Then, after losing Game Two, he won Game Five, 7-0, with a four-hitter. Two days later, he came back to win the deciding game, 2-0, on a three-hitter.

Koufax was named the Series MVP. Soon afterward, he won the Cy Young Award and was second to Willie Mays in the MVP voting.

Sandy followed his magnificent season with a 27-9 record and a 1.73 ERA while pitching in 323 innings, striking out 317, and winning his third Cy Young Award. By then, though, the pain in his arthritic elbow had become unbearable.

At the age of 30, Koufax was forced to retire. He had a 111-34 record in his last five years. It was the end of a brilliant career that had been championed by his amazing season one year earlier.

27

DON DRYSDALE

THREW SIX SHUTOUTS IN A ROW

From a pitcher's standpoint, there is almost nothing as satisfying as hurling a shutout. Firing a shutout means that at least for one game the opposition is incapable of hitting enough of your offerings to score a run, and that epitomizes the work a pitcher hopes to do every time he takes the mound.

Shutouts, of course, are about as rare these days as doubleheaders, five-dollar tickets, and players who know how to bunt. If one team pitches as many shutouts in a single season as Don Drysdale did in six games, there might be cause for a parade.

In 1968, Drysdale fired six shutouts in a row. No one had ever done that before, and no one has ever done it since. In 1904, Doc White of the Chicago White Sox hurled five straight shutouts for a major league record that stood until Drysdale broke it. In three of his six games, Drysdale beat other future Hall of Fame pitchers.

Not only did the hard-throwing right-hander of the Los Angeles Dodgers break the shutout record, but he also set a new mark with 58 2/3 consecutive scoreless innings pitched, passing the record of 56 straight scoreless innings set in 1913 by Walter Johnson.

Don Drysdale

Although Drysdale certainly carved a memorable place in the record books that season, his career was filled with sparkling campaigns. The powerful 6-5, 190-pound hurler won in double figures in 12 straight seasons, failing to do that in only his first and last years in the big leagues. He pitched in more than 300 innings four years in a row, started 40 or more times in five seasons—four of which he led the league—and had the league's highest strikeout record three times, including 1960, when he had a career-high of 246. He fanned 200 or more batters in six seasons, then a major league record until broken by Tom Seaver in 1974.

Drysdale won the Cy Young Award in 1962, when he recorded a 25-9 mark with a 2.83 ERA while leading the league in strikeouts (232), innings pitched (314.1), and starts (42). That year, he was also named the Major League Pitcher of the Year by *The Sporting News*.

Overall, Drysdale had a career record of 209-166 with a 2.95 ERA. He pitched in 518 games, completing 167 while working 3,4312.1 innings, striking out 2,486, and allowing 3,084 hits. Altogether, he registered 49 shutouts. In five World Series, Drysdale, who carried an assortment of nicknames, including "Double D," "Big D," and "The Big Warrior," posted a 3-3 record with a 2.95 ERA in seven Series games.

A pitcher in five All-Star Games and the winner in the 1967 match, Drysdale was elected to the Hall of Fame in 1984.

Although he was once described as having "the face of a choirboy," there was nothing kindly about Drysdale when he took the mound. He was tough and nasty, a hurler who was never reluctant to knock an opposing batter down and who was the cause of more than a few brawls that were initiated by his intimidating style. Drysdale's hot temper was known throughout the league, and he was never reluctant to blast opposing players, fans, and members of the Dodgers staff. Some claimed that no part of the baseball community escaped his rage, and Drysdale often paid the price with fines by the league office.

"Batting against Don Drysdale is the same as having a date with a dentist," Dick Groat once said. To that, Frank Robinson added that Drysdale was "mean enough to throw at a batter, and he did it continuously. And when he did, he just stood there on the mound and glared at you."

Drysdale, who mixed a 95-mile-per-hour fastball with a sweeping curve, holds the modern National League record for hit batters with 154. Also a good hitter who twice hit seven homers in one season, he led the league in hit batters five times, pounding as many as 20 in 1961.

It was said that Drysdale would knock down his mother on Mother's Day. To that, it was added that he had a private war with anybody who stood at the plate. "I've never seen a pitcher so unafraid of batters," Dodgers manager Walter Alston once said.

Drysdale claimed that he learned to be aggressive on the mound and to keep the batters off balance from the old brushback pitcher, Sal (The Barber) Maglie, when he was a youngster starting out with the Dodgers. "He confirmed this idea of what I had to do," Drysdale said. "It was part of the game."

The strapping hurler, born in 1936 in Van Nuys, California, had never pitched until his senior year in high school, but then he was so good that in 1954 the then-Brooklyn Dodgers readily signed him. After just two years in the minors, one at Triple-A Montreal in the International League where he went 11-11, Drysdale made the Dodgers at the age of 19 in 1956.

In his major league debut on April 23 against the Philadelphia Phillies, Drysdale struck out the side in the first inning before going on to capture a 6-1 win. Don finished the season with a 5-5 record.

The following season he jumped to a 17-9 log. He then won 57 games over the next four years leading up to his stellar 1962 season, after which he went 19-17, 18-16, and 23-12. Along the way, Drysdale beat the White Sox, 3-1, in Game Three of the 1959 World Series, the New York Yankees with a three-hitter, 1-0, in the third game of the 1963 Series, and the Minnesota Twins, 7-2, in the fourth game of the 1965 Fall Classic. Drysdale also lost once to the Twins that year and twice to the Baltimore Orioles the following year.

Through many of his years with the Dodgers, Drysdale teamed with Sandy Koufax to give the team one of the greatest right-left mound duos in baseball history. The two even staged a highly publicized joint holdout in the winter of 1965–66, each asking for a $500,000 three-year contract. After an extended battle with Dodger management, the two settled for one-year deals, with Koufax getting $130,000 and Drysdale $105,000.

Just two seasons later, the full extent of the Dodgers' bargain with Drysdale became apparent when the pitcher who Roy Campanella had called "sweet and mean—a sweet pitcher and a mean competitor" set the record for most consecutive shutouts.

In his last start before the streak began, Drysdale had lost a 2-1 decision to the Milwaukee Braves, lasting just six innings while suffering his third defeat of the season against just one win.

Four days later, on May 14 at Dodger Stadium against the Chicago Cubs, Drysdale's began his climb up the ladder of major league history. Facing Ferguson Jenkins, Don won a 1-0 victory, allowing just two hits and striking out seven.

The second shutout came on May 18, when Drysdale beat the Houston Astros, 1-0, at Los Angeles while yielding five hits and fanning six. Drysdale pitched again on May 21 at Sportsman's Park in St. Louis, where he topped Bob Gibson and the St. Louis Cardinals, 2-0, with another five-hitter that included eight strikeouts.

The streak continued on May 26 with another road win, this time beating Houston at the Astrodome, 5-0, with a six-hit, six-strikeout whitewash. Five days later back at Dodger Stadium, the San Francisco Giants fell, 3-0, as Drysdale gave up six hits and fanned seven. The run continued on June 4 with a 5-0 triumph over the Pittsburgh Pirates and Jim Bunning, when Don pitched a three-hitter and whiffed eight.

The streak finally came to an end on June 8 against the Philadelphia Phillies when reserve outfielder Howie Bedell's sacrifice fly scored Tony Taylor in the seventh inning. It was Bedell's only RBI of the season. Although Drysdale won the game, 5-3, his streak had come to an end. But Don was in the record book with a feat that stood for 20 years.

By the end of the streak, Drysdale's earned run average had fallen from 3.33 to 1.21. His record had spurted from 1-3 to 7-3.

As it turned out, from the standpoint of final records, the 1968 campaign was not one of Drysdale's best years. He ended the season with just a 14-12 mark for a team that finished in seventh place with a 76-86 record. He did, however, post a 2.15 ERA in 239 innings of work with eight shutouts. Unfortunately, the 1968 season would be Drysdale's last full year in the big leagues.

A torn rotator cuff in mid-season the following year ended his career. Drysdale was just 33 years old, but coming in the days before surgical repairs were possible, there was no hope. "It's over, baby," Don declared. Before a late-season game, the Dodgers honored him in front of 30,000 fans in attendance.

28

BOB GIBSON

POSTED A 1.12 ERA IN ONE SEASON

O f all the statistics used to gauge a pitcher's effectiveness, none is more revealing than earned run average. No matter whether he's a starter or a reliever, or what his win-loss record is, a hurler's ERA, more than any other number, clearly defines how well he does against the opposition.

By modern standards, an ERA under 3.00 is considered outstanding. ERAs seldom go under 2.00 today, but if they do, they are regarded as extraordinary. Or, in the case of Bob Gibson in 1968, his ERA was downright phenomenal.

That year, Gibson recorded an ERA of 1.12 while pitching in 304.2 innings. Since the mound was moved back to 60 feet, six inches, no one who has worked in 300 or more innings has posted an ERA that low.

Gibson's ERA came in a season when the National League had a combined ERA of 2.99. And, despite all of Gibson's other accomplishments that year, his magnificently low ERA was the figure that placed his name in baseball history.

The ERA, which originally became an official statistic in 1912 and is based on error-free runs per nine innings pitched, has been a vital statistic ever since.

The only pitchers since 1900 ever to have lower ERAs than Gibson were Mordecai (Three-Fingered) Brown (1.04 in 1906) and Hubert (Dutch) Leonard

Courtesy of Rich Westcott

(0.96 in 1914). Neither came close to pitching 300 innings, and both occurred in the deadball era.

The 33-year-old Gibson's record came during a season in which he made a profound impact on a magnificent career. In 1968, he posted a 22-9 record while completing 28 of the 34 games he started and leading the league in strikeouts (268) and shutouts (13). He gave up just 198 hits while walking 62. Gibson, who at one point pitched 48 consecutive scoreless innings, was not only named winner of the National League's Cy Young Award, but he was also voted the league's Most Valuable Player as he led the St. Louis Cardinals to the pennant. "As I recall," Lou Brock said, "he didn't make one bad pitch over the plate that year."

Gibson would have many fine seasons during a career that led to his induction into the Hall of Fame in 1981, but his work in 1968 was the best. He had truly come a long way from the days when he was also a standout basketball player who spent one year with the Harlem Globetrotters and might have even pursued a career in pro basketball.

The strong-armed right-hander, born in 1935, had suffered a number of childhood ailments, including a rheumatic heart, asthma, pneumonia, and rickets while growing up in Omaha, Nebraska. He overcame them to become a star baseball and basketball player at Creighton University before leaving school to play with the Globetrotters and eventually receiving a $4,000 bonus to sign with the Cardinals.

The intense, intimidating, fierce 6-1, 190-pounder, who glared at hitters with a look of great disdain, spent three unspectacular seasons in the minors, posting a 23-22 record before getting called up to St. Louis in mid-1959. In his first big league start, Gibson blanked the Cincinnati Reds, 1-0. But in 13 games, he went 3-5 and then was 3-6 the following year before getting sent down during the season to Rochester in the International League.

Gibson, known as "Hoot," returned to stay in 1961. He went from 13-12 that year to 15-13 and 18-9 over the next two years. In 1964, Bob's 19-12 mark helped the Cards win the pennant. In the World Series against the New York Yankees, he lost Game Two, 8-3, but came back to win the fifth game, 5-2, in 10 innings. Then, working with just two days' rest, he hurled his second complete game of the Series, beating the Yanks, 7-5, in the Series-clinching seventh game.

Hoot was 20-12 and 21-12 over the next two years, but a broken leg in 1967 after getting hit by a line drive by Roberto Clemente forced him to the sidelines, and he produced a mere 13-7 record for the season. But once again, St. Louis returned to the World Series, and while facing the Boston Red Sox, Gibson won Game One, 3-1, Game Four, 6-0, and Game Seven, 7-2. Overall, Bob pitched three complete games while allowing just 14 hits in 27 innings.

That was a perfect lead-in to Gibson's 1968 season. The campaign started slowly, with Bob getting no decisions in his first two games while yielding three earned runs in 14 innings. Bob then lost, 5-1, to the Chicago Cubs before winning his first game of the season, 2-1, over the Pittsburgh Pirates.

He followed that with a 12-inning, 2-1 victory over the Houston Astros, throwing 179 pitches while going the distance. In his next start, Gibson worked 11 innings, allowing just three hits and beating Tom Seaver and the New York Mets, 3-1. Getting virtually no support from Cardinals bats, Gibson then lost four straight games by scores of 3-2, 1-0, 2-0, and 3-1. In the 2-0 loss to the Los Angeles Dodgers, he gave up one hit in eight innings.

Teammate Joe Torre once said, "Bob wasn't unfriendly when he pitched. I'd say it was more like hateful." Gibson's reaction during the losing streak certainly confirmed that view. Bob was infuriated by the Cards' lack of offensive support.

"If you guys don't get me some runs," he grumbled, "there's going to be a fight."

Now holding a 3-5 record, despite having allowed just 15 earned runs in 88.2 innings, Gibson's season was about to turn around. Over the next 16 games, he won 15 of them, with a no-decision coming in the other. Ten shutouts, including five in a row in wins over Houston, the Atlanta Braves, the Cincinnati Reds, Chicago, and Pittsburgh, were included in the streak. A 2-0 win over the Reds on June 15 was played in one hour and 42 minutes.

Gibson pitched two three-hitters against the Astros, a two-hitter against the Philadelphia Phillies, three four-hitters, and four five-hitters. He completed every game, never allowing more than one run except in a 6-3 win over the Mets and in the no-decision game in which he gave up five runs (four earned) while pitching 11 innings in a game that St. Louis ultimately lost in the 13th, 6-5.

The hurler with the withering fastball won just four of his last eight games, but three of those games were four-hitters and Bob recorded 1-0 victories over the Reds in 10 innings and Houston in the last game of the season. Three of his losses were by one run.

Despite their frequently quiet bats when Gibson pitched, the Cardinals again won the pennant. In the World Series, Gibson faced the Detroit Tigers'

Denny McLain twice in a heroic confrontation of pitchers who had just completed spectacular seasons. In one of the greatest pitching performances in a World Series, Gibson struck out 17 and allowed just five hits to beat baseball's first 30-game winner since 1934, 4-0. Then Gibson beat McLain in Game Four, 10-1, with another five-hitter and 10 strikeouts. Bob lost the seventh game of the Series, 4-1, to Mickey Lolich, but McLain was quick to point out that Gibson's World Series work "was the greatest pitching performance I've ever seen by anybody."

Gibson's stellar pitching continued in 1969 when he went 20-13, working 314 innings for a team that fell to fourth place. He posted a 23-7 log in 1970, leading the league in wins and capturing another Cy Young Award. Then, after winning 20 or more games in five of his last six years, Gibson dropped to 16-13, although he fired a no-hitter in an 11-0 win over the Pirates. He posted a 19-11 mark in 1972, but after that he started to slow down. Gibson pitched for three more seasons, winning 26 games while losing 33.

Bob's career ended after the 1975 season. He finished with a career record of 251-174 and a 2.91 ERA. In 528 games, 482 as a starter, Gibson completed 255 games while hurling 56 shutouts. In 3,884.2 innings, he gave up 3,279 hits, struck out 3,117, and walked 1,336. Gibson pitched in six All-Star Games.

In World Series competition, Gibson won seven games, the second-most in the history of the Fall Classic, while hurling a record eight complete games. In nine starts, covering 81 innings, he struck out 92 and gave up just 55 hits and 19 runs while posting a 1.89 ERA.

"He was the best competitor I ever faced," Pete Rose once claimed. To that, catcher Tim McCarver said, "Nothing that has ever been said about Bob Gibson and his talent has ever been overstated."

That was never truer than during a 1968 season, when scoring runs against Gibson rarely happened.

29

DENNY MCLAIN

BECAME THE LAST OF THE 30-GAME WINNERS

In the last 100 years, there has been almost nothing rarer than a 30-game winner. A pitcher who won 30 games in a single season is someone who would be placed on a pedestal far above his peers.

Thirty-game winners were common in the late 1800s and early 1900s. But since then, such a record seldom appeared. In fact, in the last century, and through the dawn of the 21st century, there have been only eight 30-game winners.

Walter Johnson won 36 in 1913. Grover Cleveland Alexander won 30 or more in three straight seasons from 1915 to 1917. Jim Bagby won 31 in 1920, Lefty Grove posted 31 wins in 1931, and Dizzy Dean was a 30-game winner in 1934.

That was it until Denny McLain came along in 1968 and won 31 games while pitching with the Detroit Tigers. Due to its rarity, McLain's record was a landmark achievement that commands a special place in baseball history.

Coming in the modern era when 30-game winners had long disappeared from the game and it was highly unlikely that one would ever occur again,

McLain was the first 30-game winner in 34 years. Since then, no one has reached that level, making the right-hander the only 30-game winner in the last 80 years.

McLain's feat was widely acclaimed at the time, and with good reason. Before he ended the drought, no other pitcher had threatened to reach 30 wins. There were a few 27- and 28-game winners, but that was as close as anybody came. Nobody, of course, has come close since then, either.

Of all the pitchers regarded as likely candidates to win 30 games, McLain was certainly not one of them. In only his fourth full season in the majors, he had posted good numbers, but was not at the top of the ladder.

Denny's personality sometimes stood in the way. He was controversial, argumentative, and opinionated. Known as a party boy, he was nicknamed "Mighty Mouth." His flamboyance, outspoken habits, and frequent criticisms were often not very popular with others. Nor was his attitude about the game. "Baseball is just a means to an end," he once said, adding that he was really more interested in a career as an organist, a talent he had pursued since early childhood.

Born in 1944 in Markham, Illinois, McLain attended high school in Chicago, where he played shortstop and pitcher. Signed by the Chicago White Sox, he broke into the pros in 1962, and in his first start, hurled a no-hitter and struck out 16 for Harlan of the Class C Appalachian League. Shortly thereafter, McLain was promoted to Clinton of the Class C Midwest League.

The White Sox, however, failed to protect McLain, and that winter, he was drafted by the Tigers. After spending most of the 1963 season in the minors, he was summoned to Detroit late in the season, and made his major league debut at the age of 19 with a victory over the White Sox. In that game, he hit the only home run of his 10-year major league career.

After finishing the season at 2-1 with Detroit, McLain began the next campaign at Syracuse of the International League. Called back to Detroit in June, he posted a 4-5 record during the rest of the season.

In the majors to stay in 1965, McLain, whose wife was the daughter of Lou Boudreau, went 16-6. The following year, he posted a 20-14 log and was the American League's starting pitcher in the All-Star Game. Then in 1967, he had a 17-16 record. Still, despite immeasurable help from pitching coach Johnny Sain, there was no way to predict what was about to happen.

The 1968 season started slowly, with McLain getting no decisions in his first two outings and not notching his first win until April 21 with a 4-2 victory over the White Sox. In his next start, McLain beat the New York Yankees, 7-0, with a five-hitter.

By then, McLain was two games into a streak of five complete-game victories. The run ended on May 15 when the 6-1, 185-pound hurler made his shortest appearance of the season, lasting just two innings in a 10-8 loss to the Baltimore Orioles.

Five days later, McLain, who specialized in a strong fastball with a curveball and changeup mixed in, fired a 10-inning, three-hitter to beat the Minnesota Twins, 4-3. Two wins later, he struck out a season-high 13 with a four-hit, 3-0 victory over the California Angels.

On June 16, McLain beat the White Sox, 6-1. He followed that with a 10-strikeout, three-hit, 5-1 win over the Boston Red Sox. McLain ended June with a 14-2 record. At that point, he was in the midst of a streak of nine straight wins and seven complete games in a row.

McLain twirled two more three-hitters in July, beating the Twins, 5-1, and the Orioles, 9-0, when he became the first hurler since Alexander to win his 20th game before August. He won seven of eight games that month while building another streak of seven straight wins. Included was a four-hit, 4-0 shutout of the Washington Senators on the last day of July.

In his top games in August, McLain recorded a 13-1 victory over the Cleveland Indians, blanked the Red Sox, 4-0, and struck out 11 in a 6-1 triumph over the Angels. McLain entered September with a 26-5 record. He fanned 12 in two games in a row, in an 8-3 victory over the Twins and a 7-2 decision over the Angels. The following game on September 14, he whiffed 10 in a 5-4 win over the Oakland Athletics for his 30th victory of the season before a crowd of 33.688 at Tiger Stadium.

McLain won one more game—a 6-2 victory over the Yankees—before losing, 2-1, to the Orioles and getting no decision against the Senators in his final start of the campaign.

He finished the season with a 31-6 record. Pitching in 41 games, all as a starter, he completed 28, with six of them shutouts. In 336 innings, Denny gave up 241 hits, struck out 280, and walked 63 while compiling a 1.96 earned run average.

McLain led the league in wins, winning percentage (.838), games started, complete games, and innings pitched.

McLain beat every team in the league at least twice. He topped the Twins six times and the Angels five times. He posted a 14-4 record with a 2.47 ERA in 22 games at home and a 17-2 mark with a 1.40 ERA in 19 games on the road.

The Tigers easily captured the American League pennant, with 103 wins and a 12-game lead over the Orioles. In the World Series, they outdueled the St. Louis Cardinals in seven games, with Mickey Lolich winning three for the Tigers, including the deciding game.

McLain, however, did not fare so well. Said to be nursing a sore arm, he lasted just five innings in the opener and 2.2 innings in Game Four, losing to Bob Gibson each time. He won the sixth game with a complete game, 13-1 victory.

Denny, who had pitched in his second All-Star Game, was the unanimous winner of both the Most Valuable Player and the Cy Young Award, making him the first American League pitcher to win both trophies in the same season.

Winning for the fifth straight time in double figures, McLain followed his spectacular 1968 season with a 24-9 mark while leading the league in wins, games started (41), innings pitched (325), shutouts (nine) and hits (288). He pitched in his third All-Star Game and after the season was rewarded with a second straight Cy Young Award. But it would be his last good year in the majors.

Surrounded by controversy regarding a variety of issues, including dealings with organized crime, McLain became heavily involved in gambling, and was suspended by Commissioner Bowie Kuhn for three months of the 1970 season. He pitched in just 14 games while going 3-5, but was suspended twice more at the end of the season, one for an altercation with two sports writers, the other for carrying a gun on a team flight.

That winter, the Tigers traded McLain to the Senators in an eight-player swap. Just three years after his spectacular season, McLain's record tumbled to 10-22. ·

Traded to the Athletics, he played one more season, appearing in just 20 games with the A's and Atlanta Braves before getting released in early 1973. He then played briefly in the minors before retiring at the age of 29.

McLain finished with a career record of 131-91 and a 3.39 ERA. He pitched in 280 games, starting 264 and completing 105, with 29 of them being shutouts. In 1,886 innings, McLain gave up 1,646 hits, struck out 1,281, and walked 548.

30

ELROY FACE

CAPTURED 18 WINS AS A RELIEVER

There was a time when relief pitchers were totally unlike those of today. The old relievers didn't come in from the bullpen, face one batter, and leave. There were no one-inning specialists who ran out of gas if they worked a second inning. No one carried a label such as middle-inning reliever, setup man, or closer.

A relief pitcher was somebody who worked at any time in any situation. It didn't matter who he was facing or what inning he entered the game. His job was always to be ready and to do whatever had to be done for whatever length of time it took.

That's the way it was when Elroy Face took the mound. Relief pitchers were guys who might get into a game in the third inning and pitch the rest of the way. And if they had to pitch two or three days in a row, they did.

"Relief pitching was different when I pitched," said Face. "You might go four or five or six innings. And you'd come back the next day if they needed you. One year, I either got in the game or warmed up 110 different games. The next year, it was 112."

Pitching long and often never bothered the slightly built right-hander, who—despite his 5-8, 155-pound stature—could throw about as hard as anybody. Stan Musial once called Elroy one of the top pitchers he ever faced.

While pitching for the Pittsburgh Pirates for 14 years, the man nicknamed "The Baron" never appeared in less than 54 games in nine straight years and in 11 of 12 seasons. Twice, he led the National League with 68 appearances, and five times he marched in from the bullpen more than 60 times in one season. At one point, Elroy pitched in 98 straight games without a loss.

Overall, Face appeared in 848 games, posting a 104-95 record and a 3.48 ERA in 1,365 innings. His 96 wins in relief are a National League record. When saves were added to a reliever's record in 1969, researchers went back and credited Elroy with 193 saves. While registering double digits in saves nine times, Face led the league in that category three times and finished second twice. He was the first major league reliever to save 20 or more games more than once.

Those numbers established Face as one of the pioneers of modern day relief pitchers. Long before the term became widely used, Face exemplified the word "closer." And when Elroy came striding in from the bullpen, hitters knew they were in trouble.

Face had an especially lasting claim to fame. In 1959, he posted an 18-1 record, which is not only one of the greatest seasons ever recorded by a reliever, but an all-time record for wins by a fireman. At one point, Face won 17 games in a row, stretching his win streak (counting five wins the previous season) to an all-time baseball record for relievers of 22 straight victories.

Relief pitching was not something that Face had contemplated as a youth. Born in 1928 in Stephentown, New York, he didn't play baseball until he was 16, then became both a shortstop and a backup pitcher in high school. After graduation, he joined the Army and then played in a semipro league. When a Philadelphia Phillies scout, who was vacationing in the area, saw Face playing, he offered him a contract of $140 a month.

The 21-year-old hurler became a full-time pitcher, and in two seasons as a starter in the Phillies farm system, posted a 32-7 record. The Phillies, however, failed to protect Face, and he was plucked out of the system by the Brooklyn Dodgers and Branch Rickey. Two seasons later, going 23-9 one year at Pueblo of the Western League, Face was taken by Rickey to Pittsburgh. After serving four years in the minors, Face joined the Pirates in 1953.

He made his big league debut against the Dodgers in relief, striking out Gil Hodges, Jackie Robinson, and Roy Campanella in order. Face went on to start 13 of his 41 games, but a 6-8 record got him sent back to New Orleans the following season. One year later, despite adding a paralyzing forkball to his already dazzling fastball, slider, and curve, Face was back in the majors.

Essentially, Face became a full-time reliever in 1956 when he led the league with 68 games pitched (three as a starter). While posting a 12-13 record that year with six saves, he pitched in a major league record nine straight games.

"I enjoyed relief pitching," Face said. "I got to pitch a lot more often than I would have as a starter. And I enjoyed the competition between me and the hitter. There was never any pressure on me. The batter was the one who had the pressure. He was the guy who had to hit the ball. I had eight guys behind me. If you threw strikes and make them hit the ball, you had a chance to get them out."

Face's 1959 streak, following two campaigns in which he pitched in a combined total of 116 games and was later credited with 30 saves, began on April 22 against the Cincinnati Reds. After trailing, 7-0, the Pirates staged a seven-run rally in the seventh inning. Face allowed one run in the eighth before the Bucs came back to win, 9-8.

Elroy's run continued throughout the summer. He won five games in both May and June and pitched an entire month without yielding a run. In one game, he toiled for five innings, allowing no runs and three hits in a 4-2 victory over the Chicago Cubs. In the second game of a doubleheader against the Phillies on August 30, the Pirates trailed by one run before tying the score in the ninth and going ahead in the 10th. Face pitched two scoreless innings to give Pittsburgh a 7-6 win.

That gave Face 17 straight wins for the season, two short of Rube Marquard's single-season record, and 22 wins overall, just two behind Carl Hubbell's all-time record for consecutive victories. Elroy's streak was broken by a 5-4 Los Angeles Dodgers win after the Pirates had blown a 4-3 lead with Face giving up two runs in the ninth. The loss was Face's first in 99 appearances dating back to May 30, 1958.

Face's 18th victory arrived on September 19 against the Reds. With the score tied, 2-2, he entered the game in the ninth. He pitched three shutout innings before allowing one run in the 12th. The Pirates won, 4-3, in the bottom half on Bill Mazeroski's two-run triple.

Face, who said he weighed just 146 pounds at the end of the season, finished with an 18-1 record and a 2.70 ERA. In 57 games while pitching 93.1 innings, he allowed 91 hits, struck out 69, and walked 25. Seven times, he worked three or more innings. Later, he was credited with 10 saves and four blown saves.

For Face, the magic continued in 1960 when the Pirates won the National League pennant and a memorable World Series against the New York Yankees. Elroy was credited with 10 wins and 24 saves while hurling in 68 games during the season, and three saves in four appearances in the Series.

In the Series, the Pirates won the first game, 6-4, with Face pitching two innings and getting a save. After losing the next two games, Pittsburgh won the fourth game, 3-2, with Face again getting a save and retiring eight Yankees in a row. He notched his third save in Game Five, a 5-2 Pittsburgh win in which he hurled 2 2/3 scoreless innings.

In Game Seven after the Yankees had evened the Series in the sixth game, Face pitched three innings, giving up six hits and four runs. He departed in the bottom of the eighth during a five-run inning in which the Pirates came back from a 7-4 deficit to take a 9-7 lead into the ninth. In the bottom of the ninth, after the Yanks had gained a 9-9 tie, Mazeroski hit the memorable home run that gave Pittsburgh a 10-9 victory and the World Championship.

Face pitched in four All-Star Games. After recording 28 saves and eight wins with a 1.88 ERA in 1962 and being named the National League's Fireman of the Year, Elroy spent nearly six more seasons with the Pirates. A knee injury that required surgery after he damaged a cartilage while chasing a fly ball during batting practice limited his appearances to 16 in 1965. But he worked in 115 games the next two years before getting sold late 1968 to the Detroit Tigers. Face then spent the 1969 season with the expansion Montreal Expos, was released, and the following year played briefly with the Hawaii Islanders before retiring from baseball at the age of 42.

ANOTHER ERA OF SPECTACULAR HURLERS – 1970–1994

31

HOYT WILHELM

BECAME FIRST HURLER TO PITCH IN 1,000 GAMES

Pitching in 1,000 games during a big league career was once considered one of the most unlikely feats in baseball. To begin with, nobody played the game long enough to reach that level. Moreover, in the days before relief pitching proliferated, moundsmen didn't work in enough games each season to accumulate that many appearances over a career.

Even Cy Young, who pitched in the majors for 22 years, didn't come close. Young pitched in 906 games, and that stood as the major league record for 57 years. The record was ultimately broken in 1968 by Hoyt Wilhelm, a relief pitcher.

That was a highly significant achievement for Wilhelm. Even more noteworthy, though, was the mark he etched in the record books as the first pitcher in baseball history to appear in 1,000 games.

Wilhelm appeared in his 1,000th game in 1970 near the end of a sparkling 21-year career. At the time, it was an astonishing achievement that had long been thought to be impossible.

Hoyt reached that milestone as a pitcher stocked with unusual characteristics. He was the first great knuckleball pitcher, a breed that heretofore had not

been overly conspicuous on baseball mounds. In fact, when he was elected to the Hall of Fame in 1985, Wilhelm was not only the first relief pitcher ever to be inducted, but he was also the first knuckleball hurler to enter the baseball shrine.

The 6-foot, 190-pound right-hander was also one of baseball's oldest players. When he appeared in his 1,000th game, he was nearly 48 years old. That year, he also set a record (since surpassed by Jamie Moyer) as the oldest pitcher ever to win a major league game.

Wilhelm pitched in the big leagues from 1954 to 1972, retiring just five days short of his 50th birthday. By then, he had played for nine teams, accumulating a 143-122 record with 227 saves and a career ERA of 2.52. While playing 13 years in the American League and 10 in the National, Hoyt appeared in 1,070 games, including 1,018 in relief, while pitching in 2,254.1 innings and allowing 1,757 hits.

He won 123 games in relief and finished 651 games while holding opposing hitters to a .215 batting average, the third lowest of all time.

It had been a long, winding path before Wilhelm reached that point. Born in 1922 (not 1923 as it had been originally listed) in Huntersville, North Carolina, one of 11 children of a family of tenant farmers, Hoyt learned to throw a knuckleball as a teenager after a local newspaper ran an article about knuckleballer Emil "Dutch" Leonard and the mechanics of throwing the highly unusual pitch.

Throwing the knuckler on nearly every pitch in high school, Wilhelm was signed to a pro contract in 1942, and posted a 10-3 record at Mooresville of the North Carolina State League. After the season, he was drafted into the Army and spent three years in the service during World War II. Wilhelm fought in the Battle of the Bulge, where he was wounded and later received a Purple Heart.

After the war, Wilhelm returned to Mooresville, where he spent the next two years recording 21-8 and 20-7 records. After three years in Class D, Wilhelm was drafted by the New York Giants in 1947. He spent four more years in the minors, all as a starter. Finally, at age 29, he earned a place on the Giants' roster. Manager Leo Durocher, enamoured with Hoyt's knuckleball, made him a reliever, claiming "that knuckler can fool them for four or five innings, even if he doesn't have the hard stuff to go nine."

In his maiden season in 1952, Wilhelm appeared in 71 games, all in relief, and registered a 15-3 record with what later were counted as 11 saves. He not only set a rookie pitching record for games played, but also led the league in

ERA (2.43) and placed fourth in the voting for Most Valuable Player. And in his first major league at-bat, Hoyt hit the only home run of his career.

Wilhelm, who often took the mound in the fifth or sixth inning and worked the rest of the way, had another banner season in 1954, when he helped the Giants win the National League pennant while posting a 12-4 record with seven saves. In the World Series in which the Giants swept the Cleveland Indians, he worked in two games, allowing one hit and no runs.

Hoyt spent two more seasons with the Giants before getting traded to the St. Louis Cardinals. All the while, his knuckleball was attracting a considerable amount of attention. Many of the catchers who went behind the plate when he pitched were unhappy with the assignment and were frequently charged with passed balls. During his first 16 years in the majors, Wilhelm's teams led the league in passed balls each season. Once, while catching Hoyt, Ray Katt was charged with four passed balls in one inning. It eventually reached the point that when Wilhelm moved to the Baltimore Orioles a few years later, manager Paul Richards designed a special mitt just for catching Hoyt's knuckler.

Wilhelm spent just one season with the Cardinals before beginning a lengthy journey around the major leagues. He pitched for the Indians, Orioles, Chicago White Sox, California Angeles, Atlanta Braves, Chicago Cubs, and Los Angeles Dodgers. Along the way, he was named to eight All-Star teams and twice won his league's Pitcher of the Year award.

While he was at Cleveland in 1958, the knuckleballing fireman was occasionally used as a starting pitcher. Later that season, after getting claimed off the waiver list by Baltimore, Wilhelm grabbed the spotlight again. In a game at Memorial Stadium before a crowd of just 10,941, he pitched a 1-0 no-hitter against the New York Yankees led by Mickey Mantle and Yogi Berra and with Don Larsen on the mound. At the time, Wilhelm carried a 2-10 record.

Not only was the no-hitter Wilhelm's only win for Baltimore that season and one of only 20 complete games during his career, but also it was the first no-hitter in modern Orioles history and the last complete game no-hitter pitched against the Yankees.

Wilhelm pitched five years with the Orioles, during which time he threw a no-hitter for eight and two-thirds innings,and six seasons with the White Sox. After 1963, the year he went to Chicago, he never started another game.

With good reason, based on his success coming out of the bullpen. Over a five-year period from 1964 through 1968, Wilhelm's ERA never reached as high as 2.00, the low coming in 1967 when it was 1.31. In 1968, he set a career high with 72 appearances. Wilhelm was so good that slugger Ted Williams said, "Don't let anybody ever tell you they saw a better knuckleball than Wilhelm's."

In 1968, Wilhelm broke Young's record for most games pitched when he came out of the bullpen against the Oakland Athletics. Hoyt was not impressed. "The next 900 won't be so tough," he said.

Two years later, while a member of the Braves, Wilhelm strode to the mound for the 1,000th time in his career. Just one day before his spectacular feat, Hoyt had pitched three innings against the Cardinals, striking out Dick Allen and Joe Torre with one out and the bases loaded in the seventh, and then fanning the same duo with two on in the ninth to preserve a 5-3 Braves win.

Hurling against the Cards again the next day, May 10, at Fulton County Stadium, Wilhelm entered the game in the ninth inning with the Braves holding a 5-3 lead. St. Louis had the bases loaded and none out. Hoyt got the first batter he faced to ground out, but one run scored. Then he gave up a walk, followed by a two-run single by Jose Cardenal, and the Cards wound up with a 6-5 victory.

The ever-modest hurler always tried to minimize his success. "I never went into a game and got all flustered," he once said. "I try to take a close game and men on base in stride. I've always thought that baseball was just a game, and I enjoy it." He always threw his knuckleball, he said, "with a lot of determination."

Late in the season of his 1,000th game, Wilhelm was sold to the Cubs. Then he hurled again for the Braves before finishing his career in 1972 with the Dodgers.

By then, Wilhelm had earned a prominent place in baseball history. Although 15 other relief pitchers would appear in 1,000 or more games by 2013, with Wilhelm dropping to sixth on the all-time list, Hoyt would forever rank as the father of all ironman relievers.

32

STEVE CARLTON

REGISTERED 27 OF HIS TEAM'S 59 VICTORIES

There's not much to be said about a team that wins just 59 games in one season and finishes 37 ½ games out of first place. Teams that lose that many games over the course of a full campaign usually have few redeeming features.

A classic exception to such a paltry record was the 1972 Phillies. True, this was a club sweeping the bottom of the standings and the losers of 97 games. It had a manager (Frank Lucchesi) who on his way to being booted out the door said they weren't going to "make a scrapgoat out of me." He was replaced by the team's new general manager (Paul Owens). And the roster was glutted with highly mediocre players.

Then there was Carlton. "Lefty," as he was called, had one of the most extraordinary seasons in not only Phillies history, but in major league annuals as well.

There was nothing normal about Carlton's season. In a way, he wasn't even supposed to be playing with the Phillies. Carlton had been with the St. Louis Cardinals, but had resisted the club's contract offer after the 1971 season. He

had earned a reported $45,000 that year, and after going 20-9 and at one point striking out 19 batters in one game, was seeking a $20,000 raise.

After dividing two years between the Cards and the minors following his signing as a 19 year old in 1964, Carlton had posted a 74-59 record in five full seasons in St. Louis. By the late 1960s, the Miami, Florida native, who was born in 1944, had become one of the premier hurlers in the National League.

In 1971, Phillies star pitcher Rick Wise was also coming off a superb year, pitching a no-hit game in which he hit an unprecedented two home runs, and wining 17 games overall. He, too, wanted a raise to $65,000, an increase from $32,000 the previous year.

Neither the Phils' current general manager John Quinn nor Cards' GM Bing Devine was interested in giving in to what they considered ridiculous demands, and when the latter proposed a trade, Quinn quickly agreed. The deal was made. It was the last one Quinn ever made.

The eccentric Carlton came to the Phillies and got what he wanted. So did the Phillies. In his first season in Philly, the 6-4 southpaw won 27 of his team's 59 games. That's 46 percent of the team's victories, an unheard-of figure never equaled in the long history of the game.

Carlton's overall record was 27-10. He not only led the league in wins, but also in earned run average (1.97), innings pitched (346.1), games started (41), complete games (30), strikeouts (310), and hits (257). At one point, he won 15 games in a row, a club record that had stood since 1886. With such a performance, Carlton was, of course, named the winner of the CY Young Award, the first of four he earned during a distinguished 24-year career that led him to the Hall of Fame in 1994.

A physical fitness addict, Carlton was known to perform strenuous exercises and work out for several hours at a time, including both before and after games he pitched. "Whoever put that man together genetically did one helluva job," Phillies conditioning coach Gus Hoefling once said. "His first, last, and middle name should be consistency," added former Phillies manager and front office executive Dallas Green.

The 1972 season had started late because of a labor dispute in which players had boycotted part of Spring Training and the first week of the season. When the campaign finally began, Carlton was the Phillies' Opening Day pitcher, and in a battle of future Hall of Famers, he beat Ferguson Jenkins and the Chicago Cubs with a four-hit, 4-2 victory.

Carlton threw a laser-like fastball and a virtually unhittable slider. Trying to hit these offerings was once described by Pittsburgh Pirates slugger Willie Stargell as "like trying to drink coffee with a fork." In his next outing, Lefty fired one of his best games of the season. Pitching a three-hitter, he beat the Cardinals and another future Hall of Famer, Bob Gibson, 1-0.

Lefty got even better in his next start. Facing Juan Marichal and the San Francisco Giants, he gave up just one hit—a leadoff single by Chris Speier in the first inning—while striking out 14 and walking one to gain a 3-0 decision. In his next start, though, Carlton lost to the San Diego Padres, 4-0. Then after two more wins, incredibly he lost five straight, dropping his record to 5-6. At one point during Carlton's slump, the Phillies lost nine games in a row.

A no-decision game followed, and then the streak began on June 7. Carlton beat the Houston Astros, 3-1, with 11 strikeouts, before capturing another 3-1 decision over the Atlanta Braves. Two more no-decision games came next before he beat the Montreal Expos, 1-0, with a four-hitter on June 25. The win ran his record to 8-6.

Over a period of nearly the next 10 weeks, Carlton won 15 games with three no-decision outings along the way. Fourteen of those wins were complete games and five were shutouts. Carlton beat every team at least once, and his old St. Louis team four times while he worked nearly every fourth day. "It keeps you sharp, strong, and eager," he told reporters.

A few years later, Carlton stopped talking to reporters for the rest of his career. But many years later, he talked with the author about the streak. "I didn't get involved in the momentum of the streak," he said. "I didn't worry about what happened yesterday or what was going to happen tomorrow. Before each game, I went over the pitches I normally threw. Then I'd go out and build on that, and try not to make any mistakes.

"You just go out and be a regular pitcher on a day-to-day basis," he added. "You can't get caught up in the moment. You have to be prepared on the particular day you're pitching, and dedicate yourself to that day. Right then, that's the only thing that matters, and you have to get through it."

Game after game, Carlton got through it. He threw 160 pitches and struck out 13 in a 9-4 victory over the New York Mets. He beat the Padres, 3-2, in 11 innings. In one no-decision game against the Giants, he was lifted after pitching five innings and trailing, 4-0, but the Phils stormed back with 11 runs in the seventh inning to win, 11-4, and get Carlton off the hook.

A young catcher just coming up from the minors was behind the plate for a few of Carlton's games. "The first time I caught him," said Bob Boone, who would go on to be the Phillies catcher for the next decade, "it was like, wow, this guy is unbelievable. It was like going from a Volkswagen to a Mercedes. I can tell you, he was the best I ever caught. He was just awesome."

After the Giants debacle, Carlton hurled nine straight complete games. Included were consecutive 2-0 victories over the Los Angeles Dodgers—Lefty hit a two-run triple in the seventh—and Chicago Cubs, who got just four hits. Two weeks later, he pitched consecutive three-hitters, beating the Pirates, 2-0, with 12 strikeouts, and the Expos, 2-1.

Carlton won his 20th game on August 17, beating the Cincinnati Reds, 9-4. The streak ended in his next start when he went the distance but lost to Atlanta, 2-1, in 11 innings. Steve then won seven of his next 10 decisions, three of which were 2-1 triumphs (over the Pirates and then the Cardinals twice)—one a victory over Wise. He finished the season with an 11-1 win over the Cubs.

Carlton's magnificent season with such a terrible team was saluted far and wide. But it was just the start of a sparkling run with the Phillies during which he posted 20-7, 23-10, 24-9, and 23-11 records while winning in double figures 13 straight years and becoming the team's all-time leader in numerous categories, including wins, with 241.

Overall, Carlton finished his career with a 329-244 record and a 3.22 ERA while pitching in 741 games, completing 254 with 55 shutouts. In 5,217 innings, he gave up 4,672 hits, struck out 4,136, and walked 1,833. He is currently the second-winningest left-hander in baseball history.

"He was one tough pitcher," George Brett declared. "You couldn't give in. You had to fight. You had to grind it out. I didn't hit against him that often, but when I did, I always knew I was in for a battle."

Lots of other hitters knew that, too, including all those in 1972 who batted against one of the toughest hurlers of all time.

33

NOLAN RYAN

FIRED A RECORD SEVEN NO-HITTERS

Of all the events that happen in baseball, one of the rarest is a no-hitter. No-hitters seldom happen, and when they do, they represent one of the most spectacular achievements in the game.

Throughout baseball history, few pitchers can claim that they tossed a no-hitter. Since modern baseball records began when the pitching mound was pushed back in 1893 from 50 feet to 60 feet, six inches from home plate, there have been just 259 no-hitters thrown by one pitcher in a game. By comparison, in that same period, there have been 586 triple plays, and players have hit for the cycle 292 times.

Since 1893, there have been 21 seasons in which no big league pitcher tossed a no-hitter. And even when they did, it was likely to be the only one in a pitcher's career. Just 28 hurlers have thrown more than one no-hitter in the modern era. Only four of them—Nolan Ryan, Sandy Koufax, Cy Young, and Bob Feller—have recorded more than two hitless games.

Ryan is the king of all no-hit hurlers. During a glittering 27-year career in the major leagues—the longest of any player in baseball history—the big right-hander fired seven no-hitters, three more than his closest rivals, Koufax and

Young. Pitching seven no-hitters ranks among the most spectacular achievements in baseball.

To make Ryan's work even more amazing, the Hall of Fame hurler had 24 no-hitters broken up in the seventh inning or later. Overall, Ryan pitched 12 one-hitters, 19 two-hitters, and 30 three-hitters.

Ryan's collection of no-hitters was the crowning achievement of his career. But he had countless other highlights, not the least of which was his record-setting 5,714 strikeouts while leading the league 11 times and fanning more than 300 batters six times, including a record-setting 383 in 1973.

Standing 6-2, 170 pounds at the peak of his career, "The Ryan Express," as he was called, set 53 major league records while compiling a 324-292 mark between 1966 and 1993. Throwing fastballs that could reach speeds of more than 100 miles per hour, Ryan appeared in 807 games, working 5,386 innings and posting a 3.19 ERA. He walked 2,795. Despite often playing with lowly teams and appearing in just one World Series (with the Mets in 1969), he won in double figures 20 times. Ryan's career loss total is a big league record.

The owner of a crackling curve, Ryan, who was still throwing fastballs well over 90 mph in his mid-40s while firing an 80 mph changeup, was the kind of pitcher no batter liked to face. "When you went up to the plate, you just had to muster a little more courage," said Hall of Fame slugger Mike Schmidt. "He put everything he had into a pitch. He was what they call 'effectively wild,' but his fastball was unbelievable and his curveball looked like a fastball. It would come across the plate right in front of your face. It was scary."

Ryan struck out 10 or more batters in one game 215 times and 15 or more hitters in 26 games. He fanned 19 hitters in a game four times, 18 hitters in a game once, and 17 batters three times while averaging 9.55 kayos a game. Twice, he struck out eight batters in a row. In 1990, at the age of 43, Ryan became the oldest player ever to lead the American League in a major statistical category when he finished first in strikeouts.

"My really high totals come when hitters are looking for my fastball and I'm getting my breaking ball over the plate." Ryan once said. "I have more strikeouts than other pitchers do because of my breaking ball."

"He had a very nasty curveball," said slugger Mark McGwire, who faced Ryan as a young player. "He has one of the best fastballs I've ever seen," added Hall of Famer Joe Morgan.

"I think he threw harder than any pitcher who ever picked up the ball," said Dick Allen. "You'd come to the plate just hoping you could put the ball in play somewhere."

The first baseball player to earn $1 million a season, Ryan was born in 1947 in Refugio, Texas. As a youth living in Alvin, Texas, he followed baseball closely. "If I had an idol, it was Sandy Koufax," he said.

Ryan was a 10th round choice of the New York Mets in 1965. After starting out in the minors, Nolan posted a 17-2 record at Greenville, South Carolina of the Class A Western Carolina League. A brief trip to the Mets, nearly one year in military service, and a sore elbow kept Ryan out of the big time until he arrived back in New York in 1968.

Nolan went on to spend five unspectacular years with the Mets before joining three teammates in a trade to the California Angels for Jim Fregosi. He then played eight seasons in Los Angeles, leading the American League in strikeouts seven times while posting records that included his only seasons as a 20-game winner (21-16 in 1973, 22-16 in 1974) and two 19-16 seasons. Ryan then went to the Houston Astros as a free agent, and spent nine years in Texas, his highest win total being 16. He finished his career in 1993 with the Texas Rangers.

Ryan always had a reputation for being extremely focused when he was on the mound. "I give the team I'm pitching for the opportunity to win," he said. "I don't have much to do with the offense. I'm a defensive specialist. That's my job. If I do it, fine, we have a chance to win. If we lose, either we didn't score runs or I didn't do my job."

Ryan, also a physical fitness addict who always strived to use the proper mechanics, did his job especially well on seven particular occasions. That was when he set the all-time standard for no-hitters.

The first no-hitter came in on May 15, 1973, while Ryan was toiling in his second season with the Angeles. In what ranks as his greatest season, with 21 wins and a record 383 strikeouts, Ryan beat the Kansas City Royals, 3-0. He struck out 12 and walked three in the first big league no-hitter ever pitched in Kansas City.

Exactly two months later on July 15, Ryan became only the fourth pitcher to hurl two no-hitters in the same season, joining Johnny Vander Meer, Allie Reynolds, and Virgil Trucks, when he blanked the Detroit Tigers, 6-0, before a crowd of 41,411 at Tiger Stadium. This time, Ryan uncorked 17 strikeouts, including 12 of the first 15 outs, while walking four. In his next start, Ryan allowed the Baltimore Orioles no hits for seven innings.

En route to a 22-win season, the big flame-thrower was back on the no-hit trail on September 28, 1974, when he cut down the Minnesota Twins, 4-0, at Anaheim Stadium. In a game in which he was unusually wild, Ryan whiffed 15 but walked eight.

On June 1, 1975, Ryan became the first and only pitcher ever to hurl no-hitters in three consecutive seasons when he whitewashed the Orioles, 1-0, at Anaheim. It was a special day for Ryan, as the victory was the 100th of his career. Although hampered by injuries to his groin, leg, and elbow, Ryan fanned nine and walked four. In his next outing, he tossed a two-hitter against the Milwaukee Brewers.

It took six years for Nolan's next no-hitter to arrive. Coming on September 26, 1981, it was Ryan's first National League no-hitter, making him just the third hurler—Young and Jim Bunning were the others—to toss a no-hitter in both leagues. Pitching for Houston at the Astrodome, Ryan downed the Los Angeles Dodgers, 5-0. He struck out 11, including eight of the first nine outs, while walking three.

Number six took nearly nine more years to surface. With Ryan now pitching for the Rangers, this one was fashioned on June 11, 1990 against the defending American League champion Oakland Athletics at Oakland Coliseum. At the age of 43, Ryan became the oldest pitcher ever to hurl a no-hitter. He also became the first moundsman to fire no-hitters in three different decades. Ryan beat the A's, 5-0, with 14 strikeouts and two walks before a crowd of 33,436.

Ryan's final no-hitter came on May 1, 1991 before a crowd of 33,439 at Arlington Stadium. In his 25th season, but still throwing hard, Ryan beat the Toronto Blue Jays, 3-0, in a game in which the Jays hit just four balls out of the infield. The Blue Jays, owners of the best batting average in the major leagues, went down swinging 16 times, while drawing two walks. Ryan retired the last 19 batters in order.

For Ryan, who struck out a total of 94 batters during his seven master-pieces, his no-hit record had come to an end. But it was one of the most mag-nificent records ever compiled by a big league pitcher.

34

TOMMY JOHN

KNOWN AS THE FATHER OF ELBOW SURGERY

There once was a time when pitchers faced an uncompromising dilemma. If they had torn a ligament in their arm, and with no way to fix it, they were faced with a distressing choice. They could either suffer the pain and try to continue on, or they could look for a new job.

Legions of pitchers—as well as other players—faced this situation. Unable to struggle along, most of them turned in their uniforms and joined the everyday workforce. There was no other solution. Most of the common methods for treating the problem were usually temporary, and the patient was never again as good as he had been.

Then along came Dr. Frank Jobe. A prominent orthopedic surgeon in Los Angeles, California, Jobe had often treated players with arm and shoulder injuries. One of the most common of these was damage to the ulnar collateral ligament in the elbow. That condition resulted from excessive and highly stressful use of one's arm, for which there was no known cure.

Working hard to find a cure, Jobe came up with a surgical procedure in which the torn ligament was removed and replaced with a tendon from another part of the person's body, usually either from the wrist or forearm of his other

arm. Holes were drilled in the damaged area, and the new part was woven in through the holes. There was no guarantee that such an operation would return a pitcher to his previous level of performance. In fact, Jobe estimated that the success rate might be about five percent.

At about that time, a pitcher named Tommy John seriously damaged the ligament in the elbow of his pitching arm. John was a veteran hurler who had been pitching professionally for 14 years.

John had come out of Terre Haute, Indiana, where he was born in 1943. An outstanding basketball player in high school, he held the city's scoring record. But he was more interested in baseball and signed with the Cleveland Indians in 1961. He made his major league debut in 1963.

The 6-3, 185-pound hurler pitched in just three games with the Indians that year. He appeared 14 times the following season before getting traded to the Chicago White Sox in 1965. That year, his first as a full-time hurler, John posted a 14-7 record.

Over the following two seasons, John went 14-11 and 10-13, and was 10-5 in 1968, a year in which he recorded a 1.98 earned run average and was named to the American League All-Star team. He followed that with 9-11, 12-17, and 13-16 records with bad to mediocre White Sox teams. He pitched in 37 games in 1970 while working in a career-high 269.1 innings, and appeared in 38 contests the next season while toiling in 229.1 innings.

The White Sox traded John to the Los Angeles Dodgers in 1972 for slugger Dick Allen. Now playing with a good team, John began with an 11-5 mark and a 2.89 ERA in 29 games. He followed that with a 16-7 record and a 3.10 ERA in 31 games. Then in 1974, he had a 13-3 record with a 2.59 ERA in 22 games, but something was wrong. John's elbow was in pain, and the uncomfortable feeling just kept getting worse.

In 10 full seasons and parts of two others, John had compiled a 124-104 record. But with the injury to his left elbow, his career appeared to be over.

John was the perfect patient for Jobe's new process. "People with a torn ligament were sent back to the farm or wherever they came from," Jobe had said. "But Tommy didn't want to go."

On September 25, 1974, Jobe performed for the first time the operation he had invented. Known as ulnar collateral ligament reconstruction surgery, Jobe extracted the ligament in the elbow of John's pitching arm and replaced it with a tendon from his right forearm. The process took about three hours to complete.

It didn't appear likely that the operation would allow John ever to pitch again. No such operation had ever been done before, and because of its revolutionary method, which was enormously difficult to perform, the result was totally unpredictable.

But both Jobe and John were determined to succeed. Accordingly, John underwent a relentless rehabilitation program. He spent the entire 1975 season on the disabled list. Eventually, it took him 18 months to recover.

In 1976, John took the mound again. His motion was different. He didn't throw as hard as he once did. But he had developed some new pitches, and in his first season back he started 31 games, pitched 207 innings, and posted a 10-10 record with a 3.09 ERA. After the season, he was named the League's Comeback Player of the Year.

John's comeback was nothing short of amazing. Some called it "miraculous." But whatever the description, the surgery was a success. A new door was opened to players with damaged ligaments in their elbows.

Soon afterward, the surgery was given a name. It became known as "Tommy John Surgery." From then on, the procedure would be called that in recognition of the pitcher who pioneered one of the most successful operations in the history of sports medicine.

Since Tommy John Surgery was first performed, it has been used on thousands of athletes. It has been done on not just pitchers, but position players as well as athletes from other sports. It is estimated that more than 300 big league pitchers, many of whom went on to sign multi-year contracts, have undergone the operation, including in recent years hurlers such as Jamie Moyer, Tim Hudson, Stephen Strasburg, Eric Gagne, Chris Carpenter, Joba Chamberlain, and Matt Harvey.

The operation is now also performed by prominent surgeons, Dr. Lewis Yocum and Dr. James Andrews. Yocum is said to average about 100 operations per year, most of them being minor league baseball players and high school and college athletes.

In the early days of the surgery, most doctors told pitchers with partial tears in their ligaments that they would be most likely to recover simply by resting for a long period of time. Now, doctors do not hesitate in recommending Tommy John surgery, and players are often quick to rush to the operating tables.

The surgery now takes about one hour to perform. The success rate for pitchers is about 85 percent, most of them performing as well if not better than they did before the operation. It now takes about 12 months to rehab, and in the case of pitchers, they often throw harder and more effectively once they return to the mound.

In John's case, the slender moundsman went on to stage the best years of his career. In 1977, he vaulted to a 20-7 record. In 31 games, he worked in 220.1 innings, compiling a 2.78 ERA. The Dodgers won the West Division title, and in the League Championship Series against the Philadelphia Phillies, John, pitching throughout the game in a steady rain, went the distance to gain a 4-1 victory in the fourth and deciding game of the Series. In the World Series against the New York Yankees, however, John lost Game Three, 5-3.

John posted a 17-10 record in 1978, and again defeated the Phillies in Game Two of the LCS , 4-0, on a four-hitter. With the Dodgers again meeting the Yankees in the World Series, John won the opener, 11-5, but for the second straight year, the Yanks won the Fall Classic in six games.

Traded to the Yankees in 1979, John's career soared even higher. In 37 games, he went 21-9 with a 2.96 ERA. Then he came back with a 22-9 record with a 3.43 ERA while working in 36 games. In 1980, as was the case in 1978 and 1979, John was named to his league's All-Star team.

John then posted 9-8 and 10-10 records with the Yankees. He got the win in Game One of the 1981 ALCS against the Oakland Athletics and then captured a 3-0 victory in seven innings of work in Game Two of the World Series against the Dodgers.

During the 1982 season, John moved on to the Los Angeles Angels. He went to the Athletics during the 1985 season and then traveled back to the Yankees in 1986. In a little less than eight years with those three clubs, his record was 55-62.

John retired in 1989 at the age of 46. His final record was 288-231 with an ERA of 3.34 while appearing in 760 games and working in 4,710.l innings. He struck out 2,245, walked 1,259, and gave up 4,783 hits.

Since his surgery, John had won 164 games. What's more, thousands of other athletes had their careers extended. That was ample testimony to the incredible surgery that he had been the first to undergo and that bore the name, Tommy John Surgery.

35

DON SUTTON

WON IN DOUBLE FIGURES 21 TIMES

There is nothing unusual about a pitcher's win total reaching double figures in a single season. Over the years, hundreds of pitchers have done it, and more names are added to the list every year.

There is something very special, though, about winning in double figures 20 or more times. Cy Young never did it. Neither did Walter Johnson. Nor did Christy Mathewson nor Grover Cleveland Alexander. In fact, there is only one pitcher ever to have won in double figures that many times.

That is Don Sutton. While pitching 23 years in the major leagues, Sutton registered wins in double figures 21 times. He did it during a career that ran from 1966 through 1988, and that resulted in 324 victories and induction into the Hall of Fame in 1998.

A hurler who was known for his consistency, durability, and confidence, Sutton never spent one day on the disabled list and never missed a start during his entire career. Moreover, he failed to pitch past the sixth inning in just 17 starts. Eight times he worked in more than 250 innings, and 10 times he pitched in 35 or more games in a single season.

Sutton, who spent 16 years of his career with the Los Angeles Dodgers, wound up with a final record of 324-256. He started 756 of the 774 games in which he pitched, and finished 178 of them, 58 of which were shutouts. The 6-1, 185-pound right-hander was on the mound for 5,282.1 innings, allowing 4,692 hits, striking out 3,574, and walking 1,343.

Don struck out 100 or more batters in 21 seasons. He was Rookie of the Year in 1966, finished in the top five in the voting for the Cy Young Award five straight years, hurled eight shutout innings in four All-Star Games (and in one of which (1977) he was the Most Valuable Player), and pitched five one-hitters. Although he was a 20-game winner only once, he won 19 in one season twice, 18 once, and 17 three times.

Relying on a lively fastball, and a curve, slider, and screwball, batting against Sutton was an extremely difficult task. "He had a very good breaking pitch," said Hall of Famer Ryne Sandberg. "You never wanted to hit against that pitch. He also had an outstanding fastball that had a real jump to it and could rise up across the plate."

Sutton saw himself as a hard-worker who used all the tools of his trade. "I was a mechanic," he said. "I exhausted every opportunity. The club always knew I was going to be prepared. They were going to get the best I had to offer, and I would never shortchange them. I looked for every possible edge. I think I got the most out of everything I was given.

"I was gifted with the kind of delivery you would not wish on any 12-year-old kid learning to pitch," Sutton added. "But I was fortunate that it loaded up the big muscles in my body. Then, whether it was because of dieting, stretching, conditioning, or chiropractory, they helped me along, and along with the grace of God, I was able to stay injury-free throughout my career."

Sutton claims to have been given the start toward the road to success by his parents. Born in a tar-paper shack to teenage parents in 1945 in Clio, Alabama, he grew up in Molino, Florida, where he played football, basketball, and baseball in high school. He won considerable acclaim in baseball, twice leading his team to the state finals and twice earning all-state honors.

"I grew up the son of sharecroppers," Sutton said. "Later, my dad worked in construction. What I saw in my parents was preparation to do the job you had to do. That carried over to my discipline and preparation as a pitcher. If my dad could do what he did in the work he was in, I could darn sure do it, too."

Sutton, who attended Gulf Coast Community College for one year, started down that path when he was signed as a free agent by the Dodgers in 1964.

Afterward, he spent one year in the minors, posting an 8-1 record with Santa Barbara in the California League, and then finishing the season with a 15-6 mark at Albuquerque of the Texas League.

The Dodgers beckoned in 1966, and Sutton went 12-12 in 37 games and won the top rookie honors in the National League. More significantly, a streak was launched.

Over the next five years, while playing for mostly mediocre Dodger teams, Sutton logged records of 11-15, 11-15, 17-18, 15-13, and 17-12. In 1969, in his fourth year in the majors, he recorded career highs in games started (41) and innings pitched (293.1). In 1972, he raced to a 19-9 mark while placing first in shutouts with nine (and at one point hurling 35 straight scoreless innings), recording a career-low 2.08 ERA, and notching a career-high 18 complete games (in 33 starts).

Sutton went 18-10 in 1973. The following year, the Dodgers exploded with 102 wins and won both the West Division title and the National League pennant. Sutton posted another 19-9 record while leading the league in games started with 40.

He won twice in the playoffs, defeating the Pittsburgh Pirates in Game One with a four-hit, 3-0 shutout, and in the deciding Game Four, allowing just three hits in eight innings of a 12-1 victory. In the World Series, he won one game, a 3-2 triumph over the Oakland Athletics in the Dodgers' only victory of the Fall Classic. That was his 12th straight win of the season. Sutton got no decision after pitching five innings in the fifth and final game.

Don recorded a 16-13 mark in 1975. One year later, he posted a 21-10 record while making 34 starts and recording a 3.06 ERA. That was followed by a 14-8 log in another pennant-winning season for the Dodgers. In the NLCS, Sutton beat the Philadelphia Phillies with a 7-1 nine-hitter in the second game. In the World Series, which LA lost in six games to the New York Yankees, Don got a no-decision after hurling seven innings in Game One, and then went the distance to win the fourth game, 10-4.

In 1978, Sutton went 15-11 as the Dodgers again advanced to the World Series, but Don lost Game Three against the Phillies while pitching just 5.2 innings. He then fell twice in the World Series against the Yankees in another Dodgers loss in six games.

Over the next two years, Sutton registered 12-15 and 13-5 records. He led the league in ERA with a 2.20 mark in 1980, a year in which he pitched in more than 200 innings for the 15th straight time. At the end of that season, however,

Sutton became a free agent and ultimately signed with the Houston Astros. That ended a 15-year stint with the Dodgers.

Sutton posted an 11-9 record in his first season in Houston. Then after going 13-8 in 1882, he was traded late in the season to the Milwaukee Brewers and went 4-1 in the remainder of the campaign. Don's streak of 17 straight years of winning in double figures ended in 1983, when he slipped to an 8-13 record with the lowly Brewers. He bounced back with a 14-12 record in 1984.

That winter, Milwaukee traded Don to Oakland, where he went 13-8 before moving to the California Angels toward the end of the 1985 season. Sutton then put together double figures in the next two seasons with 16-11 and 11-11 marks. He won his 300th game in 1986, a 5-1 win over the Texas Rangers. Sutton returned to the Dodgers in 1988 before retiring at the age of 43 at the end of the season.

Sutton wound up not only with an unmatched achievement, but also the respect of the hitters who faced him.

"Young players typically don't prepare for their at-bats when they first come to the big leagues," said the powerful slugger Mark McGwire. "After they get their feet wet and get a little older, they understand that it takes more than just physical ability to be successful. It's about preparation. With Sutton, you always had to be prepared. You had to try to understand what he was trying to do to you. He was trying to understand your strengths and how they stood against his strengths. That kind of thinking on the part of a pitcher made a hitter's job all that much more difficult. Hitting against Sutton was extremely tough."

Twenty-three years' worth of major league hitters faced that situation. Given Sutton's record over 21 of those years, most of those hitters didn't handle it very well.

36

TOM SEAVER

MADE 16 OPENING DAY STARTS

Being named the starting pitcher on Opening Day is an honor that's usually reserved for a team's best hurler. Because it's a reward that's bestowed just once a year, the pitchers selected to launch season openers for their teams form a highly select group whose numbers are extremely limited.

Accordingly, over time, even a pitcher who's the best—or often in the modern era, the healthiest—has few opportunities to take the mound when the bell rings to open the season. Doing it 16 times during one's career is staggering number that is a major league record.

The owner of that record is Tom Seaver, who was his team's Opening Day pitcher in all but four years of his 20-year career. Of those 16 starts, he started 12 in a row. Ten of those came while Seaver pitched for the New York Mets, six of which were wins and four of which were no-decisions. Seaver also tossed a no-decision opener for the Mets when he returned to the team later in his career.

Overall, Seaver had a 7-2 record in the openers, with seven no-decisions. Three of those openers came while he worked for the Cincinnati Reds, and

two were in the uniform of the Chicago White Sox. He faced the Philadelphia Phillies in five openers and the Montreal Expos in three.

Opening Day starts were, of course, not Seaver's only unusual achievements during a career that led to his induction in 1992 into the Hall of Fame with the highest percentage of votes (98.84%) ever cast. In an outing against the San Diego Padres in 1970, he struck out 19 batters, including the last 10 of the game. "Tom Terrific," as he was nicknamed, earned berths on 12 All-Star teams, won three Cy Young Awards, pitched a no-hitter, and is the Mets' all-time leader in wins with 198.

Seaver posted a 311-205 career record with a 2.86 earned run average. In another amazing achievement, Tom started all but nine of the 656 games in which he appeared. While firing 61 shutouts, he worked 4,783 innings, allowing 3,971 hits, striking out 3,640, and walking 1,390. He was a 20-game winner five times, and won in double figures 17 times, including 15 in a row. He also struck out 200 or more batters nine years in a row, reaching a high of 289 in 1971. During his career, Seaver fanned more batters (3,272) than any right-hander in National League history.

The 6-1, 210-pound right-hander was noted for his sizzling two-seam fastball, sinker, and cutter.

"He had great control, he could throw to both sides of the plate, and sometimes his ball would dart away from the batter, making it very tough to hit," said fellow Hall of Famer, Ryne Sandberg. "He was a power guy who used his whole body, and his stride came right at you. My plan was always to try to get him before he got me. You just wanted to put the ball in play somewhere."

Seaver had his own plan. "Pitching is using whatever you have to work with on any particular day, or inning, or situation" he said. "It's something that can change every time you go to the mound."

Tom started going to the mound in his days as a high school hurler in Fresno, California, where he was born in 1944. An all-city basketball player, Seaver hoped to pursue a baseball career, but after graduation from high school, spent one year in the Marines before enrolling at Fresno City College. Then, after pitching in a summer league in Alaska, he won a scholarship to the University of Southern California, where he pitched for one year. Ultimately, after a highly complex set of maneuvering involving several teams and the commissioner's office, Seaver wound up with the Mets.

With his strong credentials, Seaver spent his first year in pro ball in 1966 all the way up in the International League with Jacksonville, where he posted a 12-12 record. He won a spot on the Mets' staff the following year, and his 16-13 mark earned him Rookie of the Year honors and a spot on his first All-Star team, for which he got the save for the National League in a 15-inning, 2-1 win.

Seaver pitched his first opener in 1968, but did not get a decision in a 5-4 Mets loss to the San Francisco Giants. The next two openers were no-decision outings, too, but the one in 1969 launched a season that ranks as one of Seaver's as well as the Mets' greatest campaigns. Tom won his first Cy Young Award with a 25-7 record, the best one of his career. He threw a perfect game for eight and one-third innings against the Chicago Cubs. Meanwhile, the "Miracle Mets," as they were called, went from ninth place the year before all the way to the World Series. Seaver beat the Atlanta Braves in the first National League Championship Series ever played. The Mets then downed the powerful Baltimore Orioles in five games, with Seaver winning the opener, 4-1. In Game Four, he hurled a complete game, but lost, 2-1, in 10 innings.

Seaver's reputation as a masterful moundsman had by now been clearly established. "He was strong, and he could put the ball where he wanted to, which was often inside," said Dick Allen. "He was one tough pitcher." Or, as Reds' Hall of Fame skipper Sparky Anderson said, "My idea of managing is giving the ball to Tom Seaver, and then sitting down and watching him work." Added Reggie Jackson: "Blind men come to the park just to hear him pitch."

After three straight no-decisions, Seaver finally won his first opener in 1971. He worked just five innings, but gained the victory as the Mets beat the Expos, 4-2. He won again the following year with six innings of work in a 4-0 triumph over the Phillies. Then in 1973, he went the distance and beat the Phillies and Steve Carlton, 3-0.

From 1970 through 1973, Seaver posted records of 18-12, 20-10, 21-12, and 19-10, leading the league in ERA three times, including a career low of 1.76 in 1971. In 1973, after leading the league with 18 complete games, he again helped the Mets to the World Series, winning the clinching game in the NLCS against the Reds, and dropping Game Six to the Oakland Athletics as they marched to the Series title.

Seaver's fourth Opening Day win came in 1975, when he beat the Phillies with a six-hitter, 2-1. He went on to post a 22-9 record that season. Then in 1976, he beat the Expos on Opening Day, 3-2. That was followed by another win, a 5-3 decision over the Cubs to start the 1977 season. In June that year, however, following a salary dispute, the Mets traded Seaver to the Reds for four players. With a 14-3 record for the Reds, Seaver went on to log his final 20-win season, posting a combined 21-6 mark.

While winning 75 and losing 46 in five and one-half seasons with the Reds, Seaver drew the Opening Day assignment three times, getting no-decisions against the Houston Astros in 1978 and the Phillies in 1981, and his first loss in 1979 against the Giants. In 1978, Seaver reached another career milestone. Three times, Seaver had reached the ninth inning with a no-hitter, but had to settle for a one-hitter. Overall, he had pitched five one-hitters, but on June 16, he finally twirled a no-hitter, beating the St. Louis Cardinals, 4-0. He struck out three and walked three.

After an injury-ridden season in 1982, Seaver was traded back to the Mets. Once again, he was the Mets' Opening Day pitcher in 1983. Although he got no decision in a 2-0 New York victory over the Phillies, Seaver tied Walter Johnson's all-time record with 14 Opening Day starts.

Seaver was good for only a 9-14 record in 1983 with the Mets. After finishing his 12 years with the Mets with a 198-124 record, he moved on the White Sox in 1984. He started two openers for the Chisox, earning the win in a 4-2 victory over the Milwaukee Brewers in 1985, and taking the loss the following season in his last opener, 5-3, to the Brewers.

Seaver gained his 300th win back in New York in 1895 with a complete game, six-hit, 4-1 victory over the Yankees before a crowd of 54,032. During the 1986 season, the White Sox traded him to the Boston Red Sox, and Seaver then won the final game of his career. He retired early in the 1987 season after an unsuccessful bid to rejoin the Mets for the third time.

When he retired, Seaver's name was etched among the all-time leaders of numerous pitching records. Among them was the extraordinary feat of being the starting pitcher in 16 season openers.

37

MIKE MARSHALL

PITCHED IN 106 GAMES IN ONE SEASON

Since relievers became an integral part of every team's pitching staff more than one-half century ago, the best ones have usually accumulated a large number of appearances each season. That's their job. Rush in from the bullpen and stifle opposing hitters. Put out the fire.

These firemen, as they're appropriately called, may not pitch many innings. And maybe they don't always have a fire to put out; they're just brought in because the starter—good grief—has thrown 100 pitches. But for whatever reason, a good reliever, especially if he's a closer, will often pitch in one-third or even more of his team's games.

Of course, there are some relievers who exceed that number. Over the years, a handful of bullpen artists have even climbed the mound in as many as one-half of their team's games. That hasn't happened often, but those who do appear in that many games are in a special class.

The leader of the class is Mike Marshall. A right-handed chucker, he holds a major league record that has never been approached. In 1974, Marshall appeared in the unfathomable number of 106 games while pitching for the Los

Angeles Dodgers. The total broke Marshall's previous record of 92 games, set the year before with the Montreal Expos.

Today, the number closest to Marshall's record total is 94, a figure attained by both Kent Tekulve and Salomon Torres. While that's an admirable number, it's a long way off from Marshall's record, which is even more amazing considering that it came in an era before pitch counts governed all starters' performances on the mound.

To add to that achievement, Marshall worked in 208 innings that year, which is also a major league record for relief pitchers. While appearing in all but 58 of his team's regular season games, he posted a 15-12 record and 21 saves. With a 2.42 earned run average, Marshall struck out 143, walked 56, and gave up 191 hits for a Dodger team that won 102 games during the regular season.

Marshall also made two appearances in the four National League Championship Series games, and pitched in all five games in the Dodgers' World Series loss to the Oakland Athletics, thus running his season's total to 113 games altogether.

It was a magnificent season for Marshall, capped by his becoming the first relief pitcher ever to win the Cy Young Award. He was also named by *The Sporting News* as both the National League Pitcher of the Year and Fireman of the Year, an award he also won in 1973 and 1979.

Overall, during a 14-year major league career in which he played with nine different teams between 1967 and 1981, Marshall appeared in 723 games, including 24 as a starter. He posted a 97-112 record with 188 saves and a 3.14 ERA. In 1,386 innings, Marshall gave up 1,281 hits while striking out 880 and walking 514. Mike led his league in games pitched four times, and in saves and wins by a reliever each three times.

"The whole secret of pitching to me, besides having the ability to throw the ball where you want it, which we assume every major league pitcher has," Marshall once said, "is sequencing your pitchers properly."

Controversial and often abrasive, Marshall was noted as a player who applied unconventional methods to his work on the mound. His theories on pitching, bolstered when he earned a PhD in kinesiology while playing in the big leagues, made considerable contributions to his playing career.

"He was very macho on the mound," said former standout hitter Keith Hernandez. "He strutted around—he was definitely an alpha male. But he threw really hard and had a real heavy fastball and an elusive screwball. I was young and struggling when I batted against him, so he didn't waste much time with me."

Nicknamed "Iron Mike," he was also known as an extremely hard worker who never ceased to keep himself in top condition. "I believe no baseball player was ever in better physical condition than Mike Marshall," said former major league outfielder Danny Litwhiler, who was the pitcher's coach at Michigan State University.

A native of Adrian, Michigan, where he was born in 1943, Marshall had suffered a severe back injury as a youth when a car in which he was riding was hit by a train, killing his uncle, who was driving. Mike was hospitalized and endured long periods of medical treatment.

Eventually, Marshall healed and began playing baseball. Then, after graduating from high school, he enrolled at Michigan State, where he developed an interest in the mechanics of the human body. His expertise in that field would play a major role in his later years as a major league pitcher.

Ironically, Marshall was not a pitcher in his early days of playing baseball. He began his professional career late in 1960 as a shortstop after signing as a free agent with the Philadelphia Phillies. He played that position for four years before the Phillies made him a pitcher in 1965. That year, he posted a 2-4 record in 26 games with Chattanooga of the Southern League.

In 1966, the Phillies sold Marshall to the Detroit Tigers. Then, in the midst of a three-year stint in Toledo of the International League, Marshall made his big league debut with the Tigers in 1967 and pitched in 37 games as a reliever. Two years later, he was selected by the Seattle Pilots in the expansion draft and made 14 starts before going back to the minors, and then getting sold to the Houston Astros in 1969. The following year, he was traded at midseason to Montreal, where he played for four years, twice winning 14 games and leading the league in games pitched (65) in 1972 and games pitched (92) and saves (31) in 1973.

The Expos swapped Marshall to the Dodgers for outfielder Willie Davis in the winter of 1973. During his three years in Los Angeles, the 5-10, 180-pounder won 28 games and saved 60.

The 1974 season began with Marshall pitching in each of the first five games while working a total of 8.2 innings. By the end of April, he had come out of the bullpen 15 times over a 23-day period. He had pitched 25 innings, including three innings twice and two innings in each of six other games. Only once did he hurl less than one full inning. Marshall ended the month with one loss and two saves while allowing six earned runs, striking out 16, and yielding 19 hits.

The Iron Man's relentless pace continued in May, when he pitched in 18 games, including at one point eight days in a row. During that period, he gave up just seven earned runs and 32 hits in 37.2 innings while posting a 2-1 record with six saves. Twice, he worked four innings, and in three other games he hurled at least three innings.

In June, Marshall appeared in 18 more games and captured seven wins in eight decisions with two saves. This time, he pitched in 29.2 innings while giving up 29 hits and 10 earned runs. Then in July, he relieved in 19 games, posting a 2-3 record and three saves while striking out 31 and yielding 10 earned runs in 40.1 innings. Between late June and early July, Marshall appeared in 14 straight games. On July 4, he got the win in a 3-2 victory over the Cincinnati Reds while pitching in his 20th game over a 30-day period.

Marshall's magnificence continued in August, when he again appeared 18 times, winning two, saving six, and allowing 35 hits and nine earned runs in 39 innings. He worked in 17 games in September, recording two wins, two saves, and yielding 30 hits and 13 earned runs in 34.2 innings. Marshall pitched one game in October before the season ended. Overall, he had pitched in three or more innings 22 times. He pitched six innings in one game, five frames in another, and four innings five times.

But it really hadn't ended. In the NLCS, he worked three innings in two games as the Dodgers beat the Pittsburgh Pirates in four games. Then in the World Series, he pitched a total of 12 innings in all five games. He recorded a save in the Dodgers' 3-2 victory in Game Two, but took the loss while hurling the final three innings in the deciding fifth game won by Oakland, 3-2.

For the rubber-armed hurler, it was an astounding season. Other fine seasons followed, but none matched the '74 record. After leaving the Dodgers in a mid-season trade with the Atlanta Braves in 1976, Marshall played with the Texas Rangers, Minnesota Twins, and New York Mets. His best season came in 1979 with the Twins, when he led the American League in games (90) and saves (32). Marshall's baseball career ended after the 1981 season, after pitching for 14 years.

38

RON GUIDRY

POSTED HIGHEST WINNING PERCENTAGE

Seldom does a starting pitcher who's collected a large number of decisions during a season ever win seven or eight times as many games as he lost. He's not expected to do that. If he wins two or three times more games than he lost, it's considered a commendable season.

Ron Guidry was different. Not only did he claim victory one season in nearly 90 percent of his decisions, but also he set a record in that category. It's a record that has withstood numerous unsuccessful attempts to pass it.

While winning 25 games and losing just three in 1978, Guidry compiled a winning percentage of .893. It's the highest figure ever recorded among pitchers who won 20 or more games in one season.

In just the left-hander's second full season in the major leagues, the pitcher called "The Louisiana Lightning" completed the feat and also won the Cy Young Award while leading the New York Yankees to victory in the World Series. He also finished second (to Jim Rice) in the voting for Most Valuable Player.

Guidry, who while running away with the league lead in wins and winning percentage also was first in earned run average with a 1.74 and shutouts with

nine, started 35 games and completed 16. He worked in 273.2 innings, allowed 187 hits, struck out 248, and walked 72.

During a 14-year career spent entirely with the Yankees, Guidry was a 20-game winner three times, won in double figures nine straight times, and was in the top 10 in the voting for the Cy Young Award six times. He also appeared in four All-Star Games and won five Gold Gloves.

Guidry had a career record of 170-91 with an ERA of 3.29. He pitched in 368 games, starting 323 and completing 95, with 26 shutouts. In 2,392 innings, he yielded 2,198 hits, struck out 1,367, and walked 633.

Ron was noted for a wicked slider and a relentless fastball. "He was one of the toughest lefties I ever faced," said standout hitter Harold Baines. "He had a nasty slider that was very hard to hit. And he was a competitor who never gave in."

Guidry began life in 1950 in Lafayette, Louisiana. He didn't throw a baseball in his early youth and his high school had no team. He got his first real test on the mound pitching for the University of Southwestern Louisiana. Ultimately, he was a third-round pick of the Yankees in 1971 and spent five years in the minors, mostly as a reliever, before serving brief stints with the Yanks.

The 5-11, 160-pound chucker first came to the Yankees as a relief pitcher in 1975. He pitched in 10 games, nine in relief. The following year, he appeared in seven games, all as a reliever.

In 1977, Guidry finally emerged as a starting pitcher, and posted a 16-7 record with a 2.82 ERA while appearing in 31 games, including 25 as a starter. He also won Game Four of the World Series, a 4-2 victory over the Los Angeles Dodgers. The season provided a perfect entrée into the 1978 campaign.

It began on a sour note, though, when "Gator," as he was also called, missed the early part of Spring Training because of a severe case of the flu. When he finally recovered, he was still weak and pitched poorly in the early part of the season.

In each of his first six games, including the season's opener when he held the Texas Rangers to one run in seven innings before the Yanks lost, 2-1, he lasted no more than seven innings and had a no-decision in four of those games.

He got his first win in his second start of the season while working his only complete game in his first eight outings, beating the Chicago White Sox, 4-2.

Two starts later, he won his second game, an 8-2 decision over the Baltimore Orioles, although he had to leave the game after seven innings when he became ill after swallowing tobacco juice.

But that had launched a win streak during which he won 13 straight games before losing his first game of the season on July 7. Before then, he won back-to-back 5-2 games against the Rangers and Kansas City Royals, plus a 10-1 victory over the Cleveland Indians when he struck out 11 batters and a 5-3 triumph over the Toronto Blue Jays, which was his first complete game of the season.

As June began, Guidry had successive games in which he fanned ten or more batters per outing: 11 in a 3-1 win over the Toronto Blue Jays, 10 in a 9-1 victory over the Seattle Mariners, and 11 again in his first shutout of the season, a 2-0, three-hit decision over the Oakland Athletics.

Guidry pitched his best game on June 17 against the California Angels, when he notched his second straight shutout, 4-0, gave up four hits, and struck out a whooping total of 18 batters. At one point, Gator struck out 11 of 12 hitters. His 18 strikeouts were the most ever recorded by a left-handed pitcher in the American League.

Ron ended June with a 12-0 record and then started July with a 3-2 win over the Detroit Tigers. Five days later, the streak ended with a 6-0 loss to the Milwaukee Brewers. But after a no-decision game, he came back with two straight shutouts. One was a four-hit, 4-0 win over the Minnesota Twins, while the other was a 4-0 verdict over Kansas City, which stopped the Royals' 10-game winning streak.

After a no-decision game against the Twins, Guidry finished July with a 15-1 record. He started August with a 2-1 loss to the Orioles, but then tossed two straight shutouts, beating Milwaukee with a three-hitter, 9-0, and Oakland with a four-hitter, 6-0. The whitewashes sent Guidry on a seven-game winning streak during which he had his seventh and last no-decision game of the season.

In the final game of August, he beat Baltimore, 5-4, but had to leave the game in the eighth inning when a bat flew out of the hands of Ken Singleton and slammed into his ankle. Fortunately, the ankle turned out to be undamaged, and Guidry returned five days later to beat the Tigers with a five-hitter, 9-1, for his 20th win of the season.

Afterward, Guidry fired back-to-back two-hit shutouts, both times beating the Boston Red Sox, 7-0 and 4-0. The first one was the third of a four-game sweep registered by the Yankees as they surged back to tie the Bosox for first place. The second win gave New York a two and one-half game lead.

Guidry's streak ended against Toronto when Ron, pitching on three days' rest, lasted just one and two-thirds innings and left after giving up five runs in a game won by the last-place Blue Jays, 8-1.

That was his final loss of the season. Guidry won his next two games. In his third two-hitter of the month, he blanked Cleveland, 4-0. Then he topped Toronto with a four-hitter, 3-1, in the final game of the regular season.

At one point in mid-season, Guidry's Yankees had trailed the Red Sox by as many as 15 games. But a second-half Yankee surge, accompanied by a devastating Red Sox slump, had wound up with the two teams tied for first place when the regular season ended. A one-game playoff was necessary.

Naturally, Guidry was on the mound for the Yanks. Before a crowd of more than 33,000 at Fenway Park, the Red Sox took an early 2-0 lead. Then in the top of the seventh, Bucky Dent hit his memorable three-run homer to give New York a 3-2 lead. Guidry left in the bottom of the seventh, but he got the victory, as the Yanks captured a 5-4 verdict.

The win gave Guidry his final 25-3 record. In the last two months of the season, Ron had posted a 10-2 record with a 0.91 ERA.

In the League Championship Series, Guidry was too exhausted to pitch until the fourth game. But his 2-1 victory in that outing against Kansas City clinched the pennant for the Yankees. Then in the World Series, Guidry beat the Los Angeles Dodgers, 5-1, in Game Three to help his team take a four-games-to-two victory.

Over his next seven seasons, Guidry pitched masterfully. He went 21-9 in 1983, when he led the league with 21 complete games, and 22-6 in 1985, when he topped the AL with a .786 winning percentage.

Arm and shoulder problems that had surfaced in the mid-1980s had an effect on Guidry's pitching in his final three years, and he retired after shoulder surgery following the 1988 season. Guidry's departure ended a sparkling career during which one very special season made him a significant part of baseball history.

39

JIM PALMER

WAS A WORLD SERIES WINNER IN THREE DECADES

Winning a World Series game is something for which all pitchers strive. Such an accomplishment puts a hurler in a special class that is occupied by a small group of participants.

Only those fortunate enough to be part of a team that at least that season is one of the two best in baseball can claim membership in that highly select group. And even if they do, the number of times their team travels to the Fall Classic in any given era has a definite effect on the number of games a pitcher can win.

Thus, it is quite unusual that a pitcher could be part of the same team that played in the World Series in three consecutive decades. It is even more unusual that he could win a World Series game in each of those decades.

In fact, it's only happened once since the World Series was initiated in 1903. While pitching with the Baltimore Orioles, Jim Palmer won games in the 1966, 1970 and 1971, and 1983 World Series.

As baseball's only three-decade World Series winner, Palmer accomplished this amazing feat during a career filled with special records. An eight-time

20-game winner, Palmer won three Cy Young Awards and finished second twice while posting a career record of 268-152 during a 19-year career spent entirely in Baltimore.

Palmer appeared in 558 games, including 521 as a starter. His earned run average of 2.86 was bolstered by allowing just 3,349 hits in 3,948 innings while striking out 2,212 and walking 1,311. The 6-3, 190-pound right-hander was named to six All-Star teams and won four Gold Gloves. Palmer, who never allowed a grand slam home run during his entire career, threw a no-hitter just four days after coming off the disabled list.

Outspoken, opinionated, and intelligent, Palmer is considered the greatest pitcher in Orioles history. "The problem with me," he once said, "is that everybody expects me to be perfect. They expect me to always win and never get hurt."

In postseason action, Palmer had an 8-3 record, including a 4-2 mark in six World Series. His record got a quick start in 1966, when as a 20 year old, he became the youngest pitcher ever to throw a World Series shutout when he defeated the Los Angeles Dodgers in the second game of an Orioles four-game sweep.

Coming at the end of his first full season in Baltimore when he posted a 15-10 record, Palmer hurled a four-hitter to beat the Dodgers and Sandy Koufax in his last big league game, 6-0. The complete game victory came in the midst of a streak of 33 1/3 scoreless innings by Orioles pitchers in that Series.

Palmer's next Series win came in 1970 during a season when his 20-10 record gave him his first 20-win regular season. Jim, who was noted as one who ate pancakes before every start, went 8 2/3 innings to top the Cincinnati Reds in the opener, 4-3. Palmer also pitched seven innings in Game Four, but got no-decision in a 6-5 Reds win, en route to an eventual Baltimore series win in five games.

After compiling a 20-9 record during the season and defeating the Oakland Athletics, 5-3, in Game Three of the American League Championship Series, Palmer captured another World Series win in 1971 against the Pittsburgh Pirates, working eight innings in an 11-3 victory in Game Two. Again Palmer got no decision in his second outing in a 3-2 Orioles win in the sixth game of a Series won the next day by the Pirates.

The pitcher who was known for his high kick and smooth delivery got his third decade win in 1983 in a five-game Orioles victory over the Philadelphia

Phillies. Hurling in relief in his only appearance of the Series, he registered the verdict after working two innings of a 3-2 victory over Steve Carlton.

By then, Palmer's three-decade career was just about over. It had been a brilliant career laced with special accomplishments despite repeated arm, back, and shoulder problems, which often put him on the disabled list. Through it all, Palmer won in double figures 13 times while leading the league in wins three times and in innings pitched in four seasons.

"Jim had one of the most beautiful deliveries I've ever seen," said former Baltimore pitching coach Ray Miller. "It was almost like watching ballet." Added slugger Bill Skowron, "I think he's the hardest thrower in the league."

Palmer had been playing baseball since his days as a Little Leaguer. Born in 1945 in New York City, he lived in his youth there and in several places in California and finally in Scottsdale, Arizona, where he was a high school baseball, football, and basketball star. After playing in a summer league in South Dakota, he signed with the Orioles in 1963 as a 17 year old for a reported $60,000 bonus.

Jim spent just one year in the minors, posting an 11-3 record and tossing a no-hitter in 1964 with Aberdeen of the Northern League before landing with the Orioles in 1965. That year, while used mostly in relief, he had a 5-4 record in 27 games. Then the following year, Palmer rocketed to stardom.

His 15-10 record in 30 starts ended when Palmer beat the Kansas City Royals in Baltimore's pennant-clinching game. It was then on to the World Series and the start of Jim's amazing streak.

Baltimore took a break in Series action in 1967, but early in the season Palmer pitched a one-hitter against the New York Yankees. Soon afterward, he developed arm problems and was sent back to the minors. He played at both Rochester and Miami while also spending more than one month on the disabled list before returning to the Orioles in September.

The arm and subsequent shoulder problems continued in 1968, and Palmer never pitched in Baltimore, dividing his time between the disabled list and the minors. After off-season surgery and playing winter ball, the Orioles made Palmer available, first on waivers and then through the expansion draft. But no one picked him, and he returned to the Birds in 1969.

To almost everyone's surprise, he went 16-4, despite spending 41 days on the disabled list. On August 13 in his first start since returning to action, he pitched a no-hitter against Oakland. While relying on a crackling fastball, Palmer made 142 pitches, striking out eight and walking six in an 8-0 victory. That fall, the

Orioles won their first of three straight American League pennants. Palmer beat the Minnesota Twins, 11-2, in the third and deciding game of the ALCS, but lost Game Two of the World Series to the New York Mets, 5-0.

Palmer went from there to post four straight 20-win seasons, capped by a 22-9 mark with a league-leading 2.40 ERA in 1973, when he won his first Cy Young Award. In 1970, he again beat the Twins, 6-1, in Game Three of the ALCS. In 1971, he was part of one of the greatest pitching staffs of all time when all four Baltimore starters—Dave McNally, Mike Cuellar, Pat Dobson, and Palmer (each with 20, except for McNally, who had 21)—won 20 or more games. Only one other major league staff—the 1920 Chicago White Sox—ever had four 20-game winners in the same season. And in 1972, in his third straight All-Star Game, his scoreless streak in the three games reached eight consecutive innings.

More arm trouble plagued Palmer in 1974, and with nearly two months on the disabled list, he slipped to a 7-12 record. But he bounced back with four consecutive 20-win seasons. He led the league with a 2.09 ERA and 10 shutouts in 1975, when he posted a 23-11 record and won his second Cy Young Award. With a 22-13 mark the following year, he won another Cy Young, becoming the first American League pitcher to win the award three times. That year, he led the league with a career-high 40 starts and in innings pitched (315). In 1977, his 20-11 mark led the league in wins for the third straight year, and he was also at the top in starts (39) and a career-high 319 innings pitched.

Palmer had no more 20-win seasons after his 21-12 log in 1978, but he went 16-10 in 1980 and 15-5 in 1982. With more arm trouble in 1983, he pitched infrequently (5-4), and was released early in the 1984 season after going 0-3.

Six years later, he was inducted into the Hall of Fame. "I'm here," he said, "because I played for the Baltimore Orioles. I was surrounded by great players. We had the kind of teams that if you would get in shape and go out there, you'd win close to 20 games every season."

And if your name was Jim Palmer, you'd hold an unmatched record of winning a World Series game in each of three straight decades.

40

DWIGHT GOODEN

DEFIED THE SOPHOMORE JINX

Every player in baseball who has had an outstanding rookie season faces a similar threat. It's called the Sophomore Jinx, a condition in which a player's performance in his second season is often well below that of his first year.

The record book is bloated with examples of players who were victims of the Sophomore Jinx. Some recovered in succeeding years; some didn't. Some were never heard from again, while others went on to stellar careers, the Sophomore Jinx being only a temporary setback.

And then there was Dwight Gooden. The 6-3, 190-pound fire-balling right-hander of the New York Mets had an outstanding rookie season, and he followed that with an even better second season. No Sophomore Jinx got in Gooden's way. In fact, few players ever had a second season as sensational as Gooden's.

After posting a 17-9 record and leading the league in strikeouts in 1984, Gooden compiled a 24-4 mark as a sophomore. His earned run average was 1.53. In 35 starts, he completed 16, including nine shutouts, a Mets record. He pitched 277 innings, struck out 268, allowed 198 hits, and walked 69. Eleven times, he struck out 10 or more batters in one game. From May 30 until the

end of the season, he went 18-1. Gooden led the league in wins, earned run average, innings pitched, and strikeouts.

It was truly a glittering season, one that defied the age-old threat that bad would follow good in the first two seasons of a player's career. To make it even more impressive, Gooden was just 20 years old and would become the youngest pitcher ever to win the Cy Young Award.

Gooden's success was not unexpected. A first-round pick and the fifth pick overall, the Tampa, Florida native who was born in 1964 had gone 19-4 and struck out 300 as an 18-year-old hurler with Lynchburg of the Carolina League in his second season in the minors in 1983. The following season, he came to New York, and compiled a 2.60 ERA while working 218 innings in 31 starts (seven complete games and three shutouts) and leading the National League with 276 strikeouts, an all-time rookie record. Gooden even fired a one-hitter against the Chicago Cubs. After the season, Dwight was second in the voting for the Cy Young Award.

After winning eight of his last nine starts in 1984, having become the youngest pitcher ever to play in an All-Star Game, and winning the Rookie of the Year Award, Gooden was hardly expected to better his freshman record. But he did, beginning on April 9, when he became the youngest pitcher ever to start an Opening Day game. Facing the St. Louis Cardinals at Shea Stadium, he had a 5-2 lead in the seventh inning, but was taken out, and the Cards rallied to cop a 6-5 verdict, with Gooden getting no decision.

Five days later, though, "Doc," as they would call him, bounced back with a four-hit, 4-0 victory over the Cincinnati Reds in a game in which he struck out 10 batters. He followed that with a 1-0 victory over Steve Carlton and the Philadelphia Phillies, yielding just three hits in eight innings. Then, after losing to St. Louis when his 23-game scoreless streak was broken, he won four straight games, one of which was a 5-0 victory over the Phillies, when he gave up just three hits and struck out 13.

Two losses dropped his record to 6-3, but Gooden bounced back on May 30 with a 2-1 win over the San Francisco Giants, striking out 14 and yielding six hits. For the rest of the season, Gooden would win 17 more games while losing only one. Twelve times, his opponents got one run or less, and seven of those games were shutouts.

On June 14, Gooden got a no decision in a 5-4 Mets loss to the Montreal Expos in a game in which he threw 147 pitches. Five days later, he blanked the Chicago Cubs, 1-0, with a six-hitter, to run his record to 10-3. Then after a win and a no decision, he took the mound against the Atlanta Braves, but was lifted in the third inning after a rain delay with the Braves leading, 2-1.Eventually, the game went 19 innings, with the two teams combining for 46 hits and 22 walks. The Braves won, 16-13.

Gooden, whose fastball was clocked as high as 98 miles per hour and who threw a sweeping curve, then won seven straight games before his streak was interrupted with a no decision. In one game, he captured a five-hit, 11-strikeout, 1-0 decision over the Houston Astros. In another, he went six innings and gave up two hits in a 16-4 triumph over the Braves. He fanned 10 and yielded five hits in a 2-0 whitewash of Montreal. Then he beat the Cubs back to back, with one of the wins being a five-hit, 4-1 victory.

Doc set a season's high with 16 strikeouts when he beat the Giants, 3-0, with a seven-hitter. In his next start on August 25, he won his 20th game, 9-3 over the San Diego Padres. The win made him the youngest pitcher ever to win 20 games, breaking the old record set in 1939 by Bob Feller.

The winning streak that began on May 30 finally ended for Dr. K on August 31, when he bowed to the Giants, 3-2, while working just six innings. Two games without a decision followed, after which he beat the Phillies, 9-0, while fanning 11 and allowing two hits. Next, he was touched for just four hits in a 12-1 decision over the Pittsburgh Pirates during which he hit his only home run of the season. He followed that with a 3-0 whitewash of the Cubs for his ninth shutout of the season.

From August 31 through October 2, Gooden had hurled 49 consecutive innings without giving up an earned run. He had thrown 31 straight scoreless innings and in three consecutive games had struck out a total of 43 batters. So dominant was Gooden that a sign painted on the side of a building on Times Square showed Doc with the caption, "How does it feel to look down the barrel of a loaded gun?"

Gooden wrapped up his season with a 5-2 win over the Cards. Entering the game, the Mets trailed St. Louis by just two games in the National League East, but they faded at the end and finished three games back. But it certainly wasn't Gooden's fault. The youngster had the greatest season any pitcher ever had in his sophomore year.

"I took a lot of pride in my work," he said many years later. "But I didn't feel like it was easy. To me, it felt like a concert, and I was the main event."

When Dwight finished the season, the accolades came from all directions. "I don't see why he can't be the greatest pitcher ever," said Bob Gibson.

"If nothing happens to him, he may set and break all the records within reach," added Sandy Koufax.

Gooden went on to pitch 14 more seasons in the big leagues, but none came close to his 1985 campaign. He went 17-6 in 1986 and at 21 years old became the youngest pitcher ever to start an All-Star Game. Although the Mets won the National League pennant and the World Series, Doc failed to win a single post-season game, which included a 1-0 loss in the NLCS opener with Houston and a 10-inning outing in which he gave up just one run in Game Five. He failed to get past the fifth inning in both his World Series starts.

After his spectacular 1985 season, Gooden won in double figures in seven out of eight years with the Mets, his best seasons being an 18-9 mark in 1988 and a 19-7 log in 1990. He played 11 years with the Mets, compiling a 157-85 record.

Drug and other problems waylaid the rest of Gooden's career. He was suspended for the entire 1995 season before signing with the New York Yankees, and over his final five years played for them, the Cleveland Indians, Houston, the Tampa Bay Devil Rays, and the Yanks again, the last three all in 2000, Gooden's last season in the majors.

Gooden finished his 16-year career with an overall record of 194-112. He appeared in 430 games, starting 410 and finishing 68, 24 of which were shutouts. In 2,800.2 innings, he allowed 2,564 hits, struck out 2,293, and walked 594.

41

OREL HERSHISER

RECORDED 59 STRAIGHT INNINGS WITHOUT A RUN

U p and down they came, batter after batter, inning after inning, and not one could drive in even a single run. The scoring famine lasted for 59 innings, and by the time a run finally crossed the plate, Orel Hershiser was the holder of a record that may never be broken.

It happened in 1988 during a brilliant season by Hershiser in which his work earned a special place among the ranks of baseball's most memorable pitching feats. That season, Hershiser posted a 23-8 record, led the National League in innings pitched (267), complete games (15), and shutouts (eight), and was a unanimous choice for the Cy Young Award while leading the Los Angeles Dodgers to victory in the World Series.

The season was the best in a career in which Hershiser recorded a lifetime 204-150 mark. He registered a 3.48 earned run average while pitching in 510 games, 466 as a starter. Orel worked in 3,130 innings, gave up 2,939 hits, struck out 2,014, and hurled 25 shutouts.

The 6-3, 190-pound Hershiser was known as an intense, unyielding hurler whose focus and knowledge of the game were almost immeasurable. That

attitude had been fueled in part by Dodgers manager Tom Lasorda. When the slender right-hander first arrived in the majors in 1983, Lasorda felt that he was intimidated by the hitters and pitched too carefully. "Be aggressive," Lasorda insisted. "Go after the hitters."

It worked, and Lasorda soon gave Orel the nickname of "Bulldog." Over the years, Hershiser earned a reputation for not only being a fierce competitor, but also a hurler who was noted for his mental discipline and the consistency with which he studied opposing hitters. He also developed a collection of highly effective pitches that he threw with different arm angles and varying locations. His heavy fastball and his nasty sinker were particularly tough to hit.

"He also had a great curve ball," said Keith Hernandez, one of the National League's top hitters. "And he threw a fastball that started an inch or so inside, then broke back over the corner. He put an extra three or four miles-per-hour on it, so it snuck up on you. He really knew what he was doing out there."

"Baseball is a game where you continue to put yourself in a position to have the highest percentage of chance to succeed," Hershiser said. "What I did yesterday doesn't matter other than what I learned. The key for me is to concentrate on execution. Attitude is crucial."

Hershiser never stopped learning. Born in Buffalo, New York in 1958, he grew up mostly in Cherry Hill, New Jersey, where he was the star pitcher on his high school team and played on a junior ice hockey team sponsored by the Philadelphia Flyers. He attended Bowling Green University, where he first caught the eyes of pro scouts. Orel became a 17th round draft pick of the Dodgers in 1979, and spent four years in the minor leagues before being summoned to LA late in the 1983 season. He pitched in eight games, all in relief.

Orel divided duties between starting and relieving in 1984, posting an 11-8 record in his first full season in the majors. He followed that with a 19-3 mark and a 2.03 ERA, finishing third in the Cy Young voting. Seasons of 14-14 and 16-16 followed, with Hershiser leading the league in innings pitched (264.2) in 1987.

The off-season that followed did not bode well for Hershiser's 1988 campaign. First, he underwent knee surgery. Then he suffered from appendicitis while playing golf and again needed surgery. In Spring Training, Bulldog had to work extremely hard to get ready for the season.

It was a season that began with a three-hit, 5-0 shutout of the San Francisco Giants. Hershiser won six games in a row before losing his first game. That came just two days after he'd pitched one inning in relief.

By the time his scoreless streak began, Hershiser had already hurled a two-hit, 2-0 victory over the Houston Astros and a 2-0, five-hit win over the Montreal Expos. He had beaten the Atlanta Braves' Tom Glavine twice and the Astros' Nolan Ryan three times. He won six straight games twice.

On August 30, his record was 18-8 after he beat the Expos, 4-2, with a six-hitter. Hershiser blanked Montreal over the last four innings while setting a season's high with nine strikeouts. On September 5, the streak continued with a four-hit, 3-0 victory over the Braves in a game in which he struck out Dale Murphy four times. Five days later, before a crowd of 42,393 at Dodger Stadium, Hershiser gained his 20th win of the season with a seven-hit, 5-0 decision over the Cincinnati Reds.

Claiming that "this was the most energetic I've ever been," Hershiser was gaining momentum, but on September 14, his streak nearly ended. Facing the Braves, with 42,434 jammed into the stands, he loaded the bases in the seventh inning before Ron Gant hit a towering shot to deep left that looked like it might be a grand slam. But with his back to the wall, left fielder Kirk Gibson caught the ball to save the shutout. Hershiser finished with a 1-0 victory when Mike Marshall doubled home the winning run in the ninth inning.

Another 1-0 win followed five days later when Orel pitched a four-hitter to beat Houston, on John Shelby's seventh inning home run. Then on September 23, he beat the Giants, 3-0, on Mickey Hatcher's three-run homer in the eighth inning to run his record to 23-8 and his scoreless streak to 49 innings. By then, Don Drysdale's scoreless streak of 58 2/3 innings was in sight. "I hope he breaks it," the ex-pitcher said.

On September 28, the Dodgers met the San Diego Padres. The game was scoreless after nine innings. Hershiser now had 58 straight shutout innings. In the 10th, he retired the first two batters, tying Drysdale's record. Orel wanted to be taken out of the game because he didn't want to break the record of a pitcher he admired. But better heads prevailed, and he stayed in, retiring pinch-hitter Keith Moreland on a fly to right fielder Jose Gonzalez. Hershiser had the record. He was relieved after the 10th inning, and the Padres won, 2-1, on Mark Parent's two-run homer in the bottom of the 16th.

The Dodgers won their division title and faced the Mets in the National League Championship Series. In the opener, Hershiser pitched eight more scoreless innings, taking a 2-0 lead into the ninth, before allowing one run and getting relieved. The eight shutout innings, however, did not count toward

Orel's streak because it was achieved in postseason play. Although Hershiser was also charged with a second run after he departed, the Mets won, 3-2.

Hershiser was back on the mound for Game Three, and this time left for a pinch-hitter after eight innings with the Dodgers leading, 4-3. The Mets came back with five runs to win, 8-4. Orel then pitched one-third of an inning in relief and got a save after entering the game with two outs and the bases loaded in the 12th inning of a 5-4 Dodgers victory in Game Five.

In Game Seven, Hershiser added another laurel to his season, scattering five hits in a 6-0 victory that gave the Dodgers the pennant. Hershiser, who compiled a 1.09 ERA during the NLCS, was named the Most Valuable Player.

In Game One of the World Series, Hershiser pitched one of his best games of the season, a three-hit, 5-0 victory over the Oakland Athletics. He also slammed two doubles and a single.

Next, Hershiser took the mound in Game Five. In what turned out to be the World Series clincher for the Dodgers, he pitched a four-hitter and won, 5-2. Again, Orel was named Most Valuable Player. In his last 12 games, he had won eight without a loss while posting a 0.46 ERA. In 96 of his final 100 innings, he did not yield a run.

The following year, as a lack of offensive support often spoiled his efforts, Hershiser's record fell to 15-15, although he led the league for the third straight season in innings pitched (256.2). Rotator cuff surgery knocked him out for most of the 1990 season, and he won just 35 games (and lost 37) over the next four years.

Hershiser spent three seasons (1995–97) with the Cleveland Indians, bouncing back with 16-6, 15-9, and 14-6 records. He was named MVP of the ALCS in 1995, leading the Indians to victory over the Seattle Mariners.

Orel played one year each with the Giants (11-10) and Mets (13-12) before returning to the Dodgers for his final season in 2000. When he retired, Hershiser had spent 18 years in the big leagues. None, though, matched that magnificent campaign in 1988.

42

JIM ABBOTT

PITCHED WITH ONLY ONE ARM

In baseball, as in most sports, it is extremely difficult to play with a serious disability. Few players have done it, and even fewer have done it with any degree of success.

Pete Gray was an outfielder who played one season in the big leagues with one arm. Monty Stratton pitched in the minors with one leg. And Bert Shepard appeared briefly as a pitcher after losing a leg.

No one with a physical handicap, however, has played nearly as long or as successfully in the majors as Jim Abbott.

Born with no hand on his right arm, Abbott enjoyed a 10-year career in the big leagues. During that time, he won in double figures five times, hurled a no-hitter, and landed numerous awards. Being able to perform that successfully was a magnificent achievement for a player with such a substantial disability.

At least, publicly, Abbott never seemed to let it bother him. "There are millions of people out there ignoring disabilities and accomplishing incredible feats," he said. "It's not the disability that defines you, but how you deal with the challenges the disability presents. I've learned that you have an obligation to the abilities you have, and not the disability."

AP Photo/John Hayes

Abbott's right arm extended below his elbow and down to where it became a stump. When he was pitching, the left-handed-throwing Abbott placed a right-handed fielder's glove over the stump. As he completed his delivery, he switched the glove to his left hand and with that, fielded balls hit his way. To throw the ball to a base, Abbott would stuff the glove back under his right armpit, then pull the ball out of the glove with his left hand.

The 6-3, 200-pound hurler's main problems were his fielding—batters often tried to bunt on him—and his trouble holding runners on base. Playing mostly in the American League, he never had to bat, although during a brief stint in the National League, he collected two hits in 21 at-bats.

Among his pitches early in his career, he threw a 95 mph fastball and an assortment of good breaking pitches. He had excellent control, too.

"For a guy with special needs and what he had to go through, he was a great pitcher," said the hard-hitting Harold Baines. "He was certainly tough on me. I didn't get that many hits off him.

How did most players react to Abbott's disability? "The players were amazed at how consistent he was," said Baines, who during his stellar American League career batted many times against Abbott. "He could command both sides of the plate."

Abbott's final record of 87-108 would've been much better had he not had two bad seasons at the end of his career, when he won just four of 30 decisions. Overall, he started 254 of the 263 games in which he pitched, tossing 31 complete games and six shutouts. In 1,674 innings, Jim allowed 1,779 hits, struck out 888, and walked 620. He had an earned run average of 4.25.

A native of Flint, Michigan, where he was born to teenage parents in 1967, Abbott gravitated to sports before he even started school. Jim was especially fond of baseball, and as a youngster, he would spent long hours throwing a rubber-coated baseball at a brick wall on the side of his parents' house. "I would imagine myself a major league pitcher," Abbott said.

With the help of his parents, especially his father, Abbott progressed rapidly. The first time he ever pitched in a game was for a Little League team, and he fired a no-hitter. By the time he reached high school, Abbott was not only an accomplished pitcher, but also a quarterback and punter on the football team. After graduating, he turned down an offer from the Toronto Blue Jays, instead enrolling at the University of Michigan.

After posting a 6-2 record in his freshman season, Abbott won the prestigious Most Courageous Athlete Award, presented by the Philadelphia Sports Writers Association. He pitched two more seasons with the Wolverines, leading them to the Big Ten championship one year. Along the way, Abbott won two games, including a three-hitter against Cuba, while leading the United States team to second place in the Pan American Games. He also earned the James E. Sullivan Award as the country's outstanding amateur athlete, and the Golden Spikes award as the top amateur baseball player. In 1988, Abbott beat Japan in the final game to give the U.S. team the gold medal in the Olympics.

With one year of college left and a 26-8 record in three years, Abbott was selected by the California Angels as the eighth choice in the first round of the 1988 major league draft. He signed for a $207,000 bonus, and the following spring gained a spot on the Angels' roster, even though he had no minor league experience.

In an event that was followed around the world, the 21-year-old Abbott lost in his major league debut, lasting just five innings. But he exited the field to a standing ovation from the crowd packed into Anaheim Stadium. It took another loss before he beat the Baltimore Orioles for his first win. From then on, Abbott was spectacular. He finished the season with a 12-12 record and was fifth in the American League Rookie of the Year voting.

"He probably had as strong an arm as any left-hander I ever caught," said star backstop Lance Parrish.

By now a huge national attraction, Abbott slipped to a 10-14 mark in his sophomore season. Then in 1991, he began the campaign with four straight losses, but bounced back to post the best record of his career, an 18-11 mark with a 2.89 ERA. After the season, Jim finished third in the voting for the Cy Young Award, which Roger Clemens won. He was also awarded a contract for $1.85 million.

The 1992 season proved to be one of the low points in Abbott's career. With the weak-hitting Angels winning just 72 games and finishing in sixth place in the West Division, he could only go 7-15. His 2.77 ERA, however, told a different story. That and his seven complete games were both career highs.

That winter, the Angels, deadlocked with Abbott in a salary dispute, traded him to the New York Yankees for three minor leaguers. Abbott's contract battle continued with the Yanks before he finally signed for $2.35 million. That season, he went 11-14.

But there was one high point. On September 4, Abbott pitched a no-hitter against the Cleveland Indians. Six days earlier, the Indians had raked Abbott for 10 hits and seven runs in three and two-thirds innings. But before a crowd of 27,225 at Yankee Stadium, Abbott came back to blank the sixth-place Indians, striking out three and walking five in a 4-0 victory.

Abbott posted a 9-8 record in the strike-shortened 1994 season. That winter, he became a free agent and signed with the Chicago White Sox. He logged a 6-4 mark before the Sox swapped him at mid-season to the Angels, where he went 5-4 the rest of the year to finish with an 11-8 overall record.

The following season was absolutely dreadful for Abbott. Having lost his fastball, he plummeted to a 2-18 record with a 7.48 ERA in 27 games and was released at the end of the season. Convinced his career was over, Abbott sat out the 1997 season. The following year, however, he had second thoughts and launched a comeback with the White Sox. After hurling in the minors, Abbott got a late-season call to Chicago, and posted a 5-0 record in five starts.

That winter, he won the Tony Conigliaro Award, which goes annually to the player who best overcomes obstacles and thrives despite adversity. It was a fitting award for Abbott, who throughout his career had demonstrated a high level of strength and courage. "People will tell you that I overcame obstacles," he once said. "Maybe. But the truth is, I was incredibly blessed in my life. More was given than was ever taken away."

Chicago didn't offer Abbott a contract in 1999, so he signed with the Milwaukee Brewers. In his only National League campaign, Abbott went 2-8 before getting released at mid-season. Shortly afterward, he retired for good at the tender age of 31.

When he did, Abbott ended a career that, no matter what the record was, ranked at the top of the list as one of baseball's—if not one of all of sports'—most heroic achievements.

"My career statistics weren't that great," Abbott said. "But if a career can be measured by special moments, lessons learned, and a connection with people, then I would stack mine up with anyone's."

Certainly, no one could ever argue with that.

MODERN MASTERS OF THE MOUND – 1995 TO PRESENT

43

DENNIS ECKERSLEY

WENT FROM TOP STARTER TO TOP RELIEVER

By the second half of the 20th century, the pitching staffs of most teams were clearly defined. There were starting pitchers and there were relief pitchers. Usually, a hurler was developed as one or the other, and it was highly unlikely that he would ever switch jobs.

Of course, there have always been worn-down starters who lived out the final years of their careers as relievers. And in rare instances, a younger pitcher has been converted from one position to the other. Otherwise, there has been a distinct separation between the two kinds of moundsmen, with each having his own particular role on the pitching staff.

But there have been a few noteworthy exceptions, wherein players have exhibited immense versatility as both a starting pitcher as well as a relief pitcher. No one fit this description more than Dennis Eckersley. He was originally an outstanding starter before he became an outstanding reliever. The success he had in those twin roles is unmatched in baseball annals.

Eckersley pitched 12 years as a starter and 12 years as a reliever. Altogether, he won 197 games and saved 390. He was the first pitcher ever to win 20 games

in one season as a starter and save 50 games in another season as a reliever. Eckersley's amazing record earned him induction into the Hall of Fame in 2004.

During his 24-year career, Eckersley spent 19 and one-half seasons in the American League, playing mostly with the Boston Red Sox and Oakland Athletics. Overall, he appeared in 1,071 games, of which he started 361 and relieved in 710. He fired 100 complete games, including 20 shutouts. In 3,285.2 innings, he allowed 3,076 hits, struck out 2,401, and walked 1,278, while posting an earned run average of 3.50.

A right-hander, Eckersley threw a no-hitter, was voted Rookie of the Year, won Cy Young and Most Valuable Player awards, pitched in six All-Star Games, and was twice voted Rolaids Relief Man of the Year.

At his Hall of Fame induction, where he was the first pitcher with dual careers as a starter and reliever to ever be elected, Eckersley had a special definition of his career. "I just like to think of myself as a pitcher," he said. "People think of me more as a closer because that's where I had the most success, but I like to think it was the uniqueness of my career that got me in."

Originally, Eckersley had no intentions of being a reliever. It was only after he'd been traded to Oakland that he joined the bullpen brigade after what would be known as a historic move by Athletics manager Tony La Russa, who is often credited with being the person who pioneered the idea of having a "closer" hurl the final inning of a winning game.

"Eck," as he was known, had been a starter throughout his early years, beginning with his high school team in Fremont, California. Although he hoped that he would be drafted by Oakland, where he was born in 1954, Dennis was a third-round pick of the Cleveland Indians in 1972. He spent three years in the minor leagues—two at Reno of the California League and one at San Antonio of the Texas League, where he went 14-3 in 1974.

Summoned to Cleveland the following year, Eckersley pitched a three-hit shutout in his first start, a 6-0 victory over, ironically, the Oakland A's. He went on to compile a 13-7 record, and was named the American League's Rookie of the Year. He then went 13-12 and 14-13 in the next two years, posting a career-high 200 strikeouts in 1976 and pitching two shutout innings in the 1977 All-Star Game.

Eckersley also etched his name in the record book with a no-hitter in 1977 against the California Angels. With his fastball and curve working superbly, Eck struck out 12. With two outs in the first inning, he walked his only batter of the game. In his previous start, Eckersley had not allowed a hit over the final seven and two-thirds innings. In his start after the no-hitter, he extended his hitless streak to 22.1 innings, just two outs short of Cy Young's then-record of 23 straight hitless innings.

With long hair, a moustache, and a high-kicking delivery with a blazing fastball and an excellent sinker and slider, the 6-2, 190-pound hurler was a favorite of the fans. But Cleveland stunningly traded him to Boston in 1978 in a six-player deal that, among others, brought pitcher Rick Wise and catcher Bo Diaz to the Indians.

In need of a number one starter, the Red Sox were rewarded when Eckersley posted a 20-8 record. He followed that with a 17-10 mark, which included eight straight wins. But with arm and shoulder problems surfacing, Dennis dropped to 12-14 in 1980, although he did fire a one-hitter in a 3-1 victory over the Toronto Blue Jays.

After starting 30 or more games in five consecutive seasons, Eckersley won just 35 games and lost 38 over the next three-plus years. The Red Sox, in turn, swapped him to the Chicago Cubs. Eckersley went 10-8 the rest of the season, and the Cubs made their first postseason appearance since 1945, with Dennis dropping one of those games.

Eck posted an 11-7 mark in 1985, but by this time, alcoholism was taking a heavy toll on his performance, and he slid to a 6-11 mark. Eckersley overcame his drinking problem with rehab work, but the next spring the Cubs dealt him to Oakland. After two early-season starts, the 32-year-old pitcher, who once was a superb starter, had an incredible career change. La Russa and pitching coach Dave Duncan moved him to the bullpen with the intention of making him a long-distance reliever. Soon, though, they were desperately in need of a closer after an injury to Jay Howell, and they gave the new hurler that responsibility.

It was a brilliant decision. Eckersley saved 16 games that year, en route to becoming one of the circuit's dominant closers with a league-leading 45 saves in 1988. The Athletics won the West Division title, and in the League Championship Series, their reliever recorded saves in all four games as the A's swept the Red Sox. Eckersley was named the Most Valuable Player of the ALCS. The only blot on his season came in the first game of the World Series against the Los Angeles Dodgers, when Kirk Gibson slammed a two-out, two-run homer in the bottom of the ninth inning to give a 5-4 win to LA on their way to winning the Series.

Claiming later that the incident "made me more aggressive, and the more aggressive I became, the better I was," Eckersley bounced back the following year with 33 saves and a 1.56 ERA. He saved three games in the ALCS against the Blue Jays, before earning the save in the deciding fourth game of the World Series against San Francisco.

By then, he was almost unhittable. "Eck always throws strikes, and he has the heart of a giant," Duncan said. "His natural response is to challenge a crisis head-on. That's what makes him such a great reliever."

That greatness continued as Eckersley had a miraculous season in 1990, when he saved 48 games and posted the best ERA ever recorded by a hurler who worked in 50 or more innings, a 0.61 mark. He allowed just five earned runs all season and yielded only 41 hits in 73.1 innings. He tallied 43 saves in 1991, and then in 1992 he had another spectacular year.

Eckersley saved a career-high and league-leading 51 games (while posting a 7-1 record). In a career-high 69 games, he recorded a 1.91 ERA, while allowing 62 hits in 80 innings. Eck was the winner of the American League's Cy Young and the Most Valuable Player awards, only the third reliever to win both honors in the same season.

From 1988 to 1992, Eckersley saved 220 games and posted a 2.46 ERA while appearing in 310 games, finishing 284 of them. In 359.2 innings, he gave up 247 hits and 76 earned runs. He also won 24 games and lost nine.

Then from 1993 to 1995, the relief ace had seasons of 36, 19, and 29 saves. After the '95 campaign, La Russa left Oakland to become manager of the St. Louis Cardinals, and soon after that, he acquired Eckersley in a trade. Eck saved 30 games in 1996 and 36 the following year. In 1996, he also recorded three saves in the Cards' NLDS win over the San Diego Padres. He gained another save in the NLCS to run his postseason save total to 15.

Eckersley pitched in 1998 with the Red Sox. At the age of 43, he appeared in 50 games in a mop-up role. He retired after the season, having accomplished a feat that even in modern times is virtually unthinkable.

44

GREG MADDUX

NAMED THE CY YOUNG WINNER FOUR STRAIGHT TIMES

In the 1990s, hitters were a dominant force in baseball, and the home run was a common occurrence. Scores of games were often high, and so were batting averages. As a result, pitching records were generally mediocre, and sometimes they were downright dismal.

There were, of course, exceptions. One was Greg Maddux. Unlike many of his peers, Maddux was no friend of hitters. Throughout his career, but especially in the 1990s, the stellar right-hander dominated hitters like few pitchers ever have.

During the decade of the '90s, Maddux became the first pitcher ever to win four straight Cy Young Awards. In the '90s, he was a 20-game winner twice, a 19-game winner twice, and in one season captured 18 victories. Maddux never won less than 15 games in any one season while posting a 176-88 record over the 10-year period. He also had earned run averages under 2.00 twice and led the National League in innings pitched five straight times.

It was one of the most outstanding decades ever recorded by a pitcher, who along the way set a major league record by leading the league in starts seven

straight times. The record was made even more glittering when Maddux had the highest winning percentage ever registered by a starting pitcher when his 19-2 mark in 1995 gave him a .905. *The Sporting News* named him The Best Pitcher of the Decade.

Overall, the hurler known as "Mad Dog" had a 355-227 record during a 23-year career in the majors. Only Warren Spahn has won more games since the start of the live-ball era in the early 1920s. While posting a 3.16 earned run average, Maddux started 740 of the 744 games in which he pitched, completing 109 of them and firing 35 shutouts. In 5,008.1 innings, he gave up 4,726 hits, struck out 3,371, and walked 999, never walking more than 82 hitters in a single season. Greg led the league in games started seven times, a major league record.

Chosen for the National League All-Star team eight times, Maddux also had the good fortune of playing for stellar teams through most of his career. Five of the teams for which he played went to the World Series. While being a major contributor to these teams, Maddux posted a 2.09 ERA in 38.2 innings in the World Series. He also pitched in nine League Championship Games and 11 Division Series.

Considered one of baseball's smartest pitchers, Maddux, who never put extra stress on his arm while being an outstanding control pitcher and the owner of a fastball with considerable movement, once said that what makes a pitcher look smart is "locating your fastball down and away." Some of the hitters he faced had other ways to describe the way he worked on the mound.

"He was really big on throwing a pitch and then seeing a hitter's reaction," said Hall of Famer Ryne Sandberg, who played with and against Maddux. "If he threw it on the outside corner and the batter leaned over, he was asking for the next pitch to be inside. I tried to think along with him. It was a big cat and mouse game when I faced him.

"He was very good at locating his pitches," Sandberg added. "His command was excellent. If he wanted to pitch on the inside corner, the ball ended up there. If he wanted to pitch on the outside, it was there. He also had off-speed stuff that he used very well."

"Actually, I was more comfortable hitting against him than some other pitchers because you knew he'd always be around the strike zone," said the standout hitter Terry Pendleton, who also played with and against Maddux. "You knew he was going to make you swing the bat. He was very tough. He threw everything with the same motion, but with that slider, the changeup, and his sinker, he really kept you off balance."

Maddux was also an outstanding fielder. He won 18 Gold Gloves, a record for pitchers that may never be broken. The 6-0, 170-pound right-hander holds the record for most career putouts (510) and most career double plays (89) by a pitcher.

Called the best, smartest, and most competitive pitcher he ever saw by Atlanta Braves manager Bobby Cox, Maddux came out of San Angelo, Texas, where he was born in 1966. Selected by the Chicago Cubs in the second round of the 1984 draft, he pitched three seasons in the minors, starting with Pikeville of the Appalachian League and ending with Iowa of the American Association. Over that time, Maddux, whose older brother Mike also pitched in the big leagues, posted a 33-15 record.

Called up to Chicago at the end of the 1986 season, Maddux did nothing special until 1988, when he rang up an 18-8 mark. He finished the decade with a 19-12 log, and then posted 15-15, 15-11, and 20-11 records in the first three years of the 1990s. In 1992, he worked in a career-high 268 innings while capturing his first Cy Young Award.

After nearly seven seasons with the Cubs, Maddux signed as a free agent with the Braves and in his first year in Atlanta, posted a 20-10 record and won another Cy Young Award. The following season, he went 16-6 while registering a career-low 1.56 ERA.

In 1995, Maddux had one of the most glittering seasons of any hurler in big league history. He went 19-2 with a record winning percentage for a starter of .905. His 1.63 ERA made him the first pitcher since Walter Johnson did it in 1918 to record back-to-back seasons with ERAs under 1.80. The average ERA in the National League in 1995 was 4.23.

Maddux pitched a no-hitter for eight innings against the Houston Astros before finishing with the only one-hitter of his career. At one point, he worked in 51 innings in a row without allowing a walk. He then won games in the NLDS and the NLCS before firing a two-hitter in Game One in the Braves' World Series victory over the Cleveland Indians.

During a run in which the Braves appeared in 11 straight NLDS, nine NLCS, and five World Series, Maddux posted a combined record of 11-14, with a 2.81 ERA in 35 games (including four with the Los Angeles Dodgers). He won two more Cy Young Awards (1994-95) and finished fifth, second, and fourth in the voting over the following three years. In 1995, he also placed third in the voting for Most Valuable Player.

From 1996 through 1999, Maddux posted 15-11, 19-4, 18-9, and 19-9 records. In one game in 1997, he threw just 76 pitches in a complete game victory over the Cubs. Earlier in the season, he tossed 84 pitches in a win over the New York Yankees. In 232.2 innings that year, he walked just 20 batters.

Maddux started the new century just like he'd ended the last one. He posted a 19-9 record. Over the next three years, he added 17-11, 16-6, and 16-11 marks.

During that period, he formed with Tom Glavine and John Smoltz one of the finest pitching staffs of all time.

Greg, who usually worked with his own personal catcher, became a free agent after the 2003 season. Following 11 masterful seasons in Atlanta during which he was regarded as the most dominant hurler in baseball, he returned to the Cubs. In his first season back in Chicago, Mad Dog won his 300th game, an 8-4 decision over the San Francisco Giants. Later that season, he became only the ninth pitcher in baseball history to win 300 games and strike out 3,000 hitters.

Just prior to his 300th win, Maddux had talked about that lofty plateau. "It is a significant goal," he said, "but I've always pitched for tomorrow, and never really looked past my next start. So, I haven't really thought about it."

After setting a major league record by winning 15 or more games in 17 consecutive years, Maddux tumbled to a 13-15 log in 2005. Then during the following season, he was traded to the Dodgers and finished the campaign with an overall record of 15-14. In one game that season, he threw just 68 pitches in eight shutout innings.

Joining the San Diego Padres in 2007, Maddux went 14-11 before returning to the Dodgers in the middle of the following season and winding up with an 8-13 record. At age 42, Maddux, who had trained relentlessly throughout his career, retired at the end of the season. "The game has given me more than I ever dreamed it could," he said.

The reverse could be said about Maddux, who gave back more to the game of baseball than many pitchers who have played. He put together an amazing set of numbers during a career that could lead him to the Hall of Fame in 2014. None, however, was more amazing than the ones he posted during that spectacular decade of the 1990s.

45

RANDY JOHNSON

SURPASSED 300 STRIKEOUTS IN FIVE STRAIGHT SEASONS

There is nothing unusual about a pitcher who strikes out 200 or more batters in one season. The history books are full of the names of moundsmen who sent that many hitters back to the dugout mumbling to themselves.

But 300 strikeouts in one season? Few hurlers have ever done that. Even fewer have done it more than a few times.

Since the pitching mound was pushed back to 60 feet, six inches in 1893, hurlers have struck out 300 or more hitters in a single season just 34 times. Randy Johnson did it six of those times.

Johnson's all-time record total has some remarkable numbers that no one else has achieved. Not the least of these is that Johnson is the only pitcher ever to strike out 300 or more batters in five straight seasons.

Those seasons occurred between 1998 and 2002. In consecutive years, Johnson fanned 329, 364, 347, 372, and 334 hitters. The 372-strikeout season ranks third behind Nolan Ryan and Sandy Koufax as the most whiffs ever registered in one season.

The flame-throwing left-hander, whose fastball at the height of his career often exceeded 100 miles per hour and who threw a devastating slider that he called "Mr. Snappy," which could approach the plate going up to 90 miles per hour, undeniably ranks as one of the greatest strikeout artists of all time. Along with his six 300-strikeout seasons, Johnson also struck out 290 or more batters in three other seasons.

Standing 6-10, which places him among the tallest hurlers of all time, Johnson was so intimidating that batters hated to come to the plate when he was on the mound.

"He put a lot of fear in you, and you can't hit when you have fear," said the great hitter George Brett. "At the height of his career, he was not only fast, but he had great control. He was a tough man to hit."

So tough, in fact, that Johnson led the league in strikeouts nine times. His career total of 4,875 strikeouts is the most ever recorded by a southpaw and ranks second behind Ryan on the all-time list. His 10.67 strikeouts per nine innings pitched ranks first on the all-time list.

"I don't care who I'm facing," he once said. "I am going to fail sometimes, and I'm prepared for that. But there's no challenge that's too big for me."

Johnson fanned 20 batters in one game in 2001 against the Cincinnati Reds. Twice he struck out 19 batters in one game, and in another game he whiffed 18 in eight innings. Another time, he struck out three batters in one inning on nine pitches. He also holds the major league record for most strikeouts by a relief pitcher when he whiffed 16 in a rare appearance out of the bullpen in 2001 against the San Diego Padres. He is currently the last major league pitcher to fan 300 in a single season.

The year 2001 was especially spectacular for Johnson. Not only did he fan 372 in just 249.2 innings of work, but also he racked up a 21-6 record for the Arizona Diamondbacks and won the Cy Young Award.

Overall, Johnson won five Cy Young Awards (including four straight from 1999 to 2002) and was picked for 10 All-Star Games, four of which he started. He pitched a no-hitter in 1990 against the Detroit Tigers and a perfect game in 2004 against the Atlanta Braves, a feat that at the age of 40 made him the oldest pitcher ever to toss a perfect game. Johnson struck out eight Tigers and 13 Braves.

Johnson's career marks are just as spectacular. While pitching in 22 seasons, including 10 with the Seattle Mariners and eight with the Diamondbacks, he registered a 303-166 career record, working in 618 games including 603 as a starter. He had 100 complete games and 37 shutouts. In 4,135.1 innings pitched, he gave up just 3,346 hits while walking 1,497. His career earned run average was 3.29. He led his league in earned run average, winning percentage, and complete games each four times.

"The Big Unit," as he was called, seemed destined to be a strikeout artist at an early age. Born in 1963 in Walnut Creek, California, he was striking out batters at the rate of nearly two per inning as a high school pitcher. A basketball star, too, he fired a perfect game as a schoolboy before getting drafted in 1982 by the Braves. Choosing not to sign a pro contract, Johnson accepted a baseball scholarship to the University of Southern California, where he also played basketball.

Drafted by the Montreal Expos in 1985, Johnson left USC and joined the pro ranks, appearing first with Jamestown of the Pioneer League. After going 31-30 in the minors, he made his major league debut in 1989 and posted a 3-0 record in four starts. The following season, however, he was traded to the Mariners. Wildness cost Johnson dearly, as illustrated by his 10 walks in four innings in one game. He led the league in walks three straight years and in hit batsmen twice.

"He was really wild when he came to the American League," Brett recalled. "He had much better control later in his career, but in the early years, you'd rather not face him."

The southpaw's career took a decided upswing in 1990, when he posted his first winning record (14-11). Soon afterward, he got even better with the help of Ryan, who suggested that the speedy southpaw make an adjustment in his delivery.

Starting in 1990, Johnson would go on to win in double figures 16 times. That included a 19-8 mark in 1993, when he had his first 300-strikeout season, with 308. During the season, Johnson had a no-hitter through eight innings against the Oakland Athletics.

Randy won his first Cy Young Award with an 18-2 record and 294 strikeouts in 1995. A strike-shortened season in 1994 limited his record, but he came back with a 20-4 record while striking out 291 batters.

In the midst of a contract dispute, the Mariners traded Johnson to the Houston Astros in mid-season of 1998. He posted a combined 19-11 record, including a 10-1 mark for the Astros. That season, the man nicknamed "The Big Unit" began his amazing strikeout streak with 329 Ks, including 116 in 84 1/3 innings at Houston.

After the season, Johnson became a free agent and signed a four-year contract worth $52.4 million with the Diamondbacks. In 1999, Randy went 17-9 and led the National League in earned run average (2.48), games started (35), career highs in shutouts (12) and innings pitched (271.2), and, of course, strikeouts (364).

Johnson upped his record to 19-7 in 2000 while fanning 347. A magnificent season followed in 2001, when he elevated his mark to 21-6 with 372 strikeouts. That year, he and Curt Schilling pitched the Diamondbacks to their first World Series appearance. Johnson won three games as Arizona beat the New York Yankees in the Series, including an 11-strikeout, three-hit shutout in Game Two. Overall, the D-Backs won 11 games in postseason play that year, and Johnson won five of them.

The strikeout surge continued in 2002 when Johnson fanned 334 for his record-setting fifth straight 300-strikeout season. He posted a 24-5 record and won his fourth consecutive Cy Young Award. Along with strikeouts, he led the league in wins, winning percentage (.828), innings pitched (260), shutouts (eight), and a career-low 2.32 ERA.

Johnson spent much of the 2003 season on the disabled list with arm problems, but he returned to post a 16-14 record the following year. He struck out 290, and in June against the San Diego Padres, he became only the fourth major league pitcher to reach 4,000 career strikeouts.

After the season, Johnson was traded to the Yankees, but while posting 17-8 and 17-11 records over the next two years, his strikeout totals dropped, falling as low as 172 in 2006. Then early in 2007, the Yankees traded Randy back to the Diamondbacks. He played two more years in Arizona.

Following back surgery in 2007, Johnson registered his final season in double figures in 2008, when he went 11-10. On June 3, Johnson struck out Mike Cameron of the Milwaukee Brewers to reach second place among baseball's all-time strikeout leaders, with 4,673.

Johnson spent the final season of his career in 2009 with the San Francisco Giants after signing as a free agent for a reported $8 million. That year, he won his 300th game to become only the seventh southpaw to win that many games in a career. After finishing the season with an 8-6 record, he retired at the age of 46.

Johnson departed with a truckload of spectacular achievements. None, though, was more remarkable than his recording more than 300 strikeouts in five straight seasons.

46

FRANCISCO RODRIGUEZ

COLLECTED 62 SAVES IN ONE SEASON

It would take a vivid imagination to support the premise that a pitcher could play a major role in most of his team's victories during a single season. Logic says that's simply not possible.

Or is it? In the not too distant past, there was a relief pitcher with the Los Angeles Angels who helped his team win 64 percent of its games. Nowhere else in baseball can such a record be found.

The pitcher was Francisco Rodriguez, a rambunctious right-hander from Venezuela whose unbelievable feat in 2008 helped the Angels win the American League West's division title.

During the regular season, the Angels won 100 games. Rodriguez saved 62 games and won two others. The 62 saves rank as the all-time record in that category and the only time a pitcher has passed the 60-save mark in one season.

Only three other relievers have saved 55 or more games. Just 15 altogether have saved more than 50. Rodriguez's total broke the record of 57 saves set in 1990 by Bobby Thigpen of the Chicago White Sox.

Ironically, Rodriguez had only been a full-time closer since 2005. Before that, he had closed just a few games after breaking into the big leagues in 2002. Indeed, after beginning his pro career in 1999, he was a starter in his first three years in the minor leagues. After 2001, though, he never started another game.

Originally, Rodriguez had signed a contract in 1998 as an undrafted free agent. Afterward, the native of Caracas, Venezuela, where he was born in 1982 as one of 13 siblings raised by his grandparents, traveled through the lower levels of the minors, stopping at Butte, Boise, Lake Elsinor, and Rancho Cuca, where over a three-year period, he started 42 games and relieved in four, but posted only a combined 11-12 record.

It was obvious that Rodriguez wasn't a starter, and in 2002 at Arkansas of the Texas League, he was converted into a reliever. That year, with both Arkansas and Salt Lake City of the Pacific Coast League, he appeared in 50 games, saving 15.

The 6-0, 195-pound hurler broke into the big leagues with the then-Anaheim Angels late in the 2002 season. He pitched in only five games during the regular season, but got two wins in the American League Division Series against the New York Yankees, two more victories in the Championship Series against the Minnesota Twins, and a 1-1 mark with 13 strikeouts in eight and two-thirds innings in the Angels' victory over the San Francisco Giants in the World Series. At 20 years and 286 days old, Rodriguez's victory made him the youngest pitcher ever to win a World Series game.

Since then, he has played with four other teams through 2013, pitching in a total of 727 games, finishing 480 of them and saving 304. His win-loss record is 41-35, and in 765 innings, he has struck out 932, walked 327, and yielded 569 hits. His ERA is 2.67, and he has struck out more batters than innings pitched in 11 consecutive seasons. In six postseason games, Rodriguez has a 5-3 record with three saves.

Rodriguez's record-breaking season came at the end of a four-year span, during which he established himself as one of the top closers in the game. A set up man in 2003, when he posted an 8-3 record with two saves in 59 games, and again in 2004, when he went 4-1 with 12 saves in 69 games, K-Rod became a closer in 2005 under manager Mike Scioscia. That year, despite a trip to the disabled list with a strained right forearm, Rodriguez tied with Bob Wickman for the league lead with 45 saves. He had a 2.67 ERA in 66 games.

The following season, "Frankie," as he was also known, led the majors with 47 saves in 69 games while recording a career-low 1.73 ERA. That season, Rodriguez passed the 100 mark in saves, making him, at the age of 24, the youngest pitcher in baseball history to reach that number. He was named the American League's Rolaids Relief Man of the Year and was fourth in the league's Cy Young Award voting.

After recording a save in the 2007 All-Star Game (one of the four All-Star Games in which he appeared), Rodriguez finished the season with 40 saves in 64 games, while winning five of seven decisions. He then entered the 2008 season with a new $10 million contract. It would be a season to remember.

Using a blazing fastball that averaged 95 miles per hour, plus a slow curveball and an 85 mph changeup, Rodriguez, who during his career compiled an average of 11 strikeouts per nine innings pitched, began the season with dazzling numbers.

He saved 11 games in April, 10 in May, and 11 in June. During a five-day stretch in June, he registered saves in five straight games. Later in the month, he also converted his 25th consecutive save.

K-Rod, who usually put on an annoying and what some called "unprofessional" show on the mound after each save, saved 12 games in July, nine in August, and nine in September. With the arrival of his 35th save of the season in July, he became the first pitcher ever to post that many saves before the All-Star break, eclipsing the old mark of 34 set in 2003 by John Smoltz. He was also the winning pitcher in games in August against the Baltimore Orioles and Yankees, while also losing three games during the season.

On September 8, Frankie recorded his 200th career save, becoming the youngest player in history to reach that level. Two days later, he got his 56th save of the season as the Angels beat the Yankees to clinch the American League West Division title. The following day, he tied Thigpen's record of 57 with a save against the Seattle Mariners. Then two days later on September 13, Rodriguez struck out Raul Ibanez with runners on second and third to set the all-time record as the Angels beat the Mariners, 5-2.

"It's been a spectacular year, and I'm happy for him," said Scioscia. "He's fearless. And he's as consistent as any pitcher I've ever seen."

On September 20, Rodriguez entered a game against the Texas Rangers with two on and two outs in the ninth inning. He retired Nelson Cruz on a fly ball to preserve a 7-3 Angels victory and become the first pitcher to save 60 games in one season.

"I don't have the words to describe how happy I am," Rodriguez told reporters.

K-Rod went on to post two more saves to run his record to 62 in 69 save opportunities. He wound up appearing in 76 games, closing 69 of them, and posting a 2.24 ERA. In 68.1 innings, he struck out 77, walked 34, and allowed 21 runs. Opponents had a combined batting average of just .216 against him.

In postseason play, Rodriguez lost one game to the Boston Red Sox in the Angels' losing battle in the ALDS. That season, he placed third in the voting for the Cy Young Award and sixth in the Most Valuable Player Award election.

After the season, Rodriguez became a free agent, and signed a three-year, $37 million contract with the New York Mets. That season, he worked in 70 games, but recorded only 35 saves, just the seventh-best in the league.

By then, problems with teammates and others had begun to occur. In 2010, he was suspended by the Mets after being arrested for allegedly assaulting his girlfriend's father. Also suffering from a torn ligament in his right thumb that added to Rodriguez's shortened season, he made just 53 appearances and saved 25 games.

Rodriguez pitched in 34 games and saved 23 for the Mets in 2011, but he was traded at mid-season to the Milwaukee Brewers, where he pitched in 31 games and had a 4-0 record while recording no saves. The following season, Rodriguez worked in a career-high 78 games with the Brewers, but was reduced mostly to a setup role, with John Axford serving as the team's closer. He registered just three saves, although he did not allow a run in his last 16 appearances.

In 2013, Milwaukee granted Rodriguez free agency, but then signed him to a minor league contract. He came back to begin the season with the Brewers, and saved 10 games in 25 appearances. In July, he was traded to the Baltimore Orioles, where he wound up pitching in 20 games, but collecting no saves.

47

MIKE BUEHRLE

RETIRED 45 HITTERS IN A ROW

For those who make a living trying to throw a little round object past a man who stands just 60 feet, six inches away with a long, menacing wooden stick in his hands, succeeding in that endeavor is one of the hardest jobs in baseball. Those who can do it with regularity are ranked at the top of their profession.

Seldom, however, does anyone who throws the ball do it so well that all the guys with the sticks in their hands fail so critically that not a single one reaches a canvas bag 90 feet down the first base line. When that happens, the job by the pitcher is known as a perfect game.

Perfect games are rare. So rare, in fact, that since the piece of rubber where the pitcher stands was moved back to its present location in 1893, only 21 perfect games have been recorded in the major leagues. No pitcher ever hurled two perfect games. But one came close.

In 2009, Mike Buehrle of the Chicago White Sox fired a perfect game. Then in his very next outing, he tossed another perfect game for six and two-thirds innings. Those two games, combined with his final out in a previous game, gave the left-handed hurler a record of having faced 45 consecutive batters without

Courtesy of AP Photo/Mike Carlson

allowing a single one to reach base. No pitcher in modern big league history has ever come close to that record.

Buehrle was no stranger to no-hitters. He had pitched one in 2007. When he fired his perfect game two years later, he joined Cy Young, Addie Joss, Jim Bunning, Sandy Koufax, and Randy Johnson—Roy Halladay did it later—as the only pitchers in baseball history to toss a perfect game and another no-hitter. Buehrle's perfecto was the 16th in modern baseball history. With it, he became the 24th big league pitcher to fire two or more no-hitters.

Both of the left-hander's masterpieces were thrown at Cellular Field in Chicago and were played in two hours and three minutes. The hefty 6-2, 244-pound hurler had also pitched a one-hitter in 2001 against the Tampa Bay Devil Rays.

Five days before his perfect game, in an appearance against the Baltimore Orioles, Buehrle had allowed two singles in the top of the eighth inning, then retired Nick Markakis on a fly to center field. Buehrle was then taken out of the game, but got the win, 4-3.

On July 23, the normally unflappable and extremely modest Buehrle hurled his perfect game, beating Tampa, 5-0, before a crowd of 28,036. At the time, the White Sox, who had won 19 of their last 28 games, were in the midst of a fierce fight for the lead in the American League's Central Division.

The Rays took the field with a lineup that featured the heavy bats of Evan Longoria, Carl Crawford, B. J. Upton, and Gabe Kapler. But they were no match for Buehrle. Only seven balls were hit out of the infield by the defending American League champions.

In the ninth inning, Chicago center fielder Dewayne Wise made a sensational catch to preserve the perfect game. Inserted into the lineup because of his defense, Wise raced to the wall in left-center field on a long drive slammed by Kapler leading off the inning. Jumping above the railing, Wise caught the ball as he crashed into the wall. As Wise started to fall, the ball bounced out of his glove, but the alert outfielder caught it with his bare hand. Buehrle then retired the next two batters to finish his history-making game.

While getting help from a second inning grand slam homer by Josh Fields, Buehrle, a control pitcher who mixed a modest fastball, and a curve, changeup, and slider, struck out six and threw 116 pitches. The win, registered against one of the best-hitting teams in the league, ran his record to 11-3.

"I just don't know how to explain it," he said after the game. "I never thought I'd throw a no-hitter, never thought I'd throw a perfect game, never thought I'd hit a home run. Never say never in this game, because crazy stuff can happen."

The crafty pitcher's glowing achievements were capped in his next start after the perfect game. Counting the out by Markakis, Buehrle ran his streak to retiring 45 batters in a row. Pitching against the Minnesota Twins, he sent them down in order for five straight innings, striking out three and recording 10 outs on infield grounders with just one ball hit to the outfield.

Buehrle retired the first two batters in the sixth inning to run his streak for the game to 17 consecutive outs. But the streak came to an end when he walked Alexi Casilla. That was followed by a single by Denard Span and a double by Joe Mauer. Before the inning was over, the Twins had scored three runs. Buehrle was knocked out of the box in the seventh inning and lost the game, 5-2.

Two years earlier, Buehrle had pitched a no-hit game against the Texas Rangers. Actually, that was nearly a perfect game, too. He walked designated hitter Sammy Sosa in the fifth inning, but picked him off while facing the next batter. Then, with Jim Thome hitting two home runs, the White Sox won, 6-0. The win was Buehrle's first of the season.

Buehrle, who had allowed runs in the first inning in 12 of his previous 17 starts and who was working in his third start since getting whacked by a line drive off his pitching arm, wound up facing the minimum 27 batters while striking out eight. He threw 105 pitches in a game that was played with temperatures in the low 40s. Between innings, Mark retreated to the clubhouse to stay warm.

"You don't want to make that one mistake and give up a hit," he said after the game. "I can't believe I did it."

While Buehrle guaranteed his place in baseball history with his twin gems and 45 straight outs, he was not without other noteworthy achievements. During a big league career that by 2013 had spanned 14 seasons, he had won in double figures 13 years in a row while posting a record of 186-142. In that time, he had only one losing season. During his career with the White Sox, he was the Opening Day pitcher nine times.

In 454 games during a career in which he started 429 of them, Buehrle recorded an earned run average of 3.84 while allowing 3,030 hits, striking out 1,660, and walking 655 in 2,882.2 innings. During that time, he pitched for 12 years with the White Sox and one year each with the Miami Marlins and Toronto Blue Jays.

Buehrle was born in 1979 in St. Charles, Missouri. Cut from his high school baseball team in his sophomore year, he eventually made the team; then after his graduation, he attended Jefferson College. In 1998, he was drafted by the White Sox in the 38th round.

Although he was never an overpowering pitcher, Buehrle moved quickly through the minors, spending less than two years there while pitching for Burlington of the Midwest League and Birmingham of the Southern League. After posting a combined record of 15-8 for those teams, he was called to the White Sox in the middle of the 2000 season. He made his major league debut as a 21 year old.

In his first full year in the majors, Buehrle posted a 16-8 record, at one point throwing 24 2/3 straight scoreless innings. He followed that with 19-12 and 14-14 marks before logging a 16-10 record in 2004. That year, he led the league with career highs in games started (35) and innings pitched (245.1).

Over the next seven years with the White Sox, Buehrle went 16-8, 12-13, 10-9, 15-12, 13-10, 13-13, and 13-9. He led the league in innings pitched (236.2) in 2005 and in games started (34) in 2008. In 2005, when Chicago met the Houston Astros in the World Series, Buehrle got a save and two wins in the American League playoffs. Ironically, he also led the league in hits allowed four times over that period, including in 2006, when he yielded 247 safeties in 204 innings.

Buehrle left Chicago after the 2011 season and signed a four-year, $58 million contract with the Marlins. He wound up with a 13-13 record while working more than 200 innings for the 12th straight year. After the season, he was traded to the Blue Jays as part of a 12-player trade. In 2013, he posted a 12-10 record.

A member of four All-Star teams, the winning pitcher in one, and the owner of four Gold Gloves, Buehrle has an undeniably distinguished record during his big league career. His 45 consecutive hitless innings and his two no-hitters, though, are at the top of that list.

48

ROY HALLADAY

ACHIEVED AN UNMATCHED RECORD FOR NO-HITTERS

Pitching a no-hitter is not only one of the most spectacular achievements in all of baseball, but also it is one of the rarest. Since the pitching mound was moved back to 60 feet, six inches from home plate in 1893, there have been just 249 complete game no-hitters pitched in the major leagues through the 2013 season.

Hurling two no-hitters in one season is a feat that is even rarer. Indeed, it is virtually nonexistent. It has been done only five times in modern baseball history. In addition, there have been just two no-hitters hurled in postseason play. To date, there have been only 21 perfect games pitched since 1893, and only once has there been two perfect games recorded in the same season.

Amazingly, Roy Halladay has a place in all of those categories. Pitching for the Philadelphia Phillies, he recorded two no-hitters in 2010. One was a perfect game, and one was a no-hitter fired in the National League Division Series.

The 6-6, 230-pound right-hander, born in 1977 in Denver, Colorado, was a first round draft pick of the Toronto Blue Jays in 1995. Although he originally broke into the majors in 1998 and in his second start threw a no-hitter for eight

and two-thirds innings against the Detroit Tigers, he spent all or parts of six seasons in the minors before becoming a regular starter in late 2001.

In all or parts of 16 seasons in the majors, Halladay posted a 203-105 record, with a 3.38 earned run average in 416 games. He started 390, hurled 20 shutouts, and worked 2,749.1 innings. A three-time 20-game winner, he won Cy Young Awards in 2003 and 2010, and was selected to eight All-Star teams. Twice he was the starting pitcher in an All-Star Game.

Halladay arrived in Philadelphia in December 2009 in a trade with the Blue Jays. The Phillies had just been to two consecutive World Series, winning the one in 2008. Halladay was given a three-year, $60 million contract.

Throughout baseball history, the only other pitchers with two no-hitters in the same season were Johnny Vander Meer (1938), Allie Reynolds (1951), Virgil Trucks (1952), and Nolan Ryan (1973). Don Larsen is the only other hurler to toss a no-hitter in the postseason.

Halladay's first no-hitter was a perfect game pitched in May against the Florida Marlins. The Phillies won, 1-0, scoring an unearned run in the third inning.

It was just the second perfect game in Phillies history—the first one having been tossed in 1964 by Jim Bunning against the New York Mets—but also the second perfect game in 2010. Just three weeks earlier, Dallas Braden of the Oakland Athletics had blanked the Tampa Bay Rays.

In his previous start, Halladay had yielded seven runs in an ugly five and two-third inning stint against the Boston Red Sox. But some useful tips by teammate Jamie Moyer helped Halladay straighten out a mechanical problem with his delivery, and subsequently the man they call "Doc" became a problem for the Marlins.

Halladay threw 19 pitches in the first inning, but no more than 12 in any inning thereafter. Throwing just 115 pitches, 72 for strikes, Halladay struck out 11 with a mixture of sinkers and fastballs in the low 90 mph range. Halladay went to three-ball counts on seven batters, and got eight outs on infield grounders.

Halladay was helped by several outstanding defensive plays. Shortstop Wilson Valdez went deep into the hole in the sixth inning to glove Cameron Maybin's hard grounder. Center fielder Shane Victorino caught pinch hitter Mike Lamb's deep fly on the warning track for the first out in the ninth inning. Third baseman Juan Castro made two outstanding defensive plays, including a grab of Ronny Paulino's smash into the hole and an off-balance throw to first for the final out of the game.

"I got in a groove early," said Halladay, who fanned five of the first nine batters he faced. "It's hard to explain, but there are days when things kind of click and things happen. I was just trying to go one pitch at a time."

A little more than four months later, Halladay was back in the headlines with another no-hitter. This one was pitched in the first game of the National League Division Series against the Cincinnati Reds at Citizens Bank Park. Halladay captured a 4-0 decision. Given the circumstances, a good case can be made that it was one of the greatest games ever pitched in the major leagues.

Like Larsen blanking the defending World Champion Brooklyn Dodgers with a lineup featuring four future Hall of Famers, Halladay's no-hitter was especially noteworthy because he was pitching against the team with the best offense in the National League.

While winning the Central Division title, Cincinnati led the league in batting average, runs, hits, total bases, home runs, RBI, and slugging percentage. Led by first baseman Joey Votto, later to become the league's Most Valuable Player that season, the Reds fielded a lineup that included four players with 20 or more home runs and four starters hitting above .280.

With the Phillies, then in the midst of the greatest era in team history, the expectations were especially high. And to the legions of fans in the area that had made the Phillies Philadelphia's favorite team, success was not only desirable, but also it was demanded. All of these factors rested squarely on Halladay's shoulders when he took the mound in the Phils' first step toward an appearance in a third straight World Series.

There were 46,411 people in the stands, and excitement spread across the stadium like a monumental blanket. Rally towels and red clothing clogged the seats. The noise was deafening. "It was one of the most electric atmospheres I've ever been in," Halladay said later.

As a 21-game winner, the pitcher who would later be a unanimous choice for the National League's Cy Young Award—making him only the fifth hurler to win the award in both leagues—the hard-throwing right-hander had become the most reliable winner in town.

It was Halladay's first appearance in postseason play. And although he said later that he was more "excited" than "nervous," the heavy demands of such a situation could hardly be ignored.

In a game that Phils manager Charlie Manuel called "absolutely unreal," Halladay struck out eight and walked one. Only four balls were hit to the outfield. The only Reds batter to reach base came with two outs in the fifth inning when Doc walked Jay Bruce on a 3-2 count. Halladay needed just 104 pitches in the game—79 of them strikes.

Catcher Carlos Ruiz, who threw out the final batter of the contest from his knees after fielding a dribbler in front of the plate, said that Halladay had no problems with any pitch. "Everything was working," he said. "He threw anything on any count." Halladay mixed mid-90s fastballs, curveballs, cutters, and changeups throughout the game.

As for Halladay, one of the most focused players in the game, he called the event "surreal." He added: "I was definitely aware of what was going on. But pitching a game like that, being able to win comes first. That's your only focus until after it's over."

The Phillies, who scored three runs in the second inning, with Halladay singling home one run and scoring another on Victorino's two-run single, but who collected just five hits in the entire game, went on to sweep the Reds in three games in the National League Championship Series. But the defending NL champions lost four games to two to the San Francisco Giants, the eventual World Series winners.

Halladay's performance ranks with the best of all time. A no-hitter in the playoffs with all the tension and magnified surroundings, and add to that a perfect game in the same season—nobody's ever done that before.

The astute hurler, who always arrives at the ballpark early, sits and stares into his locker before every game he pitches, totally unaware of his surroundings and avoiding conversation with his teammates, continued his outstanding work with the Phillies the following season.

He posted a 19-6 record in 2011 while placing second in the voting for the NL Cy Young Award. Then after winning 11 games in 2012, he was sidelined with an arm injury that shortened his season. He also missed most of 2013 after getting shoulder surgery.

By then, though, Halladay had added some glittering marks to his record. He had finished in the top five in the Cy Young voting seven times, had paced in the top five in ERA seven times, and had led his league in complete games seven times and in shutouts four times. Between 2002 and 2012, Halladay led all major league pitchers in wins (181), shutouts (18), complete games (63), winning percentage (.666), and innings pitched (580).

49

JUSTIN VERLANDER

WON CY YOUNG, MVP, AND ROOKIE OF THE YEAR

To win a Cy Young Award, a pitcher not only has to be good. He has to be terrific. The same can be said for winning a Most Valuable Player Award. Few pitchers have won that honor in recent years, but those who did had magnificent seasons.

Even fewer pitchers have won both awards in the same season. Add the Rookie of the Year Award to a pitcher's resume, and the number gets even slimmer. Justin Verlander is the only pitcher to have reached that plateau in recent years, and only the third pitcher in baseball history ever to win all three honors.

Arguably the best pitcher of his generation, Verlander's trophy case is filled with awards. Among the many others, he was named Player of the Year, was a six-time All-Star Game selection, and was a college All-American.

In addition to his trophies, the 6-5, 225-pound right-hander has hurled two no-hitters, won pitching's Triple Crown, and led the American League in strikeouts and innings pitched each three times, and in games started twice.

246

SD Dirk

Overall, Verlander has a career win-loss record of 137-77, with an earned run average of 3.41. He has pitched in 266 games, all as a starter, and has completed 20 games, with six shutouts. In 1,772 innings, he has allowed 1,565 hits, struck out 1,671, and walked 545. He has fanned 10 or more batters in 24 games, and won 17 or more games in six of his eight big league seasons.

The owner of a blazing fastball and a fierce curve, pitches he throws with outstanding control, Verlander is the highest-paid hurler of all time. His current contract with the Detroit Tigers, which runs through 2019, is worth $180 million.

But it is his record as the only pitcher in the 21st century to win Cy Young and MVP honors in the same season, and only the second pitcher (Dennis Eckersley was the first) since Don Newcombe did it in 1956 to win those two awards as well as being named Rookie of the Year that puts Verlander in a very special class.

Verlander was named Rookie of the Year in 2006. He added to his laurels in 2011 during a brilliant season that ended with his being named the Cy Young and MVP winner. Only nine other pitchers in baseball history have won both awards.

Since his days as a youth growing up in Richmond, Virginia, Verlander, born in 1983 in Manakin-Sabot, Virginia, seemed destined to be a pitcher. When he was just starting high school, his fastball was clocked at 84 miles per hour. After a sparkling schoolboy career, he attended Old Dominion University, where he averaged 11.5 whiffs per game and set a number of college strikeout records. He also helped the USA national baseball team win a silver medal in the Pan American Games in 2003.

With these and numerous other college records and achievements, it came as no surprise that Verlander was selected second overall in the 2004 baseball draft by the Tigers. Subsequently, he spent less than one season in the minors with a brief stint in Detroit occurring between appearances in 2005 with Lakeland of the Florida State League and Erie of the Eastern League, where he posted a combined 11-2 log.

Although he lost both of the games he started with the Tigers, Verlander was about to launch a glittering career. In his first full season in 2006, he posted a 17-9 record with a 3.63 ERA while starting 30 games. Verlander's fastball reached as high as 100 mph, and he became the first rookie pitcher in baseball history to win 10 games before the end of June. His 17 wins overall tied for fourth highest in the league. The Tigers went to the World Series that year, and Verlander won one game in the Championship Series against the Oakland Athletics, but lost twice to the St. Louis Cardinals in the Fall Classic.

Verlander came back with an 18-6 record and a 3.66 ERA in 2007. The highlight of the season occurred when he fired the first no-hitter at Detroit's Comerica Park before a crowd of 33,555. Using a sizzling fastball that reached as high as 100 mph, the 24-year-old hurler beat the Milwaukee Brewers, 4-0, while striking out 12 and walking four for the Tigers' first no-hitter since 1984. Milwaukee, the leaders in the National League's Central Division, had slammed 22 hits in their previous game.

"After the first couple of innings, I knew I had some good stuff going," Verlander told reporters after the game. "In the bullpen, it wasn't that good. But when I got out on the mound and flipped the switch, I had some good stuff. I had a good fastball with control, and I was able to throw my breaking ball and changeup for strikes."

Justin slumped in 2008, going just 11-17. But he was back in full stride the following season with a 19-9 record and league-leading totals in wins, starts

(35), strikeouts (269), and innings pitched (240), while placing third in the Cy Young voting. He followed that with an 18-9 mark in 2010.

In 2011, Verlander had the most spectacular season of his career. He posted a 24-5 record while leading the league in wins, winning percentage (.828), ERA (2.40), games started (34), innings pitched (251), and strikeouts (250), all but games started being career highs.

Twice during the season, Verlander took a no-hitter into the eighth inning before getting touched for a hit. He also compiled an 11-game winning streak and, a rarity in today's game, never had a start in which he didn't throw at least 100 pitches. In postseason games that year, Verlander beat the New York Yankees in the ALDS, and split two decisions against the Texas Rangers in the ALCS.

Verlander's most spectacular game occurred early in the season when he registered his second no-hitter during a 9-0 victory over the Toronto Blue Jays. This time, the Tigers' fireballer had a perfect game going into the eighth inning. Then, with one out and a 3-2 count, he walked J. P. Arencibia on a questionable ball four call for the Jays' only base-runner. The batter was erased on a double play, and Verlander wound up facing the minimum 27 batters while striking out four.

"I felt fantastic," Verlander said afterward. "I made a conscious effort to slow myself down to establish a rhythm, but when I needed extra juice, I had it." Some of Justin's fastballs had so much extra juice that they zoomed up to the plate at more than 100 mph.

In his next start, Verlander had a no-hitter going into the sixth inning before he gave up a hit. That gave him 15 2/3 consecutive hitless innings over three starts.

At the end of the season, Verlander had not only won the Triple Crown of pitching, but he was a unanimous pick for the American League's Cy Young Award, too. He also was voted the league's Most Valuable Player, the first pitcher chosen for that honor since Eckersley won it in 1992.

Verlander also won numerous other awards that year, including *The Sporting News'* American League Pitcher of the Year and Player of the Year awards, and the Players Choice Awards for Player of the Year and Most Outstanding American League Pitcher. No pitcher in baseball history ever collected so many honors in one season.

The decorated hurler came close to tossing another no-hitter in 2012 when he gave up a one-out single in the ninth inning of a 6-0 victory over the Pittsburgh Pirates. He posted a 17-8 record with a 2.64 ERA and league-leading totals in innings pitched (238.1) and strikeouts (239). Verlander nearly won his third Cy Young Award, finishing in second place, just four points and one first-place vote behind David Price of the Tampa Bay Rays.

Verlander won two games against Oakland in the ALDS, one being a complete game, 10-strikeout, four-hit, 6-0 victory in the deciding game. He then beat New York, 2-1, blanking the Yanks on two hits through eight innings in the ALCS to run his 2012 postseason scoreless streak to 24 innings. In the World Series, he lost the opening game to the San Francisco Giants on their way to sweeping the Series.

In 2013, while overshadowed by the pitching of teammate Max Scherzer, who had a super season with a 21-3 record, Verlander slipped to a 13-12 log while pitching in 34 games and posting a 3.46 ERA.

50

MARIANO RIVERA

SAVED 30 OR MORE GAMES IN 15 SEASONS

S aving 30 or more games in a single season is no easy accomplishment. Few
pitchers ever reach that level with any regularity. Those who do stand at the
top of their profession.

To save that many games in 15 different seasons is downright phenomenal.
It is a feat recorded just once in baseball history, by a man named Mariano
Rivera.

During a 19-year career spent entirely with the New York Yankees, Rivera
etched his name at the top of the mountain as the king of all relievers. His career
record of 652 regular season saves not only stands at the very highest peak, but
also he saved more than 40 games in one season eight times, and more than
50 twice.

Mr. Sandman. Send me a dream. Show me an arm that can stop any team.
They called Rivera "Sandman" and played the song "Enter Sandman," when he
came into games at Yankee Stadium. He put opposing hitters to sleep. To them,
facing the strong-armed right-hander was all a bad dream.

In the era of the modern reliever, when it was considered heresy if closers
pitched more than one inning in a game and they seldom entered games unless

Chris Connelly

their team was winning by three runs or fewer 116 of Rivera's saves were registered when he pitched in more than one inning. Overall, he appeared in 1,115 games, including 60 or more in 15 seasons, while posting an 82-60 record. In 1,283.2 innings pitched, Rivera gave up 998 hits, struck out 1,173, and walked 286 while compiling a career earned run average of 2.21.

Rivera's records are just as impressive in postseason games. He has a record 42 postseason saves, including 11 in the World Series and 14 when he pitched two innings, all by far the best records in baseball history. While helping the Yankees win five World Series, four of which he was on the mound for the last out, he has a win-loss postseason record of 8-1, and his 96 appearances and 0.70 ERA are both all-time records. Sandman was also selected to 13 All-Star teams and recorded four saves in eight appearances.

He has earned numerous awards over the years. He won the Rolaids Relief Man Award five times (1999, 2001, 2004, 2005, 2009), and was *The Sporting News* Pro Athlete of the Year in 2009. Rivera was Most Valuable Player in the 1999 World Series and MVP in the 2003 League Championship Series.

Twice (both in 1997) during his career, Rivera collected saves in four consecutive games. In 2009, he saved 36 games in 36 save opportunities. He posted two saves in the same day in 2010. He holds Yankees records for most saves and most games pitched, both by large margins. And he has played more years with the Yanks than any other player except Derek Jeter.

Throughout his career, the man called "Mo" has dominated hitters with a fierce cut fastball with exceptional movement that he often threw as fast as 94 miles per hour. The pitch, along with his two- and four-seam fastballs, could all be thrown with exceptional control and varying degrees of movement made possible by Rivera's long fingers. Rivera's cutter, which he claimed was a pitch that came naturally, frequently broke the bats of opposing hitters. Jim Thome said it was "the single-best pitch ever in the game." Chipper Jones called it a "buzz saw."

"It came right in on the top of your hands, and there was nothing you could do about it," said Wally Joyner, for many years an outstanding American League hitter. "He had a very comfortable delivery that lulled you to sleep. Then when he released it, the ball was on your hands in no time. It wasn't very comfortable for the hitter."

Supremely confident, Rivera, who like many great relievers, was said to have "ice-water in his veins," was an extremely focused hurler, and a fierce competitor who never showed any emotion on the mound. He was "all business," someone said. Jeter called him the "most mentally tough" pitcher he ever played with.

"When you start thinking, a lot of things will happen," said Rivera, who was also noted as a team leader and a guy with an especially calm and friendly demeanor off the field. "If you don't control your emotions, your emotions will control your acts, and that's not good. I get the ball, I throw the ball, and then I take a shower."

The ultra-durable Rivera was good at doing that, starting with his days as a youth in Panama, where he first learned the game while playing on the beach using a milk carton for a glove. The son of a fisherman, he had entered the world in 1969, and later played shortstop as a youth in his hometown of Panama City.

After being asked to throw a few pitches, he was signed by a Yankees scout as a non-drafted free agent in 1990, getting a bonus of $3,000. Converted right away to pitcher, Mo spent his first year as a professional player with the Yankees of the Gulf Coast League, where he started just one of the 22 games in which he pitched.

But Mariano was not considered a reliever at that point, and over the next four and one-half seasons in the minors, playing at various levels, he started

66 of the 80 games in which he pitched, including each of his last 51 games. Despite surgery to repair a torn ligament in 1992, he posted a combined 27-18 record in the minors and was called up to the Yankees twice during the 1995 season. He started 10 of the 19 games in which he pitched that year, but the following season, big changes were in store.

Rivera was converted into a fireman during the 1996 season and wound up relieving in 53 of his 61 games. At one point, Mo pitched three perfect innings in three straight games over a span of seven days. From then on, despite several attempts in the early years by Yanks owner George Steinbrenner to trade him, the man called "a consummate professional" was a full-time member of the bullpen, relieving in every game for the rest of his big league career and only twice—when injured—pitching in less than 60 games in a season. It was in the capacity that he set his amazing record of 30 or more saves in 15 different seasons.

In 1997, having moved from setup man to closer, Rivera recorded 43 saves in 66 games. Although he would appear on the disabled list six times during his career and lost a substantial amount of work time during three seasons, Mariano went on to record no fewer than 36 saves each season over a five-year period. He led the American League with 45 saves in 1999, a year in which the Yankees swept the Atlanta Braves in the World Series and Rivera recorded two saves. In 2001, he finished on top again, this time with 50 saves.

After missing nearly two months with a shoulder strain, Rivera posted just 28 saves in 2002. He then registered at least 30 saves every season for the next nine years while going below 2.00 in ERA eight times. The 6-2,195-pound hurler went over the 50 mark for the second time in 2004, when he led the league with 53 saves in a career-high 74 games.

In 2005, while recording 43 saves in 71 games, Rivera set a personal record with a career-low 1.38 ERA. That season, he also tied a career high with seven wins (while losing four). Later, in 2009, 2011, and 2013, he saved 44 games in each season. At the age of 41 in 2011, Rivera became the oldest pitcher ever to save 40 or more games in one season.

His brilliant run was waylaid in 2012, when he was idled virtually the entire season with a torn ACL in his knee and pitched in only nine games. Then after the following season, he retired at the age of 43, going out with tributes throughout the league and a glowing record that made him the greatest reliever of all time.

Throughout his career, Rivera, the last player to wear Jackie Robinson's retired number 42, was the epitome of what a great relief pitcher could be.

"He was the best ever, no doubt," said Hall of Famer Dennis Eckersley.

"He's the best I've ever been around," added one-time Yankees manager, Joe Torre.

Although a good bit younger than Rivera, Phillies catcher Carlos Ruiz also grew up in Panama and knew the hurler well. "He was a great pitcher," Ruiz described. "What more can I say? He was just a very great pitcher."

And so he was. His amazing record of 30 or more saves in 15 seasons provided ample proof of that.

HONORABLE MENTION

51

OTHER PITCHERS WHO HAVE ACHIEVED OUTSTANDING FEATS

The achievements cited in the previous 50 chapters are ranked here as the most unusual pitching performances in baseball history. There have, however, been numerous other special achievements on the mound that should be mentioned. Accordingly, this chapter focuses on 50 of those additional noteworthy feats.

PRE-1920

Jack Taylor usually completed what he started. Complete games were expected from pitchers in those days. During a 10-year career, Taylor finished 278 of the 286 games he started. In 1901, he hurled a complete game that began a streak of 186 consecutive complete games over a five-year period. The high point of that streak came in 1904, when Taylor completed all 39 games he started for the St. Louis Browns. In 1899, he had also completed all 39 starts.

Joe McGinnity bore the nickname "Iron Man," and with good reason, too. In nine of his 10 years in the big leagues, he pitched more than 300 innings, twice exceeding 400. In 1903, McGinnity pitched both games of five separate doubleheaders. Three times, he won both games of those twin-bills, and won one in each of the other two. In his three winning doubleheaders, all coming in the same month, he beat Boston, Brooklyn, and Philadelphia.

Chicago Daily News, Inc.

Deacon Phillippe was the winning pitcher for the Pittsburgh Pirates in the first World Series game ever played when he beat Cy Young and the Boston Pilgrims, 7-3, in 1903. He gave up six hits and struck out 10. Phillippe had an outstanding 13-year career during which he never had a losing season while posting 189 victories, including six out of seven seasons with 20 or more wins. Phillippe had his best season in 1903, when he won 24 games.

Courtesy of Rich Westcott

Addie Joss had immaculate control during his illness-shortened career in the big leagues. That was never more evident than in 1908, when he walked just 30 batters in 325 innings pitched. He also won 24 games and posted a 1.16 earned run average that year. Overall, in 2,336 innings pitched, he walked just 370 hitters. While winning 160 games, including four straight seasons with 20 or more, he walked more than 50 hitters only twice in eight full seasons.

Courtesy of Rich Westcott

Ed Walsh never shied away from taking the ball. In fact, he did it so often that in five different seasons he pitched more than 300 innings. His top work came in 1908, when he set an all-time record of pitching 464 innings. Just the year before, he had worked 422 frames. Walsh's 1908 season with the Chicago White Sox came in a year when he posted a 40-15 record. Walsh appeared in 66 games, starting 49 and completing 42, with 11 shutouts.

Courtesy of Rich Westcott

Rube Marquard appeared during 18 seasons in the big leagues. His premier season came in 1912, when he set a modern record with 19 straight wins. During that streak he recorded 16 complete games and allowed just 49 runs in 206 innings. He had one win in relief and another (which would've brought his streak to 20) taken away from him due to what was later revealed as a scorer's mistake. Marquard won 26 games that year and 201 overall.

Courtesy of Rich Westcott

Dutch Leonard pitched in the big leagues for 11 seasons, during which he won in double figures nine times, but had losing records in four of them. In 1914, though, Leonard posted a 19-5 record while starting 25 of 36 games in which he pitched. His earned run average that season was an incredible 0.96, an all-time record. Seven of his wins were shutouts, and he gave up just 139 hits in 224.2 innings pitched.

Bain News Service

1920–39

Dazzy Vance captured 197 wins and led the National League in strikeouts seven straight years. The records could've been better, but Vance got a late start. After playing 10 years in the minors and failing to make it in three major league trials, Vance became a 31-year-old rookie in 1922. That season, he won 18 games for the Brooklyn Dodgers. Two years later, he went 28-6 and became the first National League pitcher to win the Most Valuable Player Award.

Courtesy of Rich Westcott

Howard Ehmke won seven games in 1929, his 14th season in the big leagues. But toward the end of the season, Philadelphia Athletics manager Connie Mack wanted to send him down to the minors. When Ehmke refused to go, Mack made him a scout. A few weeks later, the A's went to the World Series, and with no other hurlers available, Ehmke was asked to start the first game. He not only won the game, 3-1, but also he set a then–World Series record with 13 strikeouts. It was his last big league win.

Courtesy of Rich Westcott

Wes Ferrell won 193 games during a 15-year career in the big leagues, including 20 or more seven times. Ferrell was equally good with the bat. In 1931, while winning 22 games for the Cleveland Indians, he hit nine home runs, an all-time record for pitchers. Ferrell was one of those rare moundsmen who was often used as a pinch hitter. One season, he even played in the outfield in 13 games. Ferrell hit a pitchers-record 38 home runs during his career.

Courtesy of Rich Westcott

Dizzy Dean became noted for numerous activities while spending 12 years as a big league pitcher. The most noteworthy was in 1934. That year, Dean became the only pitcher over a 51-year period, from 1917 to 1968, to win 30 games. Dean pitched in 50 games for the St. Louis Cardinals, starting 33 of them, and completing 24. Incredibly, he also pitched in relief 17 times. Four of his wins came as a reliever. He was later credited with seven saves.

Paul Derringer had an excellent career, during which he was a 20-game winner four times and in 15 years won 223 games overall. Derringer also had a special milestone during his career. In 1935, while pitching for the Cincinnati Reds, he won the first night game ever played. President Franklin Roosevelt had pressed a telegraph key in the White House to signal workers to turn on the lights. Derringer beat the Philadelphia Phillies on a six-hitter, 2-1, at Crosley Field.

Bobo Newsom pitched for 20 years in the big leagues, winning 211 games. During that time, he played for seven different teams, including five of them more than once. That was amazing in itself, but even more astounding was the fact that Newsom played for the same team five different times. He played with the Washington Senators in 1935–37, 1942, 1943, 1946–47, and 1952. Between each stint with the Nats he was traded to some other team.

Courtesy of the Boston Public Library, Leslie Jones Collection

1940–59

Rip Sewell was pitching with the Pittsburgh Pirates when his career almost ended in 1941 after he was accidentally shot while hunting. Initially, Sewell couldn't walk. Later, he was unable to put much weight on the foot he pitched off. Sewell had to change his style, and in the process developed a blooper pitch that rose 25 feet in the air before descending to the plate. Called an eephus pitch, it was an odd but effective pitch for the rest of Sewell's big league career.

Courtesy of Rich Westcott

Mort Cooper made pitching a family affair. During the top four years of his 11-year career, his catcher was brother Walker Cooper. This was the best of all family batteries. When Walker was behind the plate, Mort went 13-9, 22-7, 21-8, and 23-9. The pair was together when the St. Louis Cardinals won three pennants and two World Series. In 1942, Mort, whose career record was 128-75, was the NL's MVP. One year later, Walker was second in the MVP voting.

Joe Nuxhall pitched for 16 years in the big leagues and won 135 games. With major league rosters depleted by World War II, he threw his first game in 1944. Nuxhall was just 15 years old, making him the youngest player ever to perform in the majors. The Cincinnati Reds were losing, 13-0, when Nuxhall was called in from the bullpen. He proceeded to give up five runs on five walks and two singles in two-thirds of an inning. Afterward, he was sent back to the minors.

AP Photo

Red Barrett performed what would be regarded in today's era, when pitch counts seemingly dominate a hurler's work, as an unfathomable feat. In a game in 1944, Barrett pitched the Boston Braves to a 2-0 victory over the Cincinnati Reds. The game lasted just one hour and 15 minutes. What made it even more amazing is that Barrett threw just 58 pitches. No one ever threw that few pitches in a complete-game win. That year, Barrett had a 9-16 record.

Dave Ferriss had only four full seasons in the big leagues, but he won 46 games in his first two years with the Boston Red Sox. As a rookie in 1945, Ferriss set an all-time record of not allowing a run in his first 22 innings in the majors. Ferriss pitched a two-hit, 2-0 win in his first start and a 7-0 triumph in his second start. He went on to win his first 10 starts, four of which were shutouts, before finishing the season with 21 wins and five shutouts.

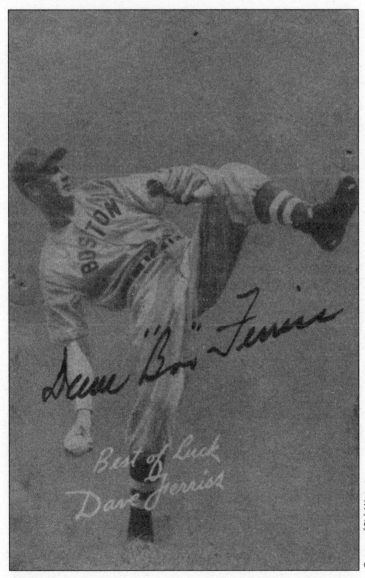

Dick Fowler had just been discharged from the Canadian Army when he reported back to the Philadelphia Athletics in 1945. Fowler had pitched for the A's in the early 1940s before entering the service in 1942. When he returned to Philadelphia, after two relief appearances, he got his first start just nine days after his discharge against the third-place St. Louis Browns. Fowler pitched a no-hitter, striking out six and walking four in a 1-0 victory for the A's.

Courtesy of Rich Westcott

Floyd Bevens had a brief career of four years with the New York Yankees that ended in 1947, when he posted a 7-13 record. In the final start of his career, in Game Four of the World Series, Bevens came within one out of pitching a no-hitter. In the ninth inning against the Brooklyn Dodgers, Bevens gave up a two-out, pinch-hit double to Cookie Lavagetto. The blow drove in two runs and gave the Dodgers a 3-2 victory. Bevens struck out five, but walked 10.

Courtesy of AP Photo

Satchel Paige was a player whose age was never known with any degree of certainty. He pitched Negro League baseball for more than 20 years before breaking into the majors in 1948 with the Cleveland Indians. At the time, it was believed that Paige was 42 years old, making him by far the oldest rookie in the history of the game. He pitched a five-hit shutout in his first start, and one week later fired a three-hit shutout while posting a 6-1 record that season.

LEROY "Satchell" PAIGE

AP Photo

Johnny Sain made his mark as one of the best pitchers in Boston Braves history, during which time he was a 20-game winner in three out of four years, and with 24 wins pitched his club to the National League pennant in 1948. Sain won 139 games during 11 years in the big leagues. Ironically, as a young player, Sain was cut four different times by Class D minor league teams before he finally got his start in the majors in 1942.

Courtesy of Rich Westcott

Jim Konstanty was the first reliever to win the Most Valuable Player Award when he won 16 games and saved 22 in 74 outings for the Philadelphia Phillies in 1950. That season, Konstanty, who had last started a game in the majors in 1946, was the Phils' starter in the opening game of the '50 World Series. Konstanty, who had pitched nine innings in relief in a 17-inning game, worked eight innings and gave up four hits in a 1-0 loss to the New York Yankees.

Courtesy of Rich Westcott

Ned Garver had the misfortune of playing mostly for low-level teams during his 14 years in the majors. A fine hurler, he won 129 games during a 14-year big league career. His top season came in 1951, when he became the first pitcher ever to win 20 games for a team that lost 100. Garver posted a 20-12 mark for a St. Louis Browns team that lost 102 games. That year he led the league with 24 complete games and was the starting pitcher in the All-Star Game.

Courtesy of Rich Westcott

Allie Reynolds is one of just six pitchers who have thrown two no-hitters in the same season. In 1951, the New York Yankees hurler blanked the Cleveland Indians, 1-0. A little more than two months later, he no-hit the Boston Red Sox, 8-0 in the first game of a doubleheader. The win clinched no worse than a tie for first place. The Yanks went on to win the second game to capture the American League pennant, and Reynolds finished the season with a 17-8 record.

Courtesy of Rich Westcott

Bobby Shantz stood just 5-6. But in a world that dwells on much taller pitchers, he took a strong stand for the little guy in 1952, when he became the shortest pitcher ever to win a Most Valuable Player Award. Shantz had a 24-7 record
with the fourth-place Philadelphia Athletics. He completed 27 of his 33 starts,
posting a 2.48 ERA. In the All-Star Game that season, he struck out Whitey
Lockman, Jackie Robinson, and Stan Musial in order.

Courtesy of Rich Westcott

Bobo Holloman may have had one of the all-time greatest starts. Having spent seven years in the minor leagues, Holloman made it with the St. Louis Browns in 1953. After four unimpressive relief appearances, he got a start against the Philadelphia Athletics. In his first big league start, Holloman pitched a no-hitter, beating the A's, 6-0. In his only big league season that year, Holloman made 10 starts and completed just one—his no-hit game.

Courtesy of Rich Westcott

Johnny Podres had just a 9-10 record in his third year in the big leagues when he started the third game of the 1955 World Series for the Brooklyn Dodgers. Coming on his 23rd birthday, Podres beat the New York Yankees, 8-3. Five days later, he started Game Seven, and again beat the Yankees with an eight-hitter, 2-0. The win was the first World Series victory for the Dodgers since the club joined the National League in 1890. Podres struck out four and walked two.

Courtesy of Rich Westcott

1960–79

Juan Marichal didn't take long to demonstrate how good he was. The pitcher who won 243 games during all or parts of 16 years in the majors broke in spectacularly in 1960 when in his first start, he pitched a one-hitter against the Philadelphia Phillies. On the way to a 2-0 victory, Marichal had a no-hitter going for seven and two-thirds innings. The six-time winner of more than 20 games, Marichal finally did fire a no-hitter in 1963 against the Houston Colt .45s.

Courtesy of The Jon B. Lovelace Collection of California Photographs in Carol M. Highsmith's America Project, Library of Congress, Prints and Photographs Division.

Tom Cheney was not in the headlines too often during an eight-year career in which he lost more games than he won. But there was one time when his name was at the top of the sports pages. That occurred in 1962, when Cheney set an all-time record with 21 strikeouts in one game. He did it while pitching all 16 innings of a Washington Senators' 2-1 victory over the Baltimore Orioles. He threw 228 pitches while allowing 20 hits and walking four.

Courtesy of the Baseball Hall of Fame

Jim Maloney threw two extra inning no-hitters in one season. But only one of them counted. In 1965, Maloney no-hit the New York Mets for 10 innings before yielding a hit in the 11th inning and losing, 1-0. Two months later, he hurled a 10-inning no-hit, 1-0 victory over the Chicago Cubs. The first one didn't count as a no-hitter because major league rules say a pitcher must hurl a complete game win to get one. Maloney also fired a no-hitter against the Houston Astros in 1969.

AP Photo/Harold P. Matosian

Tony Cloninger was a solid pitcher who in back-to-back seasons in the mid-1960s won 43 games. As a batter, he hit just .192 during a 12-year career. But in 1966 he became the first batter in National League history to hit two grand slams in the same game. Adding an RBI single, he drove in nine runs in an Atlanta Braves 17-3 rout of the San Francisco Giants. Just two weeks earlier, Cloninger had also hit two homers in the same game. He had 11 career homers.

AP Photo

Paul Lindblad played 14 years in the major leagues, working almost entirely as a middle-inning relief pitcher. Lindblad pitched in 655 games in his career, once leading the American League with 66 appearances. It was as a fielder, though, that Lindblad performed an amazing feat. Over a nine-year period from 1966 through 1974, he played in 385 games without making an error. Lindblad had a lifetime fielding average of .977, making just six errors in his entire career.

Paul Lindblad (Left). AP Photo

Vida Blue was brought up from the minors by the Oakland Athletics in late September of 1970. The 21 year old won his first start with a one-hitter against the Kansas City Royals. Then, just 18 days after being called up, Blue got his second win with a no-hitter against the Minnesota Twins. After allowing just one hit in two games, Blue blazed through his first full season in 1971, posting a 24-8 record, at one point winning 10 straight games, four of them shutouts.

AP Photo

Rick Wise proved that a pitcher can help himself in a lot of different ways. In 1971, a few months before the Philadelphia Phillies traded him for Steve Carlton, Wise pitched a no-hitter against the Cincinnati Reds. Wise hit two home runs and collected three RBI in the 4-0 victory. No other pitcher has ever hit two home runs when he hurled a no-hitter. Wise, who homered twice in another game later in the season, finished the campaign with a 17-14 record.

Philadelphia Phillies

Jim Kaat earned a reputation as a savvy pitcher who was one of only 29 players ever to appear in the majors in four different decades. Pitching from 1959 to 1983, he posted a 283-237 record in 898 games. Kaat was also an accomplished fielder. From 1962 through 1977 he set an all-time record by winning 16 straight Gold Gloves. Amazingly, Kaat wore the same glove for 15 of those years. During his 25-year career, he made just 56 errors in 1,062 chances.

Philadelphia Phillies

Gaylord Perry had one of the longest careers of any pitcher in big league history, appearing in 22 seasons between 1962 and 1983. He won 314 games, and had five seasons when he won more than 20. While pitching for the Cleveland Indians in 1972, Perry posted a 24-16 record and won the Cy Young Award. In 1978, Perry recorded a 21-6 mark with the San Diego Padres and won another Cy Young. He was the first pitcher ever to win a Cy Young Award in both leagues.

1980–99

Tom Glavine was one of baseball's finest left-handed pitchers. But it nearly didn't happen. Glavine might've become an NHL ice hockey player. A hockey star in high school who was his league's Most Valuable Player, Glavine was a fourth-round draft pick of the Los Angels Kings. Chosen 69th overall, he was picked two rounds ahead of future Hall of Famer Brett Hull. Instead, Glavine chose baseball, and won 305 games and two Cy Young Awards during 22 years in the majors.

2 on a Whim Creations

Bret Saberhagen got an early start in his career when he broke into the majors in 1984 at the age of 20 and won 10 games. It got even better for Saberhagen the following season, when he posted a 20-6 record with a 2.97 earned run average while walking just 38 batters in 235 innings with the Kansas City Royals. After the season, Saberhagen was named winner of his league's Cy Young Award. He was just 21 years old, the youngest Cy Young winner in history.

Kansas City Royals

Mike Scott was struggling along when he was traded to the Houston Astros. There he learned to throw a split-fingered fastball, and his career took a quick turn upward. In 1986, he pitched a no-hitter against the San Francisco Giants. The win clinched the West Division title for the Astros. Scott, who struck out 13, had an 18-10 record that season, while leading the league with 306 strike-outs. Although the Astros lost in the playoffs, Scott won the Cy Young Award.

AP Photo/Eric Risberg

Roger Clemens had many accomplishments during his 24-year career, not the least of which was winning 354 games and seven Cy Young Awards. One of his other major deeds was striking out 20 hitters in one game. Clemens was the first hurler to do it in a nine-inning game, and he did it twice. As a 23 year old in 1986, he broke the record of 19 by fanning 20 batters in a 3-2 victory over the Seattle Mariners. Ten years later, he whiffed 20 again to beat the Detroit Tigers.

New York Yankees

Greg Harris was a right-handed pitcher who alternated during his 15-year career between starter and reliever. Harris was ambidextrous, and in the majors, he often threw left-handed in batting practice. Finally, in 1995, he threw left-handed in a game, making him the only player in history to pitch with both arms. In his last major league game, he pitched part of the ninth inning against the Cincinnati Reds as a southpaw, retiring one batter and walking the other.

Philadelphia Phillies

2000 TO PRESENT

John Smoltz spent his time on the mound in ways unlike most other hurlers. Over a 21-year career, he went from starter to reliever, and then back to starter. In so doing, he won more than 200 games as a starter and saved more than 150 games as a reliever, making him the only pitcher in history to have that high of a record in both categories. Smoltz finished his career, spent almost entirely with the Atlanta Braves, in 2009 with 213 wins and 154 saves in 723 games.

U.S. Air Force photo/Don Peek

Octavio Dotel had to always keep his bags packed. That's because he was constantly on the move. In 15 years in the majors, he played with 13 different teams. No one else ever played with that many teams. Dotel also played with six different minor league teams, giving him a total of 19 teams. A relief pitcher who had 109 career saves and in 2002 worked in 83 games, Dotel originally signed at the age of 17, after which he was traded six times and six times signed as a free agent.

AP Photo/Gene J. Puskar

Al Leiter pitched in 19 big league seasons, dividing his time almost equally between the American and National Leagues. That was a special advantage because it allowed Leiter to perform an extremely unique feat. While posting a 162-132 career record, Leiter became the only hurler ever to defeat every one of the 30 teams in the big leagues. Leiter, who arrived in the majors in 1987, reached that plateau when he beat the Arizona Diamondbacks, 10-1, in 2002.

Florida Marlins

Eric Gagne was originally a starter, but in 2002 was converted to a reliever. At mid-season that year, he began a streak that became a major league record of 84 saves in 84 save opportunities. The streak extended into 2003, when Gagne converted all 55 save opportunities. That year, while working in 77 games, registering a 1.20 ERA, and winning the Cy Young Award, Gagne became the first reliever to have more than 50 saves in two different seasons.

AP Photo/Kathy Willens

Tim Lincecum began his career the way every pitcher would like to, but none ever have before. In his first two full seasons with the San Francisco Giants, Lincecum won Cy Young Awards each time. He won the first Cy Young in 2008 after posting an 18-5 mark for a club that had a 72-90 record. The second Cy Young Award followed in 2009, when Lincecum went 15-7. He led the National League in strikeouts in both seasons while starting 65 games.

SD Dirk

Trevor Hoffman spent 18 years as a relief pitcher and along the way set a then-record with 40 or more saves nine times. He reached a personal high of 53 saves in 1998 with the San Diego Padres. In 2007, Hoffman became the first reliever to record 500 career saves. Then in 2010, he became the first fireman to save 600 games. Hoffman, who saved 30 or more games in 14 different seasons, retired in 2010 with 601 saves while striking out 1,133 in 1,089.1 innings.

San Diego Padres

Jamie Moyer pitched for 25 years in the majors, winning 269 games while playing for eight teams from 1986 to 2012. During that time, Moyer played in 50 different major league ballparks. In 2010 with the Philadelphia Phillies, he beat the Atlanta Braves with a two-hitter, 7-0, making him at 47 the oldest pitcher ever to throw a shutout. Then in 2012 at age 49 1/2, he became the oldest pitcher ever to win a game when he pitched the Colorado Rockies to a 6-1 win over Arizona.

Seattle Mariners

R. A. Dickey is one of the few modern hurlers whose main pitch is a knuckleball. It works well for him. In 2012, he fashioned a 20-6 record with the New York Mets while leading the league with 33 starts and setting career highs with 230 strikeouts and 233.2 innings pitched. Dickey's season was climaxed when he won the Cy Young Award. In the long history of the award, he was the first knuckleball pitcher ever to win that honor.

James_in_to on Flickr (Original version) UCinternational (Crop)

SOURCES

Allen, Lee and Meany, Tom – *Kings of the Diamond*, G. P. Putnam's Sons, 1965

Buckley, James, Jr. – *Perfect, The Inside Story of Baseball's Twenty Perfect Games*, Triumph Books, 2002

Buckley, James, Jr. and Pepe, Phil – *Unhittable: Reliving the Magic and Drama of Baseball's Best-Pitched Games*, Triumph Books, 2004

Caruso, Gary – The Braves Encyclopedia, Temple University Press, 1995

Charlton, James – *The Baseball Chronology, The Complete History of the Most Important Events in the Game of Baseball*, Macmillan Publishing Company, 1991

Curran, William – *Strikeout, A Celebration of the Art of Pitching*, Crown Publishers, 1995

Eisenbath, Mike – *The Cardinals Encyclopedia*, Temple University Press, 1990

Gallagher, Mark – *The Yankees Encyclopedia*, Leisure Press, 1982

Gilbert, Bill – *Now Pitching, Bob Feller*, Harper Perennial, 1990

Honig, Donald – *The Greatest Pitchers of All Time*, Crown Publishers, 1988

Holtzman, Jerome – *The Chicago Cubs Encyclopedia*, Temple University Press, 1997

Kaplan, Jim – *Lefty Grove, American Original*, Society of American Baseball Research, 2000

Kerrane, Kevin – *The Hurlers: Pitching Power and Precision*, Redefinition, 1989

Levy, Alan H. – *Rube Waddell: The Zany, Brilliant Life of a Strikeout Artist*, McFarland & Company, 2000

Lindberg, Richard – *The White Sox Encyclopedia*, Temple University Press, 1997

Litwhiler, Danny – *Living the Baseball Dream*, Temple University Press, 2006

Mack, Connie – *My 66 Years in The Big Leagues*, Dover Publications, 2009

McNeil, William – *The Dodgers Encyclopedia*, Sports Publishing, 2003

Meany, Tom – *Baseball's Greatest Pitchers*, A. S. Barnes and Company, 1951

Nemec, David – *Great Baseball Feats, Facts & Firsts*, Signet Books, 2011

Redmount, Robert – *The Red Sox Encyclopedia*, Sports Publishing, 2002

Reichler, Joe – *Baseball's Great Moments*, Rutledge Books, 1983

Reidenbaugh, Lowell – *100 Years of National League Baseball*, The Sporting News, 1976

Ritter, Lawrence S. – *The Story of Baseball*, Morrow Books, 1999

Robinson, Ray – *Matty, An American Hero*, Oxford University Press, 1993

Salant, Nathan – *Superstars, Stars, and Just Plain Heroes*, Stein and Day, 1982

Schechter, Gabriel – *Unhittable! Baseball's Greatest Pitching Seasons*, Charles April Publications, 2002

Schneider, Russ – *The Cleveland Indians Encyclopedia*, Temple University Press, 1996

Smith, Ron – *The Sporting News Chronicle of Baseball*, BDD Illustrated Books, 1993

Society for American Baseball Research – *The SABR Baseball List & Record Book*, Scribner, 2007

The Sporting News – *Baseball's Hall of Fame: Cooperstown, Where the Legends Live Forever*, Gramercy Books, 1999

Thomas, Henry W. – *Walter Johnson, Baseball's Big Train*, Farragut Publishing, 1995

Wallace, Joseph, et al. – *Baseball, 100 Classic Moments in the History of the Game*, Dorling Kindersley, 2000

Westcott, Rich – *Diamond Greats, Profiles and Interviews with 65 of Baseball's History Makers*, Meckler Books, 1988

Westcott, Rich and Lewis, Allen – *No-Hitters: The 225 Games, 1893–1999*, McFarland and Company, 2000

Westcott, Rich – *Splendor on the Diamond: Interviews with 35 Stars of Baseball's Past*, University Press of Florida, 2000

Westcott, Rich – *Winningest Pitchers: Baseball's 300-Game Winners*, Temple University Press, 2002

Westcott, Rich and Bilovsky, Frank – *The Phillies Encyclopedia*, Temple University Press, 2004

Westcott, Rich – *The Fightin' Phils: Oddities, Insights, and Untold Stories*, Camino Books, 2008

Other Sources

Baseball-almanac.com

Baseball-reference.com

Baseball, The Biographical Encyclopedia, Sports Publishing

Hardballtimes.com

Major League Baseball team media guides

National Baseball Hall of Fame and Museum Yearbook, 2012

Phillies Report

Retrosheet

SABR BioProject:

    Jim Abbott by Rick Swaine
    Lou Brissie by Bill Nowlin
    Jack Chesbro by Wayne McElreavy
    Dennis Eckersley by Joseph Wancho
    Lefty Grove by Jim Kaplan
    Carl Hubbell by Fred Stein
    Firpo Marberry by Mark Armour
    Joe Oeschger by John F. Green
    Jim Palmer by Mark Armour
    Ed Reulbach by Cappy Gagnon
    Amos Rusie by Ralph Berger
    Babe Ruth by Allan Wood
    Hoyt Wilhelm by Mark Armour
    Cy Young by David Southwick

SI Vault

The Baseball Encyclopedia, Macmillan Publishing Company

The Sporting News Official Baseball Guide

The Sporting News Official Baseball Register

Total Baseball, Total Sports

USAToday.com

Wikipedia.org

Yahoosports.com

ABOUT THE AUTHOR

Rich Westcott is the author of 23 previous books. A newspaper and magazine writer and editor for more than 40 years, he has written for publications throughout the country and has appeared in ten film documentaries about baseball. He was the founding publisher of *Phillies Report*, a newspaper that covered the team for 14 years. A special advisor to the Philadelphia Sports Hall of Fame and the Phillies Wall of Fame, he has been inducted into three halls of fame himself. A native Philadelphian, he has taught journalism at two Philadelphia universities, and is holder of a bachelor's degree from Drexel University and a master's degree from Johns Hopkins University. He is the immediate past president of the Philadelphia Sports Writers' Association.

OTHER BOOKS BY
RICH WESTCOTT

The Phillies Encyclopedia (with Frank Bilovsky), first, second, and third editions

Diamond Greats: Profiles and Interviews with 65 of Baseball's History Makers

Phillies '93: An Incredible Season

Masters of the Diamond: Interviews with Players Who Began Their Careers More Than 50 Years Ago

Mike Schmidt

Philadelphia's Old Ballparks

No-Hitters: The 225 Games, 1893–1999 (with Allen Lewis)

Splendor on the Diamond: Interviews with 35 Stars of Baseball's Past

A Century of Philadelphia Phillies Baseball: 1900–1999

Great Home Runs of the 20th Century

A Century of Philadelphia Sports

Winningest Pitchers: Baseball's 300-Game Winners

Tales from the Philadelphia Phillies Dugout, first, second, and third editions

Native Sons: Philadelphia Baseball Players Who Made the Major Leagues

Mickey Vernon: The Gentleman First Baseman

Veterans Stadium: Field of Memories

Phillies Essential

The Mogul: Eddie Gottlieb, a Philadelphia Sports Legend and Pro Basketball Pioneer

The Fightin' Phils: Oddities, Insights, and Untold Stories

Philadelphia Phillies: Past and Present

Back Again: The Story of the 2009 Phillies

Shibe Park—Connie Mack Stadium

Philadelphia's Top 50 Baseball Players